Advanced Game Development

with Programmable Graphics Hardware

Advanced Game Development

with Programmable Graphics Hardware

Alan Watt

University of Sheffield

Fabio Policarpo

CRC Press
Taylor & Francis Group
Boca Raton London New York

CRC Press is an imprint of the
Taylor & Francis Group, an **informa** business

AN A K PETERS BOOK

First published 2005 by A K Peters, Ltd

Published 2019 by CRC Press
Taylor & Francis Group
6000 Broken Sound Parkway NW, Suite 300
Boca Raton, FL 33487-2742

© 2005 by Taylor & Francis Group, LLC
CRC Press is an imprint of Taylor & Francis Group, an Informa business

First issued in paperback 2019

No claim to original U.S. Government works

ISBN 13: 978-0-367-44647-5 (pbk)
ISBN 13: 978-1-56881-240-3 (hbk)

**Visit the Taylor & Francis Web site at
http://www.taylorandfrancis.com**

**and the CRC Press Web site at
http://www.crcpress.com**

Watt, Alan H., 1942–
    Advanced game development with programmable graphics hardware / Alan Watt, Fabio Policarpo.
      p. cm.
    Includes bibliographical references and index.
    ISBN 1-56881-240-X
      1. Computer games—Programming. 2. Computer graphics. I. Policarpo, Fabio. II. Title.

QA76.76.C672.W42 2005
794.8'151--dc22

                                                                    2005045895

Contents

Acknowledgements

We would like to thank (in no particular order):

- James Edge and Manuel Sanchez for their generous contributions to Chapter 10 (Facial Animation) and Michael Meredith for his equally generous contribution to Chapter 9 (Character Animation).

- Hoplon Infotainment for Figures 6.5, 6.7, 11.3 and 11.18 and their project 'Taikodom' that uses our system. Many thanks for all the testing, suggestions and investment on the library.

- TV Globo for figures used on the cover, Figure 8.12, 11.10 and the project 'Conquista de Titan' using our system for a TV show.

- Tony Lupidi and Roberta Brandão for Figures 9.10, 9.12, 9.13 and 9.14, their controversial project 'Hook Up 3D' and all the investment on the character animation system.

- Intel for a reliable computer system we used through the development of this book.

- nVidia and all its team members for the video cards that we used to develop the engine and demos for the book (the fastest and most flexible graphics hardware to date!) and for the excellent developer support and best high-level shading language so far (Cg).

- Simon Green from nVidia for his cool demos and the code ideas used in Listing 8.6.

- Gilliard Lopes and Francisco Fonseca for all their huge additions to the system and many of the functionality included in the editors.

- Finally, thanks are due to our publishers for their speedy production of the book and for their perseverance of late edits.

Preface

This book addresses the new possibilities that are becoming available in games technology through the development of programmable hardware. This is a rapidly evolving technology, and we have chosen to describe the basic techniques of game creation emphasizing this new hardware.

We decided to approach this topic by using Cg, C++ and OpenGL. We have chosen Cg, one of three shader languages, because it is well established, straightforward to use and perhaps the most popular. Whether this situation persists in the long term is difficult to predict at the time of writing.

Although we provide a brief introduction to Cg, we assume that the reader already has programming experience and some knowledge of 3D computer graphics. As a result, the book can be used by students of game technology or equally by established game programmers and developers who want to update their expertise to the new technology.

The topics we have included go beyond the implementation of basic shading on GPUs, described in the early chapters and include implementation of advanced algorithms using, for example, ray tracing to achieve innovative surface effects. Character animation, which forms a large proportion of contemporary games culture, is treated comprehensively in four chapters. Although we have described how to implement individual effects using shaders, we also include a treatment of the important topic of shader management in a game in the final chapter. This enables the reader to put together a system for a particular game.

Inevitably, as hardware evolves, more complex algorithms will be implementable. We have exploited the very latest hardware available for our advanced algorithms and trust that the utility of the text will survive for some time.

Most of the techniques described in the book are implemented on the included CD-ROM which comprises an advanced library of tools suitable for game development using Cg/C++/OpenGL. This system has already been used in the production of two commercial games, and we believe that it is straightforward and simple to apply. Included demos using the library will help you understand how the render and GUI object manager interfaces work.

Alan Watt
Fabio Policarpo

May 2005

Chapter One

Introduction and Cg Programming Overview

The text is mainly addressed to programmers and developers who already have some knowledge of three-dimensional (3D) graphics, programming in C-like languages and a 3D graphics Applications Programming Interface (API) such as OpenGL or Direct3D. Although a Cg text, such as [FERN03] would be required as a reference, this book is meant to stand alone for games practitioners with the aforementioned experience. It could be looked upon as a conversion text for professionals who want to progress to Graphics Processing Unit (GPU) programming.

The text is a treatment of techniques that are commonly used in games and similar real-time 3D applications. The presentation style will be description of algorithm/technique followed by pseudocode followed (*possibly*) by Cg code. Cg programs are generally quite short, and the presentation of code samples seems sensible.

The text is mainly addressed to GPU techniques, and most example code is given in Cg. So as to address the generality of the topic, techniques that are important but which do not fit easily onto a GPU code are given in C++ and OpenGL.

In the course of the text we will describe the design of programs and systems that can be used to implement games and other systems: Computer Aided Architectural Design (CAAD), for example whose requirements are to render real time animation sequences (such as walks through complex scenes) at the high quality now available in real time.

The Hardware Model

We begin by detailing a model for GPU hardware. This is a necessary prerequisite to programming a GPU, and we take the approach of describing this separately to the nature of the programming language. A hardware model does not necessarily bear much relationship to the actual hardware architecture but is a conceptual model that aids the programmer's perception of the hardware. It is also intended to be independent of hardware differences between manufacturers.

The evolution of GPU hardware has seen a shift from configurability to programmability. Although early GPUs could execute 'programs' of some complexity, by configuring the hardware in different states between passes in a multipass program, the rendering effects achievable with this technology were somewhat limited. Nevertheless quite complex algorithms, such as specular per-pixel lighting with normal maps have been implemented successfully using this technology. Now GPUs are highly programmable, and the fact that their performance is now much faster than Central Processing Units (CPUs) means that they are being increasingly exploited to carry out general computation.

One of the important implications for the games industry of this new power, is that it should be possible to perform all lighting calculations in real time, enabling more exotic dynamic lighting effects and the elimination of precalculated lighting (light maps). The shift of expensive algorithms, such as skinning, onto the GPU frees more CPU time for other aspects of a game and should eventually result in games that are more complex, and more interesting, than current titles.

Programming GPUs is different to programming CPUs, and many would say more difficult. This difficulty is minimized by the development of C-like high-level languages and compilers, principally, NVIDIA's Cg, OpenGL 2.0's Shading Language (GLSL) and DirectX 9's High Level Shading Language (HLSL). At this stage in their development, these languages are very similar, and learning to program in any one of them should enable fluency in the other two. And writing code in Cg can produce shaders, which with the appropriate compiler, will work as HLSL shaders. In this text we will concentrate mainly on Cg; although it is an NVIDIA project, it is extremely well established and in our opinion simpler than GLSL.

Along with the evolution of hardware, there is a change in the semantics of 'shader'. Before, a shader was loosely used to describe an entity that is bound to an object or part of it. With its utility exposed through a 'shader editor' it became to be used by the games industry in particular to describe an implementation that used multipass rendering or multitexture rendering, where different texture maps

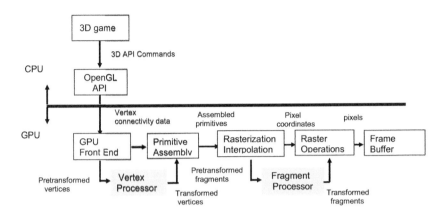

Figure 1.1. Highlighted boxes show the programmable part of the graphics pipeline.

could be combined in various ways and accept very simple animation facilities. Such shaders conformed exactly to R. L. Cook's famous shade trees [COOK84], which preceded and inspired RenderMan. Now 'shader' signifies a vertex, or a fragment program or both together. The term persists because although we can have a 'non-rendering' shader (one which does not calculate the colour of a pixel representing a point on the surface of an object); the output from a fragment program is always a shade for a pixel. For example, we may have a shader that performs two-dimensional (2D) image processing operations, as we demonstrate in Chapter 2.

The first thing to know about programming GPUs is that usually two programs are required: a vertex program and a fragment program.[1] Highlighted in the graphics pipeline shown in Figure 1.1 are the units that execute these programs. Another important aspect to bear in mind is that the hardware is designed specifically to optimize the processing required to convert the data and command stream from the CPU to render 3D scenes into the frame buffer. And indeed, the main application of this technology is rendering. However, Cg is designed to be as general-purpose as is possible with the hardware and is thus not application specific in the way that RenderMan is. In fact, as we shall see in Chapter 6, we can write programs in Cg that will enable us to implement nonrendering algorithms, such as search methods, on the GPU. This has come to be known as GPGPU (General Purpose computation on a GPU).[2]

. . . .

[1] We can have a vertex program without a fragment program (or vice-versa) on more recent hardware – the 'normal' pipeline is used on the missing component.

In Figure 1.1, the GPU accepts data that comprises a set of vertices defining the object currently being rendered. This data is a set of vertex attributes consisting of:

vertex position (x,y,z,w)
colour(s) (diffuse and possibly specular) (RGBA)
texture coordinate(s) (u,v)
vertex normal (x,y,z)
tangent (x,y,z)
binormal (x,y,z)

The vertex processor executes a program for every vertex and this will consist, at least, of transforming vertices from object space into clip space, by multiplying the position by the concatenation of the `modelview` and `projection` matrices. Other operations may be performed on the vertices depending on the nature of the program, but performing the object to clip space transformation is mandatory.

Input data for the vertex processor—the vertex attributes—are contained in read only vertex attribute registers. The output registers are write only and will contain the transformed/processed vertex attributes. Vertex processors sequentially execute instructions in the vertex program until completion. Read/write registers are available for intermediate results within the program. Flow control structure (branching and looping) are available in the latest hardware. Specialised maths operations on vectors (two, three or four components) are implemented as well as other utilities—such as swizzling—all of which we examine later in the chapter.

Associated with the vertex data is the primitive assembly information or connectivity information that is used to assemble the transformed vertices into the appropriate primitive. This activity is performed in the primitive assembly unit. The output from this stage is a stream of triangles, lines or points.

These primitives are then clipped against the view frustum and any enabled application clip planes. This will then be followed by whatever culling is specified to the API. The primitives are then rasterised resulting in a set of pixel locations and fragments. A fragment at this stage is a 'potential' pixel—it may or may not result finally in a pixel depending on subsequent operations. A colour for each fragment is determined by standard linear interpolation of the vertex attributes: colour and texture coordinates (also using perspective correction to resolve non-linearity from perspective cameras).

We now examine the role of the fragment processor in all this. Just as in the case of the vertex processor, the fragment processor has to perform 'conventional' fragment operations such as texture mapping, together with any more elaborate application

....
[2] See www.gpgpu.org for links to applications.

dependent operations that may be required at this stage. All processing results in a single fragment colour which may update the frame buffer. Also, the z value associated with the fragment in the Z-buffer can be updated by the fragment program.

Just like the vertex program, a fragment program contains a set of instructions fetched sequentially by the fragment processor and executed to completion for every fragment. The processor contains read-only input registers, read/write temporary registers and write-only output registers. Again, specialised maths operations are available together with texture mapping utilities. Flow control (branching and looping) is now implemented on the latest hardware.

In an application, we may require both a vertex program and a fragment program or one of these. If neither a vertex nor a fragment program is present then the GPU behaves as a conventional graphics pipeline. A familiar example is Gouraud versus Phong shading. Gouraud shading calculates reflected light only at the vertices of an object. The vertex program would consist of the appropriate vector operations (normalization and dot product) required to implement the standard Gouraud shading equation. The fragment program required for Gouraud shading has no further calculations to perform and simply has to pass the input colour to the output register (a so-called 'pass-through'). Phong shading, on the other hand, would be implemented by a fragment program. Here we need to apply a shading equation at each fragment. The accompanying vertex program for a Phong fragment shader is almost a pass-through—all we need to do is to implement the transformation described above. These two standard shading procedures are implemented in Chapter 2.

The final unit in the pipeline (raster operations) converts fragments to pixel updates providing they pass the tests implemented by the unit. These tests are set up by API commands, and this is where depth testing occurs together with scissor, alpha and stencil tests. Passing all tests means that the fragment becomes a pixel update and the depth of the fragment may replace the pixel's current depth value. A pixel update does not necessarily imply a replacement but may involve a blending of the fragment colour and the current pixel colour.

Programming Overview

The Programming Model

Programming a GPU is somewhat different to programming a CPU. The difference is a consequence of the hardware architecture. GPUs are highly optimized for graphics calculations, in particular the operations involved in rendering a 3D scene.

The CPU is a serial processor, fetching and executing instructions one at time, reading from and writing to memory as it goes. The GPU is a stream processor designed to exploit the implicit characteristics of 3D rendering—parallelism and locality. This imposes constraints on the nature of the programming.

If we consider the fragment program we can conceptualise its operation by considering the model shown in Figure 1.2, a standard model for a stream processor. In this model, data is streamed into the processor and operated on by a kernel function—the fragment program. Many (currently up to 16) arithmetic processors operate on the stream, and each data element is processed in parallel. Thus, there can be no dependencies between elements, a property explicit in mainstream rendering methods. The notion of locality is exploited by the input and output records.

Another common abstraction of this type of hardware is SPMD (Single Program Multiple Data). A shader is written to operate on a single vertex or fragment and is executed for every vertex or fragment.

The parallelism is not exposed to the programmer, who simply writes a program to operate on a single, and by implication every, fragment in the input data stream. Fragment (and vertex) programs can contain flow control structures–branches and loops—and we would, for example, use a deterministic loop to calculate the contributions of a scene lit by more than one light in a program that implemented Phong shading.

Parallelism works in rendering and related applications because rendering a 3D object is an inherently parallel operation. Most importantly, we require that there is no communication between processes. Communication between processes executing simultaneously is, of course, the main difficulty of parallel processing. At this stage we can note that some rendering algorithms do require

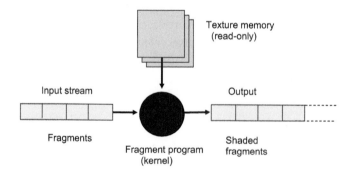

Figure 1.2. A fragment program as a stream processor.

communication between processes. Most global illumination algorithms usually cannot invoke per-fragment operations that proceed independently of each other.

Fragment program operations can execute reads (random) from texture maps which in general terms can be considered read-only memory—the analogue of 2D arrays in conventional programming with the texture coordinates as the array indices. This is important in GPGPU applications, which may in many cases require a write to memory. Since in GPUs the output is always written to the frame buffer, we can only update the texture memory either by copying the contents of the frame buffer to texture or by rendering to texture. Unlike CPUs, GPUs do not virtualise their resources, and this fact means there are hardware constraints that impact on the concept of the language as a high-level language.

Each hardware will have different limits on the maximum number of instructions it can execute, the number of registers it can use and the number of texture accesses available. Hardware limits are expressed by profiles. Some hardware profiles even have separate limits for each type of instruction like arithmetic, conditional tests, texture access, etc. The idea is that the language contains facilities that are currently available on some, but not all, hardware and even utilities that are not currently available on any hardware. These are reserved for future development.

The Languages

Shading languages are sometimes called Domain Specific Languages (DSLs) because they are designed to expose the semantics of an architecture designed around the requirements of an application—in this case rendering. As well as their domain specifics utilities, shading languages have always incorporated general programming language features of C and C++ (such as structures, functions, overloading, etc.).

All current shading languages (or you could equally say all current shading hardware) attends to three concurrent processes: application program running on the CPU, a vertex shader executing per vertex and a fragment shader executing per fragment. The similarity between the shading languages listed in the next paragraph is a consequence of this model.

Currently the main languages are Cg, OpenGL Shading Language (GLSL) and DirectX 9's HLSL. In this chapter we will discuss the first of these. The aim of the following sections is to give a brief taste of the language and to introduce its key concepts. As we progress through the text, more advanced aspects will be introduced.

As we have already mentioned, the immediate predecessor of high level shading languages for GPUs was the use of multi-pass techniques, where fairly complex shaders, such as shadow volumes, could be implemented. Unfortunately for efficiency this technology required high memory bandwidth. Hardware evolution, however, saw a substantial growth in arithmetic processing power compared to off-chip bandwidth and this limits the eventual efficacy of the multi-pass technique. This then led to the emergence of programmable functionality in the vertex and fragment processors.

In a key paper describing the design philosophy of Cg, W. Mark *et al.* [MARK03] list the design goals of the language as:

- ease of programming;
- portability across hardware;
- complete support for the hardware functionality available in assembly language;
- performance…equal to or better than handwritten assembly code;
- minimal interference with application data, making it usable in existing applications;
- ease of adoption;
- extensibility for future hardware; and
- support for non-shading uses of the GPU…should be a general-purpose language rather than a domain specific language;

A key design decision concerning the fact that the programmable units— the vertex and fragment processors—each require their own program was to adopt a multiprogram rather than a single or unified program model, where the control of both processors would be in the same program. The main reason for this was to avoid the problem of flow control that would otherwise occur with a unified program model.

Cg Overview

Very Simple Programs

We begin with a simple example of a vertex program shown in Listing 1.1. The entry point for a vertex shader is the function `main` (any name can be chosen for the entry point method as this name is passed to the compiler by the application on compile time, but if entry point is not specified it will default to `main` as in regular C/C++ programming). The first two parameters define the input from the application, and the next two define the output from the vertex shader. The final parameter is also input from the application, `uniform float4x4 modelviewProjection` is somewhat different to the first two parameters and will be described shortly.

Listing 1.1

A very simple
vertex program.

```
void main ( float4 iPosition     : POSITION,
            float4 iColour        : COLOR,
            out float4 oPosition  : POSITION,
            out float4 oColour    : COLOR,
            uniform float4x4 modelviewProjection)
{
   oPosition = mul(modelviewProjection, iPosition);
   oColour   = iColour;
}
```

All that the vertex program does is to transform a vertex from object space to clip space by effecting a matrix multiplication between the modelviewProjection matrix of the object and the object space position of the vertex. It also assigns the input colour of the vertex to the output colour. Thus, a stream of data units—the vertex's position in clip space and its colour —are passed to the next stage in the pipeline (Figure 1.1).

The input to the fragment program after primitive assembly, rasterisation and interpolation is a stream of fragments having colours interpolated from the vertex colours. If the fragment program is just a pass-through as shown in Listing 1.2, then these two programs will produce the image shown in Figure 1.3. In fact, exactly the same output would be produced if no vertex and fragment programs were present, but the idea is to start with the simplest program that takes control of the two processors.

Listing 1.2

A very simple
fragment program.

```
void main (float4 iColour     : COLOR,
           out float4 oColour : COLOR)
{
   oColour = iColour;
}
```

The cube has different colours assigned to each vertex. Bilinear interpolation across each face of the cube takes place in the rasterisation/interpolation unit, producing a different colour for each fragment. These fragments are then fed as input to the fragment processor and subsequently to the frame buffer as pixel updates.

Figure 1.3. The output produced by our first vertex and fragment programs.

We can make a number of simple observations from these two programs.

Outputs

First note that the vertex program produces two outputs, whereas the fragment program will only produce one. The fragment program has to produce a single fragment colour, which in conventional shading will be calculated from a shading equation and (usually) a texture map read. The vertex program may calculate a number of outputs from operations on the vertex input attributes. It could, for example, change the position of the vertices as part of a soft object animation procedure. It may also pass through texture coordinates, or it can operate on them.

Semantics

Input and output parameters are followed in their declarations by semantics. Note that preceding an input parameter by **in** is nonmandatory. Semantics enable vertex programs and fragment programs to connect to the rest of the graphics pipeline, and they define the special input and output registers that we mentioned above. Semantics mostly used by a vertex program are **POSITION, COLOR** and **TEXTCOORD** (but others are available and will be shown later). Input and output semantics may have the same name and may or may not contain the same value. In the case of **POSITION**, for example, the input parameter – the position – will be that supplied by the application, and the output will be the transformed value. The register into which the transformed position is written is then used by the rasterizer.

In the case of **COLOR**, the input and output values may be the same as in Listing 1.1. Since semantics reflect the actual hardware, there are constraints. For example, a fragment program must calculate a single fragment colour with which to update the frame buffer. It may also output a modified depth value.

Input semantics in a vertex program have values set by the application via the graphics API, as we explain later. Output semantics in a vertex program enable results calculated by the vertex program to be sent down the pipeline and into the fragment processor.

Types and Library Functions

Cg has native support for vector types as in

```
float4    clipPosition : POSITION;
```

reflecting the hardware support for vectors. It also supports matrices as in

```
float4x4 modelviewProjection;
```

which declares a 16 element matrix.

The Cg standard library (see also Appendix 1.1) contains built-in functions that operate on scalars and vectors. Many of these map to a single GPU function and are thus very efficient. For example,

```
mul(modelviewProjection, oPosition);
```

Specifies a matrix multiplication; in this case multiplying the 4×4 modelviewProjection matrix by the 1x4 oPosition.

Varying and Nonvarying Parameters

The declaration

```
uniform float4x4 modelviewProjection;
```

specifies a variable as **uniform** which means that it is allocated a value by the application (i.e., not within the Cg program), and this value must persist during the processing of a batch of vertices. That is, it will be constant for a batch of vertices until it is changed by the application. The only variable type in Cg that is not allowed to vary is **const**.

The other variables in our first vertex program:

```
    float4 oPosition    : POSITION,
    float4 colour       : COLOR,
out float4 clipPosition : POSITION,
out float4 oColour      : COLOR,
```

are bound to the input and output registers and will in general have changing values per vertex–the input vertex stream receiving data from the application interface and the output stream receiving the results of the calculation(s) of the vertex program.

Shaders and Application Programs

In this section, we look at the business of running the C++/OpenGL application that uses the vertex and fragment programs to render the cube in Figure 1.3. At this stage, the additions to the basic application are somewhat more involved than the simple Cg code, but of course we will progress to develop vertex and fragment programs of far greater length and complexity.

Again the style is that of an overview, dealing mainly with the function of the commands and with the absolute minimum of detail. More detail can be obtained by consulting [FERN03]. As is the way with such topics, some require more words than others to explain.

In the listing, bold type is used to highlight the commands whose function we explain.

Listing 1.3

A simple OpenGL application that renders the cube shown in Figure 1.3.

```
#include <math.h>
#include <stdio.h>
#include <stdlib.h>
#include <GL/glut.h>
#include <Cg/cg.h>
#include <Cg/cgGL.h>

static CGcontext context = NULL;
static CGprogram vertexProg = NULL, fragmentProg = NULL;
static CGparameter modelViewProjParam = NULL;

GLint CubeFaces[6][4] =
{
    {0, 1, 2, 3}, {3, 2, 6, 7}, {7, 6, 5, 4},
    {4, 5, 1, 0}, {5, 6, 2, 1}, {7, 4, 0, 3}
};

GLfloat CubeVertices[8][3];
```

```
#define MATRIX_INDEX(i, j) (j + i * 4)

static void DrawCube(void)
{
        /* Enable profile and bind vertex program */
        cgGLEnableProfile(CG_PROFILE_VP20);
        cgGLBindProgram(vertexProg);

        /* set the parameters used by it */
        cgGLSetStateMatrixParameter(modelViewProjParam,
                        CG_GL_MODELVIEW_PROJECTION_MATRIX,
                        CG_GL_MATRIX_IDENTITY);

        /* the same with fragment program */
        cgGLEnableProfile(CG_PROFILE_FP20);
        cgGLBindProgram(fragmentProg);

  /* render primitives as normal */
  for(int i = 0; i < 6; i++)
   {
    glBegin(GL_QUADS);

    glColor3fv(&CubeVertices[CubeFaces[i][0]][0]);
    glVertex3fv(&CubeVertices[CubeFaces[i][0]][0]);
    glColor3fv(&CubeVertices[CubeFaces[i][1]][0]);
    glVertex3fv(&CubeVertices[CubeFaces[i][1]][0]);
    glColor3fv(&CubeVertices[CubeFaces[i][2]][0]);
    glVertex3fv(&CubeVertices[CubeFaces[i][2]][0]);
    glColor3fv(&CubeVertices[CubeFaces[i][3]][0]);
    glVertex3fv(&CubeVertices[CubeFaces[i][3]][0]);

    glEnd();
   }

        /* disable profiles and return control to default programs */
        cgGLDisableProfile(CG_PROFILE_FP20);
        cgGLDisableProfile(CG_PROFILE_VP20);
}
```

```
static void Display(void)
{
  glClear(GL_COLOR_BUFFER_BIT | GL_DEPTH_BUFFER_BIT);
  DrawCube();
  glutSwapBuffers();
}

static void InitializeGlut(int *argc, char *argv[])
{
  glutInit(argc, argv);
  glutInitDisplayMode(GLUT_DOUBLE | GLUT_RGB | GLUT_DEPTH);
  glutInitWindowSize(512, 512);
  glutCreateWindow(argv[0]);
  glutDisplayFunc(Display);

  InitializeCube(CubeVertices);

  glDisable(GL_LIGHTING);

  /* Use depth buffering for hidden surface elimination. */
  glEnable(GL_DEPTH_TEST);

  /* Setup the view of the cube. */
  glMatrixMode(GL_PROJECTION);
  gluPerspective( /* field of view in degree */ 40.0,
                  /* aspect ratio */ 1.0,
                  /* Z near */ 1.0, /* Z far */ 10.0);
  glMatrixMode(GL_MODELVIEW);
  gluLookAt(0.0, 0.0, 5.0,  /* eye is at (0,0,5) */
            0.0, 0.0, 0.0,  /* center is at (0,0,0) */
            0.0, 1.0, 0.);  /* up is in positive Y direction */
}

int main(int argc, char *argv[])
{
  InitializeGlut(&argc, argv);

  context = cgCreateContext();
```

```
/* loading programs from files*/
vertexProg = cgCreateProgramFromFile(context,
                        CG_SOURCE, "vertexProg.cg",
                        CG_PROFILE_VP20,
                        NULL, NULL);

  fragmentProg = cgCreateProgramFromFile(context,
                        CG_SOURCE, "fragmentProg.cg",
                        CG_PROFILE_FP20,
                        NULL, NULL);

if(vertexProg != NULL && fragmentProg != NULL)
{
// load progs and retrieve references to non-standard parameters
 cgGLLoadProgram(vertexProg);
 ModelViewProjParam =
                cgGetNamedParameter(vertexProg,"modelViewProj");

  cgGLLoadProgram(fragmentProg);
 }

glutMainLoop();

cgDestroyProgram(fragmentProg);
cgDestroyProgram(vertexProg);
cgDestroyContext(context);

 return 0;
}
```

Runtime Library

```
#include <Cg/cg.h>
#include <Cg/cgGL.h>
```

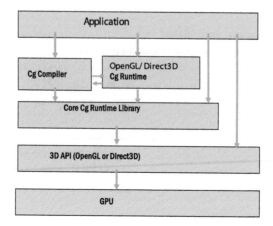

Figure 1.4. Cg system architecture.

Note that the functions used in Listing 1.3 are of the form **cg<name>()** or **cgGL<name>()**. These are functions from the Cg runtime library consisting of API specific (OpenGL) functions. The form **cg<name>()** specifies functions from the API independent or core part of the library. The Cg runtime library is itself an API that enables an application to compile and link programs at runtime. How everything fits together is shown in Figure 1.4.

We now explain the highlighted elements in the code.

Context

We need to declare a Cg-specific global variable which functions as a 'container' for multiple Cg programs. It may also contain multiple profiles.

```
/* Test cgContext creation */
context = cgCreateContext();
```

Compiling and Loading from File

The purpose of a compiler is to map your specification, in the form of Cg code, into highly optimised assembly code. Optimisation is critically important in shading language compilers, and the compiler makes choices, within the current profile, on how best to translate your code into executable instructions.

Loading programs from files is straightforward as the extract in Listing 1.4 demonstrates. **CgCreateProgram()** causes the named source file to be compiled.

Compilation is therefore dynamic, although static compilation can be used when you want to check Cg programs without running the application.

Runtime compilation is preferred to enable generic shaders to be targeted to different hardware at runtime. However, there is a disadvantage to this: as the hardware becomes more and more powerful, so shaders are becoming longer and more complex (with loops and true if/else statements). The compiler must produce highly optimised code, and this will inevitably lead to longer compile times.

Listing 1.4

Loading and compiling a vertex and fragment program.

```
/* loading programs from files*/
vertexProg = cgCreateProgramFromFile(context,
            CG_SOURCE, "vertexProg.cg",
            CG_PROFILE_VP20,
            NULL, NULL);
fragmentProg = cgCreateProgramFromFile(context,
            CG_SOURCE, "fragmentProg.cg",
            CG_PROFILE_FP20,
            NULL, NULL);
```

Profiles and Binding

A profile must be specified when a Cg program is compiled—one for the vertex processor and one for the fragment processor as shown in Listing 1.5.

Listing 1.5

Specifying vertex and fragment profiles and binding the programs.

```
/* Enable profile and bind vertex program */
cgGLEnableProfile(CG_PROFILE_VP20);
cgGLBindProgram(vertexProg);

/* set the parameters used by it */
cgGLSetStateMatrixParameter(modelViewProjParam,
                CG_GL_MODELVIEW_PROJECTION_MATRIX,
                CG_GL_MATRIX_IDENTITY);

/* the same with fragment program */
cgGLEnableProfile(CG_PROFILE_FP20);
cgGLBindProgram(fragmentProg);
```

A profile, **cgGLEnableProfile()**, specifies a particular combination of GPU hardware and graphics API facilities, and your Cg program must limit itself to facilities contained by the profile. Thus, a programmer can adopt one of two strategies: write for the lowest common denominator profile, or write to target a particular profile. Writing programs beyond the limits of the profile will cause a profile dependent error. Such errors divide into three categories:

1. **Capability**—attempting to do something beyond the (current) capability of the GPU; for example, texture access from within a vertex program on older hardware.

2. **Context**—not incorporating a mandatory operation such as outputting a parameter to the **POSITION** semantic in a vertex program.

3. **Capacity**—exceeding the capacity of the hardware by, for example, in a fragment program attempting to make more texture accesses in a single pass than the hardware is capable of.

Profile errors are detected by the Cg compiler at compile time. In the above example **vp20** is used to compile the Cg source code into a vertex program which is then used by an NVIDIA OpenGL extension. Profiles may be manufacturer specific (as in the case of **vp20**) or they may be multivendor. For our simple example, we could have used **arbvp1**, a multivendor profile. The binding semantics for the inputs and outputs of the different profiles are given in [FERN03] and these give information on the relationship between the Cg semantic and the API command. For example, **POSITION** in a vertex program is the vertex position passed by glVertex(). Output semantics of the vertex processor together with the input semantics of the fragment processor enable the communication of processed vertex attributes into the fragment processor.

As the name implies, **cgGLSetStateMatrixParameter()** communicates the OpenGL state to the Cg runtime state. The modelviewProjection matrix is an example of a uniform parameter or state whose value persists over many invocations of the vertex program, until it is changed by the application program. This contrasts with a varying input parameter, such as vertex position and texture co-ordinate, which in general changes with every vertex. Clearly, the distinction between a uniform and varying parameter is critical to generate efficient assembly code.

Binding the vertex and fragment programs is accomplished by **cgGLBindProgram().** We can only bind a single vertex and fragment program at any instant. When bound, a program will load all its uniform parameters as they wore last set. But the stardard pipeline will only be replaced by the programmable pipeline after the profile is enabled using **cgGLEnableProfile().** Disabling a profile with **cgGLDisableProfile()** will return processing to the standard pipeline functionality for that stage.

Loading and Activating

Loading a vertex program and/or a fragment program causes the compiled code to be passed to the 3D API that is being used. The code in Listing 1.6 should be self-explanatory.

Listing 1.6

Loading, activating and destroying.

```
if(vertexProg != NULL && fragmentProg != NULL)
{
 /*  load progs and retrieve references
     to non-standard parameters */
 cgGLLoadProgram(vertexProg);
 ModelViewProjParam = cgGetNamedParameter(
                     vertexProg,"modelViewProj");
  cgGLLoadProgram(fragmentProg);
}


glutMainLoop();


cgDestroyProgram(fragmentProg);
cgDestroyProgram(vertexProg);
cgDestroyContext(context);
```

Cg Functionality

The purpose of this section is to give a painless introduction to Cg functionality. At this stage, we will deal with expressions, vectors and variables. As we develop more complex shaders, we will introduce more and more of Cg. Again, we assume knowledge of C or C++ and thus we do not pretend (or intend) to present a comprehensive reference. For example, we assume that you will understand

Figure 1.5. 3D object without vertex program (left) and with inflate program activated (right).

what a type specifier such as **float4** means (a four component vector made of floats with *x*, *y*, *z* and *w* components).

We begin by presenting a vertex program (Listing 1.7) which 'inflates' an object by moving each vertex along the associated vertex normal giving the effect shown in Figure 1.5.

Listing 1.7

Vertex program to inflate a 3D object.

```
struct app2vert
{
        float4 pos       : POSITION;
        float4 color     : COLOR;
        float4 normal    : NORMAL;
        float4 texcoord  : TEXCOORD0;
};

struct vert2frag
{
        float4 hpos      : POSITION;
        float4 color     : COLOR;
        float4 texcoord  : TEXCOORD0;

};

vert2frag main_vert( app2vert IN,
                     uniform float4x4 modelviewproj,
```

```
                      uniform float inflate_factor)
{

        vert2frag OUT;


        float4 pos = IN.pos + IN.normal*inflate_factor;
        pos.w=1;
        OUT.hpos   = mul(modelviewproj,pos);


        OUT.pos    = pos;


        OUT.color    = IN.color;
        OUT.texcoord = IN.texcoord;
        OUT.normal   = IN.normal;


        return OUT;

}
```

This vertex program illustrates some functionality (arithmetic expressions involving vectors and scalars) and variables of different categories. You can see from this the similarity to C and C++.

More on Variables

In Listing 1.1, the binding semantics were specified on program parameters (the function return type was void). Cg supports structures the same way as C does, and we can optionally use a structure and specify the binding on structure elements. In the function body in Listing 1.7, all the statements are using structures.

Note that we now have another **uniform** parameter **inflate_factor** which is constant for the execution duration of the vertex program and is changed by the application.

As we have seen, variables can be **uniform** or varying. We can also define a constant type as in

```
const float pi   = 3.14159;
```

As is the convention in all high-level languages, a constant type cannot be assigned to or modified in any way. It should be clear that there is a difference between **uniform** and **const: uniform** indicates that the variable's value comes from the application and can be changed by the application (but not in the vertex or fragment program); a **const** can never be changed.

Precision and range of floating point numbers in Cg are determined by the profile, and two types are available: **half** and **float.** Integer data types are **int, long, short** and **char.** Current GPU hardware only use float numbers internally (half 16 bit and float 32 bit) so although integer types are available in Cg internally, they will map to float variables and will be treated as floats.

Maths Expressions

In the above vertex program:

```
float4 pos = IN.pos + IN.normal*inflate_factor
```

assigns the result of an expression involving the sum of a position **IN.pos** and a vector **IN.normal** which has been multiplied by a scalar **inflate_factor.** This assignment statement is also a vector constructor. In general, a vector constructor can appear anywhere in an arithmetic expression.

Cg has the same operators as C (**+, -, *, /**) and as you would expect, these exhibit the same precedence and associativity as C. Boolean types are allowed together with relational operators (**<, <=, >, >=, ==, !=**) and Boolean operators (**&&, ||, !**). Conditional expression operators (**?, :**) and assignment expressions (**=, +=, -=, *= ,/=**) are supported. A full list is given in Appendix 1.1.

Standard library built-in functions considerably simplify GPU programming. We have already used **mul()** which multiplies two matrices together. A complete list is given in Appendix 1.1. These functions are divided into two categories, mathematical and geometric. There is a comprehensive (51) library of mathematical functions consisting of the expected trigonometric functions and other common mathematical operations. Also included are functions commonly required in rendering, such as **lit()** which performs the comparisons

$$N \cdot L < 0 \text{ and } N \cdot H < 0$$

and evaluates Boolean expressions of these comparisons.

There are six geometric functions and again these are operations commonly required in rendering such as **reflect()** which calculates a reflected vector given an incoming vector and a surface normal.

Texture map functions will be introduced in Chapter 3. Partial derivative functions **ddx()** and **ddy()**, available only on advanced fragment profiles, calculate an approximate derivative of a fragment with respect to screen space coordinates **x** and **y**.

The Cg Standard library features function overloading in most of its routines. As in C++, overloading is both by the number of operands and their type.

Overloading means that a function, which conceptually performs the same task on objects of different types, can have the same name. The compiler must select the appropriate routine for the function call by examining the number of arguments and their type as in, for example

```
mul(matrix,matrix);
mul(matrix,vector);
mul(vector,matrix);
```

which are used for, as the parameters imply, multiplying matrices by vectors and matrices by matrices.

Vectors and Matrices

In Cg we can operate on both vectors and scalars. Examples of vector operations will follow in due course in Chapter 2. In Cg, **float2**, **float3** and **float4** are vectors and **float2x2**, **float3x3**, **float4x4** and **float4x3** are matrices.

Component by component operations ($*$, $/$, $-$, $+$) use the same operators as scalars and dot and cross product are implemented by the standard functions **dot()** and **cross()**. These functions exploit the hardware architecture, as you would expect, and are more efficient than writing a dot product of a pair of four component vectors, for example, as an expression with four multiplies and three additions.

Note that the standard arithmetic operators do not support matrix operands; matrix multiplication is implemented by **mul()** introduced in the previous section.

Of course, in practice we do not only consider 'actual' vectors as **float4**, but also quantities such as position (of a particle, say) which would be a **float3** and can use the vector hardware of the GPU. This is important for the point of view of efficiency.

A 'swizzling' operator '.' enables the components of a vector to be rearranged to form a new vector as in

```
float4(a,b,c,d).wzyx  produces  float4(d,c,b,a)
```

Characters **r,g,b,a** can also be used (instead of **x,y,z,w**), but these sets cannot be mixed. More complicated swizzling operations are available for matrices.

Write masking enables selected components only to be updated by an assignment. For example:

```
// assume vect1  =  (7.0,4.0,2.0,5.0)
// and    vect2  =  (1.0,3.0)
vect1.gb = vect2;   //vect1 = (7.0,1.0,3.0,5.0)
```

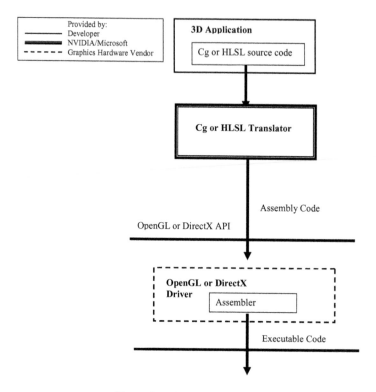

Figure 1.6. Cg/HLSL execution environment.

Features Not Supported

Finally because it is a high-level language for graphics-specialized hardware, there are many high-level language constructs and facilities not supported by Cg. Cg has been described as "programming in the small" and in this respect has no support for "C++ programming in the large" concepts such as classes, templates, operator overloading exception handling and name spaces. Cg does not support string processing, file input/output and memory allocation.

Cg, GLSL and HLSL

As we have already pointed out, all three languages are similar because they all conform to the CPU, vertex shader, fragment shader model. All three languages share a set of generic features. The differences are thus in the detail and the execution environment.

One of the most important aspects of Cg, in the context of other environments, is that the Cg compiler can generate DirectX or OpenGL vertex shader (or fragment shader) assembly code. This is facilitated by calls to Cg Runtime library.

Although in the preceding text we have loosely used the term "compiler", both Cg and HLSL shaders are *translated* into assembly code, which is then input to the OpenGL or Direct 3D API as shown in Figure 1.6. This contrasts with GLSL, where the compiler is part of the driver. (In this case, the compiler is supplied by the manufacturer.)

Appendix 1.1: Mathematical and Geometric Functions

Portions copyright (c) NVIDIA Corporation, 2001-2005. Reprinted with permission.

Mathematical Functions	
Function	**Description**
abs(x)	Absolute value of x
acos(x)	Arccosine of x in range $[-\pi/2, \pi/2]$, x in $[-1,1]$
all(x)	Returns true if every component of x is not equal to 0. Returns false otherwise.
any(x)	Returns true if any component of x is not equal to 0. Returns false otherwise.
asin(x)	Arcsine of x in range $[0, \pi]$; x should be in $[-1,1]$.
atan(x)	Arctangent of x in range $[-\pi/2, \pi/2]$
atan2(y, x)	Arctangent of y/x in range $[-\pi, \pi]$
ceil(x)	Smallest integer not less than x
clamp(x, a, b)	x clamped to the range $[a,b]$ as follows: • Returns a if x is less than a. • Returns b if x is greater than b. • Returns x otherwise.
cos(x)	Cosine of x
cosh(x)	Hyperbolic cosine of x
cross(a, b)	Cross product of vectors a and b; a and b must be 3-component vectors.
degress(x)	Radian-to-degree conversion
determinant(M)	Determinant of matrix M
dot(a, b)	Dot product of vectors a and b
exp(x)	Exponential function e^x
exp2(x)	Exponential function 2^x
floor(x)	Largest integer not greater than x

Mathematical Functions	
Function	**Description**
`fmod(x, y)`	Remainder of x/y, with the same sign as x. If y is zero, the result is implementation-defined.
`frac(x)`	Fractional part of x
`frexp(x, out exp)`	Splits x into a normalized fraction in the interval $[1/2, 1)$, which is returned, and a power of 2, which is stored in exp. If x is zero, both parts of the result are zero.
`isfinite(x)`	Returns `true` if x is finite
`isinf(x)`	Returns `true` if x is infinite
`isnan(x)`	Returns `true` if x is NaN (not a number)
`ldexp(x, n)`	$x * 2^n$
`lerp(a, b, f)`	Linear interpolation: $(1-f)*a + b*f$ where a and b are matching vector or scalar types. f can be either a scalar or a vector of the same type as a and b.
`lit(ndotl, ndoth, m)`	Computes lighting coefficients for ambient, diffuse, and specular light contributions. Returns a 4-vector as follows: • The x component of the result vector contains the ambient coefficient, which is always 1.0. • The y component contains the diffuse coefficient which is zero if $(n \bullet 1) < 0$; otherwise $(n \bullet 1)$. • The z component contains the specular coefficient which is zero if either $(n \bullet 1) < 0$ or $(n \bullet h) < 0$; $(n \bullet h)^m$ otherwise. • The w component is 1.0. There is no vectorized version of this function
`log(x)`	Natural logarithm $\ln(x)$; x must be greater than zero.
`log2(x)`	Base 2 logarithm of x; x must be greater than zero.
`log10(x)`	Base 10 logarithm of x; x must be greater than zero.
`max(a, b)`	Maximum of a and b

Mathematical Functions

Function	Description
min(a, b)	Minimum of a and b
modf(x, out ip)	Splits x into integral and fractional parts, each with the same sign as x. Stores the integral part in ip and returns the fractional part.
mul(M, N)	Matrix product of matrix M and matrix N, as shown below: $$mul(M, N) = \begin{bmatrix} M_{11} & M_{21} & M_{31} & M_{41} \\ M_{12} & M_{22} & M_{32} & M_{42} \\ M_{13} & M_{23} & M_{33} & M_{43} \\ M_{14} & M_{24} & M_{34} & M_{44} \end{bmatrix} \begin{bmatrix} N_{11} & N_{21} & N_{31} & N_{41} \\ N_{12} & N_{22} & N_{32} & N_{42} \\ N_{13} & N_{23} & N_{33} & N_{43} \\ N_{14} & N_{23} & N_{34} & N_{44} \end{bmatrix}$$ If M has size AxB, and N has size BxC, returns a matrix of size AxC.
mul(M, v)	Product of matrix M and column vector v, as shown below: $$mul(M, v) = \begin{bmatrix} M_{11} & M_{21} & M_{31} & M_{41} \\ M_{12} & M_{22} & M_{32} & M_{42} \\ M_{13} & M_{23} & M_{33} & M_{43} \\ M_{14} & M_{24} & M_{34} & M_{44} \end{bmatrix} \begin{bmatrix} V_1 \\ V_2 \\ V_3 \\ V_4 \end{bmatrix}$$ If M is an AxB matrix and v is an Bx1 vector, returns an Ax1 vector.
mul(v, M)	Product of row vector v and matrix M, as shown below: $$mul(v, M) = \begin{bmatrix} V_1 & V_2 & V_3 & V_4 \end{bmatrix} \begin{bmatrix} M_{11} & M_{21} & M_{31} & M_{41} \\ M_{12} & M_{22} & M_{32} & M_{42} \\ M_{13} & M_{23} & M_{33} & M_{43} \\ M_{14} & M_{24} & M_{34} & M_{44} \end{bmatrix}$$ If v is a 1xA vector and M is an AxB matrix, returns a 1xB vector.
noise(x)	Either a 1-, 2-, or 3-dimensional noise function depending on the type of its argument. The returned value is between zero and one and is always the same for a given input value.
pow(x, y)	x^y
radians(x)	Degree-to-radian conversion

Mathematical Functions	
Function	**Description**
`round(x)`	Closest integer to x
`rsqrt(x)`	Reciprocal square root of x; x must be greater than zero.
`sign(x)`	1 if $x > 0$; -1 if $x < 0$; 0 otherwise.
`sin(x)`	Sine of x
`sincos(float x,` `   out s, out c)`	s is set to the sine of x, and c is set to the cosine of x. If `sin(x)` and `cos(x)` are both needed, this function is more efficient than calculating each individually.
`sinh(x)`	Hyperbolic sine of x
`smoothstep(min,` `   max, x)`	For values of x between min and max, returns a smoothly varying value that ranges from 0 at $x = min$ to 1 at $x = max$. x is clamped to the range $[min, max]$ and then the interpolation formula is evaluated: $-2*((x\text{-}min)/(max\text{-}min))^3 + 3*((x\text{-}min)/(max\text{-}min))^2$
`step(a, x)`	0 if $x < a$; 1 if $x >= a$.
`sqrt(x)`	Square root of x; x must be greater than zero.
`tan(x)`	Tangent of x
`tanh(x)`	Hyperbolic tangent of x
`transpose(M)`	Matrix transpose of matrix M. If M is an A×B matrix, the transpose of M is a B×A matrix whose first column is the first row of M, whose second column is the second row of M, whose third column is the third row of M, and so on.

Chapter Two

Light/Object Shaders

Introduction

In this chapter, we will introduce basic shaders that implement local reflection models, calculating the light reflected from a vertex or a fragment. Most rendering applications will contain some kind of local reflection model, and such applications are the mainstream use of the new hardware. The new language features introduced will be flow control: conditional statements and deterministic loops.

Also in the chapter, we will look at using some of the more advanced techniques that are beginning to be used with the aid of GPUs; in particular, deferred shading and using GPUs in shading complex scenes with multiple lights.

Per-Vertex Shading

In this section, we implement Gouraud shading introducing flow control in the form of an `if` statement. Gouraud shading can easily be incorporated in a vertex program. First, we remind ourselves of the rationale of Gouraud shading. We calculate the reflected light at each vertex of an object due to incident light in the form of a point source using the following equation:

$$I = k_a I_a + I_i \left(k_d (\mathbf{L} \cdot \mathbf{N}) + k_s (\mathbf{R} \cdot \mathbf{V})^n \right)$$

The definitions of all the parameters in the equations are as follows:
- k_a is the ambient reflection coefficient;
- I_a is the colour and intensity of the ambient component;
- I_i is the colour and intensity of the (point) light source;

- k_d is the diffuse reflection coefficient;
- **L** is the normalised vector from the vertex to the light source;
- **N** is the normalised vertex normal;
- k_s is the specular reflection coefficient;
- **R** is the normalised reflection vector;
- **V** is the normalised view vector; and
- n is the shiniess index.

That is, we calculate a linear combination of the ambient reflectance, the diffuse reflected light and the specular contribution:

reflected_light = ambient + diffuse + specular

The behaviour of this equation is illustrated in Figure 2.1, which shows the light intensity at a single point P (the vertex) as a function of the orientation of the viewing vector **V**. The figure is a cross-sectional slice through a function which is a hemisphere, centred on P, with a reflection lobe superimposed. The semicircle is the sum of the constant ambient term and the diffuse term, which is constant for a particular value of **N**. Addition of the specular term gives the profile shown in the figure. As the value of n is increased the specular bump is narrowed.

Usually we make geometric simplifications that reduce the complexity of the equation but which do not visibly affect the quality of the shading. First, if the light source is considered a point source located at infinity, then **L** is constant over the domain of the scene. Second, we can also place the viewpoint at infinity making **V** constant. (Of course, for the view and perspective transformation, the viewpoint needs to be firmly located in world space, so we end up using a finite viewpoint for the geometric transformations and an infinite one for the shading equation.)

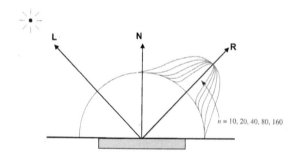

Figure 2.1 A visualisation of the shading equation used in Gouraud and Phong shading for a varying specular index.

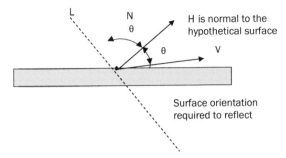

Figure 2.2. The halfway vector H.

Another common approximation is to replace **R**, which is a variable vector with **(N · H)**. **H** is the 'halfway' vector which is the unit normal to a hypothetical surface that is oriented in a direction halfway between the light direction vector **L** and the viewing vector **V** (Figure 2.2). **H** is defined as

$$\mathbf{H} = \mathbf{L} + \mathbf{V}$$

This is the orientation that a surface would require if it were to reflect light maximally along the **V** direction. Our shading equation now becomes

$$I = I_a k_a + I_i\left(k_d(\mathbf{L}\cdot\mathbf{N}) + k_s\,(\mathbf{N}\cdot\mathbf{H})^n\right)$$

because the term **(N · H)** varies in (approximately) the same manner as **(R · V)**.[1] We can implement the diffuse component in the shader as

```
float3  L        = normalize(lightPosition - P);
float3  diffuse = kd*Ii*max(dot(N,L),0);
```

and the specular term as

```
float3 V  =          normalize(eyePosition - P);
float3 H  =          normalize(L + V);
float   specular  =  ks*Ii*pow(max(dot(N,H),0),ns);
```

This immediately raises the question: why calculate the specular component and possibly set it to zero, why not position an **if-else** statement with the else part containing the specular calculation as follows?

....

[1] Note that some texts refer to Phong shading as the calculation of the specular term using **(R · V)** and using **(N · H)** as Blinn shading (Blinn was the originator of the halfway vector). In fact, the two methods give slightly different results, with the **(N · H)** term resulting in larger highlights. This means that for particular orientations of **V** you may see a highlight using **(N · H)** but not one using **(R · V)**. We adhere to the traditional definition—Gouraud shading as a per-vertex calculation and Phong shading as a per-fragment computation.

```
if (diffuse == 0)
    specular = 0;
else
    specular = <specular calculations>;
```

The answer is that it does not make any difference to the efficiency of the program. Both branches of an **if-else** statement are executed. If the result of the Boolean comparison is true, then the instructions following the **else** part, when executed, will have any output masked out. Thus it is immaterial whether we use an **if-else** before the specular calculation or a simple if statement after.

The complete Cg code for the Gouraud shader is Listing 2.1.

Listing 2.1

A vertex shader implementing Gouraud shading.

```
void Gouraud_vertex(
    float4 iPosition : POSITION,
    float3 N         : NORMAL,

    out float4 oPosition : POSITION,
    out float4 oColour   : COLOUR,

    uniform float4x4 modelviewProjection,
    uniform float3   Ia,
    uniform float3   Ii,
    uniform float3   lightPosition,
    uniform float3   eyePosition,
    uniform float3   ke,
    uniform float3   ka,
    uniform float3   kd,
    uniform float3   ks,
    uniform float    ns)
{
    oPosition = mul(modelviewProjection,
                    iPosition);

    float3 P = iPosition.xyz;

    // calculate ambient contribution
    float3 ambient = Ia*ka;
```

```
//calculate diffuse contribution
float3 L = normalize(lightPosition - P);
float3  diffuse = kd*Ii*max(dot(N,L),0);

//calculate specular contribution
float3 V  = normalize(eyePosition - P);
float3 H  = normalize(L + V);
float  specular = ks*Ii*
      pow(max(dot(N,H),0),ns);

if (diffuse == 0)
   specular = 0;

oColour.xyz  = ambient+diffuse+specular;
oColour.z  = 1:
}
```

No fragment program is required following this vertex shader: the vertex calculations are interpolated in the rasterizer and interpolator part of the pipeline.

Finally, we could have used the library function `lit()` to replace the diffuse and specular contribution calculations as follows:

```
float4 shading_geom = lit(dot(N,L),dot(N,H),ns);
diffuse  = kd * Ii * shading_geom.y;
specular = ks * Ii * shading_geom.z;
```

From which you can deduce that the four-component vector `lit()` returns in its y component

a value 0 if $(\mathbf{N} \cdot \mathbf{L}) < 0$ otherwise $(\mathbf{N} \cdot \mathbf{L})$

and returns in its z component

a value 0 if $(\mathbf{N} \cdot \mathbf{L}) < 0$ otherwise $(\mathbf{N} \cdot \mathbf{H})^n$

(the x and w components return 1.0).

Using `lit()` is more efficient and compiles to a single assembly language instruction. As a general rule, library functions should be used as much as possible as they produce highly optimised code. Such efficiency considerations are critically important, particularly in fragment programs which, by definition, will process far more fragments than a vertex program processes vertices. (Typically a fragment program will process millions of fragments per frame, whilst a vertex program, tens of thousands.)

Per-Fragment or Phong Shading

In this section, we implement Phong shading and find out how to carry out vector interpolation.

It is well known that Gouraud shading suffers from poor quality specular highlights as a function of the polygonal resolution of the object, and although it may be used for pre-viewing, nowadays the *de facto* standard for basic shading is Phong shading, which is a per fragment operation and is thus implemented as a fragment program. The shading equation remains exactly the same but is applied at each fragment using an interpolated vertex normal **N**. The fragment program (Listing 2.2) is thus almost exactly the same as the Gouraud vertex program.

```
void   Phong_frag(
           float4 iPosition      : TEXCOORD0,
           float3 N              : TEXCOORD1,
       out float4 oColour        : COLOR,

           uniform float3    Ia,
           uniform float3    Ii,
           uniform float3    lightPosition,
           uniform float3    eyePosition,
           uniform float3    ke,
           uniform float3    ka,
           uniform float3    kd,
           uniform float3    ks,
           uniform float     ns)
{
    float3 P = iPosition.xyz;
    float3 N = normalize(N);

    // calculate ambient contribution
    float3 ambient = Ia*ka;
    //calculate diffuse contribution
```

```
float3 L = normalize(lightPosition - P);
float3 diffuse = kd*Ii*max(dot(N,L),0);

//calculate specular contribution
float3 V  = normalize(eyePosition - P);
float3 H  = normalize(L + V);
float   specular = ks*Ii*
                 pow(max(dot(N,H),0),ns);

oColour.xyz  =  ambient+diffuse+specular;
oColour.z  = 1:
}
```

The important difference is the appearance of the semantics **TEXCOORD0/1**. Listing 2.3 is the vertex program that is required for this particular fragment program. In this, we can see that the vertex normal has been bound to the output semantic **TEXCOORD1,** and the effect of this is that the vertex normals associated with a primitive are interpolated as if they were texture coordinates. The fragment program thus receives an interpolated vertex normal for each fragment. The only other slight difference in the fragment program is the addition of a normalisation operation on the interpolated normal (which will have become denormalised in the linear interpolation process).

Listing 2.3

```
void Phong_vertex(
    float4 iPosition   : POSITION,
    float3 iN          : NORMAL,
out float4 oPosition   : TEXCOORD0,
out float3 oN          : TEXCOORD1,

uniform float4x4 modelviewProjection)
{
    oPosition = mul(modelviewProjection,
                      iPosition);

    oN = iN;
}
```

The vertex program required by the Phong fragment shader.

Figure 2.3. The usual suspects. Clockwise from top left: per-vertex Gouraud (diffuse only), per-vertex Gouraud (with specular), per-pixel Phong (two lights), and per-pixel Phong (one light).

A selection of different shading options is shown in Figure 2.3. Here can be seen the familiar inadequacy of the specular highlight in Gouraud shading.

This occurs as a consequence of the fact that we are only applying the shading equation at vertices. The extreme example is when a polygon is larger than a highlight. In that case, it will not be rendered because no specular component will be calculated at the polygon's vertices. The interpolator simply interpolates the diffuse component—the specular component being zero. Thus, it is a function of the polygonal resolution of the model—if the polygons are sufficiently smaller than the smallest highlight, then this effect will not occur, and Gouraud shading approaches the quality of Phong shading.

Multiple Lights

In this section, we look at the use of loop structures, arrays and internal functions to extend the basic shading model to include multiple light sources and multiple object materials. Arrays are the same as in C and C++ with the exception that pointers cannot be used. We will also briefly discuss the profile-dependent implementation of loops.

We begin by defining an internal function (Listing 2.4) that calculates the diffuse and specular contribution due to each light source, considering only the intensity of the light and the relative geometry of the vertex position with respect to the light and the view vector. That is a material independent calculation which excludes *kd* and *ks*.

Listing 2.4

```
void per_light_contribution(
    Light  light,
    float3 P,
    float3 N,
    float3 eyePosition,
    float3 ns,
out float3 diffuse_component,
out float3 specular_component)
{
  float3 L = normalize(light.position - P);
  float3 V = normalize(eye.position - P);
  float3 H = normalize(L + V);

  float4 shading = lit((dot(N,L),dot(N,H),ns);

  diffuse_component  = light.Ii * shading.y;
  specular_component = light.Ii * shading.z;
}
```

This is then called in the body of the vertex shader, which loops over all the lights for a single object (Listing 2.5).

Listing 2.5

```
void multiple_lights(
    float4 iPosition : POSITION,
    float3 N         : NORMAL,

out float4 oPosition : POSITION,
out float4 oColour   : COLOR

uniform float4x4 modelviewProjection,
```

```
uniform float3    eyePosition,
uniform float3    Ia,
uniform Light     Lights[5],
uniform float     ns,
uniform Material material)
{
  oPosition = mul(modelviewProjection,
                    iPosition);
  float3 ambient = material.ka*Ia;

  float3 diffuse_component;
  float3 specular_component;
  float3 diffuseSum = 0;
  float3 specularSum  = 0;

  for(int  i  =  0;  i < 5; i++)
  {
    per_light_contribution(lights[i],
        iPosition.xyz,N,eyePosition,ns,
        diffuse_component,specular_component);

    diffuseSum  += diffuse_component;
    specularSum += specular_component;
  }

  // apply material reflection coefficients
  float3  diffuse  = material.kd*diffuseSum;
  float3  specular = material.ks*specularSum;

  oColour.xyz = ambient+diffuse+specular;
  oColour.z = 1;
}
```

Finally, we consider the distance attenuation which can be used in the final assignment of a shader to weight both the specular and ambient component. Because a simple distance squared factor does not produce realistic results for nearby point sources, the conventional attenuation factor uses the sum of constant, linear and quadratic coefficients:

$$attenuation\ (d) = \frac{1}{a_c + a_l d + a_q d^2}$$

where:

a_c, a_l and a_q are attenuation constants that can relatively adjusted for different effects, and d is the distance to the light source.

This is implemented as an internal function as follows:

```
float attenuation(float3 P, light light)
{
    float d = distance(P, light.position);
    return 1/(light.ac + light.al*d +
            light.aq*d*d);
}
```

In the above, **distance()** is a library function that returns the Euclidean distance between two points in 3D space.

Using Control Structures

There is an important issue of efficiency when control structures are used in Cg. In older hardware, any loops in the vertex and fragment program must be deterministic, that is, a constant number of loop cycles. This is because there is no actual loop instructions in the hardware assembler, and all loops are unrolled by the compiler so it must know the number of loops at compile time.

In more recent hardware, we can use conditional loops, as this hardware supports such instructions in its assembler. This means we can have the number of loop cycles passed in as a parameter or even calculated inside the program.

Using conditional loops in current hardware incurs a high cost overhead. Conditional loops by definition imply a change in execution flow (jump) which empties the execution pipeline and in most cases will be much slower than an equivalent unrolled version. The trade off between using such features or not depends on the size of the code inside the loop compared with the overhead added by the conditional jumps.

At the moment, conditional statements are implemented in two ways, either as described above, where both the **if** and **else** part are executed, or in more recent hardware, where a jump takes place preventing one part or the other from being executed. We can refer to these two options as *conditional if statement* (using a mask at some instruction outputs) or as *true if statements* (where a conditional jump is used).

Unfortunately, we cannot distinguish between these two strategies in Cg, and currently we must use compiler options to determine what strategy to use. A future feature to be included in Cg is the supporting of compiler 'hints' inserted into code that will select the desired methods to be used at different parts in the program. Such planning needs to be done by considering the relative costs of the alternative options.

Table 2.1 shows the costs associated with such structures that make use of conditional jumps (in assembler format).

Table 2.1

Instruction	Cost (Cycles)
if / endif	4
if / else / endif	6
call	2
ret	2
loop / endloop	4

This table shows, for example, that for a given **if-else** statement; in order for it to be worth using the true **if-else** statement, the number of cycles for the instructions being avoided by the jumps must be much higher than the associated cost of 6.

Light Source Considerations

Light Source Objects

The two types of the most commonly used light source–a point source and a directional source–are defined as follows. A point light source is a source that is near to the surface of the object. In this case, we take into account its position and the direction ($\mathbf{L}$) of the source from the point being rendered. That is, in the fragment shader we recalculate $\mathbf{L}$ for every fragment. We term a directional light source to be a source located very far away, in which case we assume that $\mathbf{L}$ is constant. All light rays hitting the surface are parallel for an infinite source, or nearly so for a source such as the sun.

In third place in popularity is the spotlight, which can take different forms. The easiest spotlight to construct is a cone emanating from a point. In this case, a point is illuminated or not depending on whether it is contained within the cone. This calculation uses the vectors $\mathbf{D}$ and $\mathbf{L}$, the point being rendered P and a cone (cut-off) angle θ (Figure 2.4).

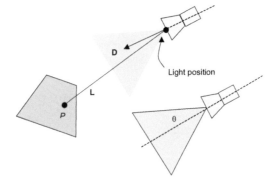

Figure 2.4. The simplest spotlight.

That is:

if $\mathbf{D} \cdot \mathbf{L} < \cos(\theta)$ **then** P is contained by cone

Using **Phong_frag** we can define an internal function **Ispot()** which checks for a spotlight contribution, calls the function in the shader and simply replaces every occurrence of **Ii** with **Ispot*Ii** in **Phong_frag**.

```
float3 Ispot(float3 P, spot S)
{
    float3 L = normalize(P-S.lightPosition);

    if (dot(S.D,L)<=S.cosTheta)
        return 1;
    else
        return 0;
}
```

Of course this is a zero/one light with an abrupt cut-off resulting in a sharp boundary between points on the surface illuminated by ambient light and those illuminated by both ambient light and the spot light. A better effect is obtainable by considering that the intensity in the cone of a spotlight is not constant but drops off as a function of increasing angle. This can be implemented by using two concentric cones—an inner one of constant intensity and an outer. If P falls in the outer cone, the intensity is reduced as a function of the distance between P and the inner cone. An example of a simple scene illuminated by such a light object is shown in Figure 2.5.

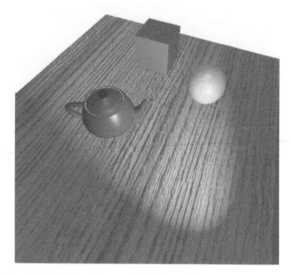

Figure 2.5. A simple scene illuminated by a fall-off spotlight.

Light versus Surface Shaders

An idea that W. Mark *et al.* [MARK03] suggest you borrow from RenderMan is to split the notion of a shader into a light shader and a surface shader.[2] The 'workings' of the light are separated from the surface shader, which performs the basic shading calculation. Thus, we can use the same generic surface shader and loop over light sources of different types.

A light source shader calculates the intensity (and colour) emitted by the light source object that arrives at the point on the surface currently being rendered. A surface shader calculates the light reflected from the surface of an object using the light arriving at the point as calculated by the light shader. Thus, a surface shader invokes one or more light shaders.

The vertex program in Listing 2.6 partially illustrates this concept. This is based on the example of Mark *et al.* in [MARK03]. The calculations that evaluate the contribution due to the geometry of the surface and light must be independent of the properties of the light since we are using the internal function for all the lights. We can make this separation more explicit by having separate light and surface shaders. This is particularly important when the type of light varies—for example, a point source or a spotlight.

....

[2] RenderMan categorises five types of shaders: surface, light, displacement, volume and image shaders.

This idea can be implemented in a single shader by using interfaces (similar to virtual function in C++). We can define a base light object with *direction* and *illuminate* methods and then implement deriving objects for different light types that will implement the methods differently. Thus, the application can pass in different light objects in a light array to the vertex program, and the vertex program will use them all as base light objects not knowing their specific different illumination functions.

.... Listing 2.6

```
// base light object
interface light
{
  float3 get_light_dir(float3 p);
  float4 get_light_properties(float3 p,
                              out float3 light_dir);
};


// point light object (light shader)
struct light_point : light
{
  float3 pos, color;

  float3 get_light_dir(float3 p)
  { return pos - p; }

  float3 get_light_properties(float3 p,
                              out float3 light_dir)
  {
    light_dir = normalize(get_light_dir(p));
    return color;
  }
};


// directional light object (light shader)
struct light_directional : light
{
  float3 dir, color;
```

Implementing surface and light shaders.

```
float3 get_light_dir(float3 p)
{ return dir; }

float3 get_light_properties(float3 p,
                            out float3 light_dir)
{
  light_dir = normalize(get_light_dir(p));
  return color;
}
};


// main program (surface shader)
float4 main(appin IN, out float4 OUT,
            uniform light lights[])
{
  ...

  // for each light
  for (int i=0; i < lights.Length; i++)
  {
    // get dir/color
    light_color = lights[i].
                  get_light_properties(IN.pos, L);
    // compute illumination
    color += light_color *
             illuminate(L,IN.normal);
  }
  OUT = color;
};
```

Structural Efficiency Considerations in Basic Shading

Efficiency considerations in GPU programming are extremely important, and we refer to such factors from time to time in the context of the technique currently being discussed. In this section, we look at structural considerations in basic rendering.

A powerful way to structure the rendering process is to use double-speed Z-only rendering together with early Z rejection. Here we first draw the scene masking out the frame buffer writes (that is, a render pass without any material information, texture map, etc., which in some hardware executes at double fill-rate speed). Then we draw the lighting pass using all material and light information masking out the depth buffer writes and using a equal depth test option. This will mean that fragments hidden by other geometry will not invoke the fragment shader due to the early Z rejection (only visible fragments will run the illumination program). The pseudocode for this process is as follows:

```
color_write=false
z_write=true
z_test=less
draw_scene_no_materials() // no shaders
color_write=true
z_write=false
z_test=equal
draw_scene_with_materials() // with lighting shader
```

Another possibility is to carefully consider "batching". This term means grouping geometry so that as many primitives or triangles are sent down the pipeline per API call. The general aim is to use as small a number of large batches as the application allows. There are many problems associated with good batching. For example, geometry with different material properties can not be batched together; different shaders/lighting must also be separated into different batches. Another problem is view culling; we cannot cull within a batch. Batches can not be dynamically altered on a per-frame basis and are preprocessed at load time.

Finally we consider the best coordinate space in which to embed rendering calculations so as to minimize the number of transformations that we have to perform. We will approach this by considering object space, world space and eye space and the three matrices M_{model}, M_{view} and $M_{projection}$. Each space possesses the following attributes and requirements:

- **Object space** is the space that is local and unique to each object. Although we tend to use the singular, there are as many object spaces as there are objects. The origin of the space is the origin of the object and its orientation is the object rotation. If we use object space to render, then we need to apply the appropriate transformations to the light(s) and camera. TBN space (discussed in Chapter 3) is by definition object space, and so when we apply the TBN transformation to the normals in a normal map, they are in object space. Note that the TBN transformation of the normals is mandatory–it has to be done whatever space we choose.

$$[L_{\text{position}}] = [L_{\text{position}}][M_{\text{model}}]^{-1}$$

$$[C_{\text{position}}] = [C_{\text{position}}][M_{\text{model}}]^{-1}$$

These transformations are applied only once per object.

- **World space** is a general space that is not biased towards any entity. Its origin is (0,0,0) and orientation is the identity matrix. The light(s) and camera are already in world space. If we work in world space, we have to transform vertices, pixels and positions from object space to world space applying the model transformations so that we can generate the **L** and **V** vectors. After applying the TBN to the normal map we have to rotate it into world space using the rotation part of the model transformation matrix.

$$[P_{\text{position}}] = [P_{\text{position}}][M_{\text{model}}]$$

$$[N_{\text{position}}] = [N_{\text{position}}][M_{\text{model}}]^{3\times3}$$

These transformations have to be performed per vertex.

- **View space** originates at the camera position and its orientation is defined by the camera rotation. View space does not have any scaling because of the view angle and perspective transformation–it does not include the projection matrix. When working in view space, we have to transform light positions, vertex positions and the normals. Note that in view space **V** the view vector is simply the normalised vertex position.

$$[L_{\text{position}}] = [L_{\text{position}}][M_{\text{view}}]$$

$$[C_{\text{position}}] = [C_{\text{position}}][M_{\text{view}}]$$

These need only be applied once per frame.

$$[P_{\text{position}}] = [P_{\text{position}}][M_{\text{model}}][M_{\text{view}}]$$

$$[N_{\text{position}}] = [L_{\text{position}}][M_{\text{model}}]^{3\times3}[M_{\text{view}}]^{3\times3}$$

These are applied once per vertex.

Figure 2.6. Part of a typical game level.

Whatever space we use the result is exactly the same, but from an efficiency point of view it is best to use object space. Note that these considerations apply to lighting; other applications may be better in another space.

Lighting in Games

Light/Object Structures

The evolution of computer games has seen the emergence of a computer graphics requirement that is common to many games and genres: that is, complex static environments or levels containing dynamic objects under control of the player and other dynamic game objects. An example of a typical game level is shown in Figure 2.6.

To shade the static levels, precalculation in the form of light maps have traditionally been used. Indeed, this classic technique enabled early 3D games to exhibit a visual complexity that was no doubt important in the amazing growth in popularity of computer games. Unfortunately precalculated lighting engenders certain restrictions. Static objects (levels) are lit by both static and dynamic lights, but light maps can only cache light/object interaction for static lights. To calculate the light/object interaction between a dynamic light and a static level requires that we update the light map dynamically per frame. For example, in [WATT01] we suggested a method that accomplishes this using a sphere of influence that interacts with a secondary data structure (Binary Space Partitioning tree, say) to identify those polygons that need to be considered in the lighting update.

Using this technology, we end up with a somewhat unsatisfactory mix of procedures that sit on top of basic light/object interaction calculations as summarised in Table 2.2.

Table 2.2

Light/object interaction type	Method	Frequency
Static light/static object	Light maps	Off line
Static light/dynamic object	Vertex light	Per frame
Dynamic light/static object	Update light map	Per frame
Dynamic light/dynamic object	Vertex light	Per frame

Ideally, we would like the second column in the table to be the same for all interactions as this removes the need for special procedures and the problems that emerge from them. For example, in implementing switchable or destroyable light sources there is a problem in recalculating the light map if the original values have reached saturation due to more than one light source having illuminated the same light map pixel. If one of the contributing lights is turned off, what value is to be used to subtract its contribution from the light map?

We would like to be able to use the basic light/object interaction introduced in this chapter for all of the four possibilities, unifying the approach to light/object interaction and eliminating the problems that arise from special algorithms. Also, this should remove the different look that results from using different techniques for different object/light interaction modes. Thus, we would like to use the same shader(s) in each case irrespective of whether the light and/or the object are dynamic or static.

When rendering scenes with multiple objects and multiple lights, we can consider two structures:

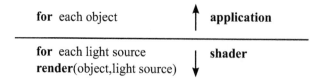

for each object   ↑ **application**

---

    for each light source   ↓ **shader**
    render(object,light source)

This is multipass object with single-pass lighting—all the lighting for each object is carried out by a single shader pass. The disadvantages of this structure are, of course, the wasted effort shading fragments eliminated by the depth test (unless the double-speed Z-only rendering is used). This inefficiency becomes more and more severe as a function of shader complexity. Also, it is difficult to integrate with shadows; we cannot use stencil shadows or shadows maps as we would have to reprocess the shadow for every object when we return to the same lights again and again. Thus, this structure is only useful if we are not rendering shadows.

Alternatively, we could reverse the structure:

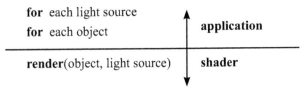

This structure (multipass object, multipass lighting) potentially suffers from the same wasted effort expended on hidden surfaces. In addition, there is computation wasted on repeated vertex transformations, but this can also be minimized by using Vertex Buffer Objects (VBOs). Another problem is the high number of batches generated by the application (one batch per object per light source). However this approach allows us to do efficient per-light shadows. So in the application light loop, before we process each object, we generate the shadow map or shadow volumes once per light and shadows from each object will project onto the others and itself correctly. Shadow areas from one light might be illuminated by other lights, thus generating a composite shadow area.

The implementation of both the above structures is discussed in Chapter 11.

Deferred Shading

Deferred shading, as the name implies, means rendering the parameters required by a shader, such as position, normal, texture coordinates, material coefficients etc., to buffers and calculating lighting as a two-dimensional post process using the information stored in these buffers. Rendering attributes to multiple buffers is called rendering to Multiple Render Targets (MRT).

Using this approach, we replace the previous nested loops with the following structure:

for each object
    render attributes to multiple targets

for each light
    apply lighting parameters to each fragment's attributes

Now shading is no longer applied to pixels eliminated by the Z-buffer. In addition this structure enables good batching to be achieved.

The attributes rendered into target buffers are light independent, and in this way we separate the (final) lighting calculation from the geometry calculations (compare the lighting/surface shader distinction in the section entitled "Light v. Surface Shaders" in this chapter). The price paid for this is the size of the target buffers, each of which has frame resolution and higher-than-normal pixel depth (say 64 bits/pixel). For example, for a set of attributes, say position, normal, diffuse colour and material coefficients (usually collapsed into alpha channels), this would add up to 256 bits/pixel.

Expanding the previous structure we now have the following:

> **for** each object
> > **render** attributes to multiple targets
>
> **for** each light source
> > **render** a full screen quad applying the same shader to all pixels
> > accumulating light in the framebuffer

In the light loop, the shading is effectively an image processing operation in 2D space.

See Chapter 11 for more details on implementing this structure. An implementation (particle system) using MRT is given in Chapter 8.

Deferred Shading and High Dynamic Range

High Dynamic Range (HDR) rendering is an important technique that is implementable using deferred shading. Dynamic range in a scene is the ratio of the highest to the lowest value of luminance of the reflected or emitted light. In real life, dynamic range can be as high as $10^5{:}1$. The importance of handling HDR images correctly can be gauged from the fact that compared with the aforementioned ratio, computer monitors have a dynamic range of around 500:1.

HDR rendering means calculating (in floating point) pixel values in that range, then mapping these values into the two orders of magnitude displayable on a monitor. This transformation is called *tone-mapping*. HDR requires deferred shading because we need to render the HDR image, calculate parameters required for the tone mapping as a function of the image properties, then apply the mapping to achieve a displayable range so that both the very dark parts of the image and the very bright are represented on the display screen in a satisfactory manner.

The problem is: what do we mean by "satisfactory"? This is really a perceptual issue and traditional photographers, who developed such methods as dodging and burning in print development, have explored it at length. In dodging and burning more light is withheld (or added) to selected regions in the image to darken (or lighten) these regions, giving an effect different to what would be achieved if the same development process were used for all of the print.

E. Reinhard *et al.* [REIN02] have explored the automation of this, and most of the work in tone mapping uses the formulae given in this paper. We also use Reinhard *et al.*'s definitions and begin defining luminance—the amount of visible light leaving a point on a surface in a given direction—as:

$$L = 0.27R + 0.67G + 0.06B$$

This corresponds loosely to brightness, and as you may have surmised from the disparate values of the constant factors, also relates to human colour perception. Tone mapping simply means choosing and evaluating a suitable mapping function for the luminance of each pixel in the HDR image to enable it to be displayed.

A global measure, or a calculation based on all pixels, is the log-average luminance:

$$L_{key} = \exp\left(\frac{1}{N}\sum_{x,y}\log(\delta + L(x,y))\right)$$

where $L(x,y)$ is the calculated pixel luminance, N is the number of pixels, and δ is a small number (to cover the case of $L(x,y) = 0$).

This is a quantative measure of a traditional subjective measure called a key indicating the overall lightness or darkness. Reinhard *et al.* suggest using this parameter in a tone mapping:

$$L(x,y) = \frac{\alpha}{L_{key}}L(x,y)$$

where $\alpha = 0.18$ typically.

The process is almost exactly analogous to setting the exposure and aperture on a normal camera according to the measurement made by an exposure or light meter. We can display $L(x,y)$ but Reinhard *et al.* point out that in most images high dynamic range exists only in small areas in the image: for example, areas of sky or those surrounding specular highlights. They suggest a further mapping that compresses mainly the high luminance areas:

$$L_{display}(x,y) = \frac{L(x,y)}{1 + L(x,y)}$$

A context dependent technique, equivalent to dodging and burning, where different areas are subject to different mappings, can be implemented using Gaussian convolution to find areas of distinct dynamic range [REIN02].

When post-processing HDR images, it is also important to take gamma correction into account. The effect of gamma correction is to apply a contrast and chromaticity shift. It is necessary because there is not a linear relationship between the values in the frame buffer and the luminance produced on a computer monitor. For example, if we consider the red channel, R_i we have

$$R_m = K(R_i)^\gamma \tag{2.1}$$

where γ is the monitor gamma (normally 2.2 to 2.8), R_m is the monitor luminance and R_i is the value in the frame buffer.

To linearise the relationship we apply gamma correction to R_i

$$R_i' = k(R_i)^{\frac{1}{\gamma}}$$

so that when it is used in Equation 2.1, the relationship is linear. Full details of determining gamma for your system are given in [BERG03]

Processing High Dynamic Range (HDR) Images

In this section, we will look at the postprocessing of existing HDR images. HDR images consist of floating point numbers for each colour component. Two types of float numbers are used for HDR images: full (32 bit) or half (16 bit). An image with RGBA components in half format takes 64 bits/pixel, and in float format, 128 bits/pixel. In practice, we could use the Cg `half` type which is a 16 bit format. Images with a range as high as $10^5:1$ can be comfortably represented with this data type.

To post-process HDR images as part of a rendering operation, we would want to implement a shader to do this. In our implementation we have used existing images in the OpenEXR format available from the OpenEXR web site.[3] In this image file format, each pixel is made of 64 bits encoding RGBA components in half floating-point format equivalent to Cg `half` type.

In practice, we would post-process an HDR image rendered into floating-point texture maps and use a similar fragment program to modulate its high colour values, transforming it into Low Dynamic Range (LDR) in order to be displayed in a monitor (tone mapping).

The following fragment shader takes an HDR image as input together with some parameters and transforms it into LDR. The parameters used in the tone mapping are *exposure, gamma, contrast* and *defog*.

....

[3] Images available at http://www.openexr.com/samples.html. This format created by ILM is an open source HDR image file format called OpenEXR, and several tools/libraries for loading and saving the EXR images are available.

```
// HDR Tone Map
// Converts a HDR image to LDR
// Parameters: exposure, contrast, defog and gamma

struct v2f
{
        float4 hpos : POSITION;
        float2 texcoord : TEXCOORD0;
};

struct f2s
{
        float4 color : COLOR;
};

f2s main_hdr_tonemap(v2f IN,
        uniform samplerRECT image:TEXUNIT0,
        uniform float3 defog,
        uniform float contrast,
        uniform float exposure)
{
        f2s OUT;
        const float gamma=0.4545;
        const float3 zero=float3(0.0,0.0,0.0);

        float3 c = f3texRECT(image,IN.texcoord);

        c = max(zero, c - defog);
        c*= exposure;
        c = log(c * contrast + 1) / contrast;
        c = pow(c, gamma) * 0.3333;

        OUT.color = float4(c,1.0);
        return OUT;
}
```

Ignoring for a moment the *defog* parameter, we multiply the float colour by the *exposure* parameter and apply the log function to modulate the contrast (setting

(a)   (b)   (c)

Figure 2.7. HDR OpenEXR image (a) low exposure, (b) high exposure and (c) high exposure with defog and contrast.

contrast to almost zero means no contrast balance is applied) and then apply the gamma correction using a power function (usually $0.4535 = 1/2.2$). Results are shown in Figure 2.7, which consists of an OpenEXR image at low exposure, high exposure and high exposure with *defog* and *contrast* active.

The *defog* option works by removing some of the average colour intensity from the scene before doing the tone mapping. The *defog* shader parameter is a multiplication of a *defog* factor (range from 0 to 0.01) and the average image colour. This average is calculated by summing the pixels in each channel and dividing by the total number of pixels. This remarkably simple operation does exactly what the name implies; the effect of *defog* is shown in Figure 2.8.

In the likely event that the subtle differences in HDR post-processing are not apparent in print, the reader can experiment with the HDR processor/viewer on the CD-ROM (Figure 2.9).

(a)   (b)

Figure 2.8. An image without (left) and with (right) defog applied.

Figure 2.9. OpenEXR processor available on CD-ROM.

Light Volume Culling

One of the main problems we encounter with dynamic lights in games is determining the extent of their influence. Just as we try to cull scenes from a visibility point of view, we would also like to cull scenes against the range of influence, or volume, of a light source. And if we are not using light maps then this technique also applies to interactions between static objects and static lights.

In [WATT01], we introduced the idea of considering lights as objects. In particular, we used a sphere as the light object or volume associated with a point source. Consider Figure 2.10.

This shows a spherical light object that intersects a planar surface such as a wall or floor. The light object is invisible but has the effect of lighting the values on the area of intersection between the sphere and the surface to be lit. In the example to find the intersection surface (bold line in the illustration) we define four areas on the surface of the light object (the sphere) as follows:

- A and B are front facing;

- C and D are back facing and C' is that part of C obscured by B;

- B and C are behind the wall and have z values greater than the corresponding current Z-buffer values that contain the depth values for the wall/floor object; and

- A and D have z values smaller than the corresponding current Z-buffer values

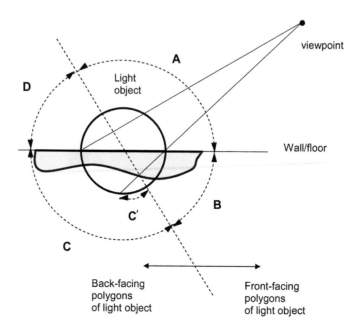

Figure 2.10. A spherical light volume intersecting a static planar surface.

We can see from this that lighting the intersect area is defined by the projection of those faces of C that are not obscured by B. In [WATT01], we implemented this approach with a multi-pass algorithm using a stencil buffer. This required one rendering pass for the object and two passes for the light object. The limitation of these simple tests that use back face culling is that they only work if the light object is convex.

With deferred shading and MRT things are much simpler. We can render the light object into a separate buffer and use the 2D intersection between the projection of the light object and the projection of the geometry of the scene to finally render the scene. We find the light volume/scene intersect area by simply rendering the geometry of the light object, with the appropriate Z-buffer tests into a memory buffer. We note that using Z-buffer comparisons to find the curve of intersection between two volumes produces aliasing, but in this case the visibility of such artefacts depends on the contrast between lit and ambient lit regions. The intersection curve is the boundary between these two regions.

Chapter Three

Texture Mapping

Introduction

From their first appearance as colour maps, there has been a steady evolution in the disparate uses to which texture maps can be put. The early stages of this evolution saw the development of bump mapping and environment mapping. Later, we have the use of texture maps to cache precalculated lighting in games, and later still, their usage in GPGPU to store the intermediate results of, say, iterative calculations. In all of these applications, the underlying motivation of their usage is to achieve an effect or make a calculation in a way that is straightforward to implement and economical.

In general, texture map facilities on GPUs are increasingly being used beyond shading applications. A fragment shader can sample a texture map, and perform calculations on the returned value and write the result in the frame buffer. The results in the frame buffer can then be copied back into a texture map and used in a second pass and so on. Thus, for example, iterative algorithms on images can be mapped onto a GPU.

In this chapter, we will look at basic mapping technology and its application in games. Chapter 5 deals with more advanced GPU techniques that exploit texture mapping.

Colour Mapping using a Two-Dimensional Map

In this section, we introduce conventional colour or texture mapping. Colour mapping[1] is an ancient technique that modulates the diffuse reflection coefficient

....
[1] We use the term "colour mapping" interchangeably with "texture mapping" as is the convention in computer graphics, but colour mapping is clearly a more appropriate term for the original and simplest form of texture mapping.

k_d with a colour derived from a texture map (Figure 3.1). Originally invented to diminish the somewhat boring effect of single colour shading, it continues to evolve, and we will introduce various advanced ways of using texture mapping throughout the text.

In conventional texture mapping, two processes are involved: the interpolation of the vertices' texture map coordinates and the use of the interpolated coordinate to access the texture map. Nowadays vertex texture coordinates are authored as part of the modeling process. The fragment program receives the interpolated map coordinates from the rasterizer/interpolator (see Figure 1.1); all we have to do is to replace the uniform parameter k_d with:

```
float3 kd  = tex2d(mapName,texCoord);
```

The texture map `mapName` is a uniform parameter of type **sampler2D** that is an object that Cg can sample. The library function **tex2d()** accesses the texture map using, as you would expect, two parameters–the name of the map and the texture coordinate of the current fragment. There are 24 texture map functions (see Appendix 3.1) mainly differentiated by the dimensionality of the map being sampled (1, 2 or 3). We will be using more of these functions throughout the text as well as detailing anti-aliasing utilities.

Listing 3.1 is the vertex program that is required for a fragment program that implements simple colour mapping.

```
void  Simple_texture_vertex(float4 iPosition : POSITION,
                                float3 iTexcoord : TEXCOORD0,
                   out float4 oPosition : POSITION,
                   out float4 oTexcoord : TEXCOORD0,

          uniform float4x4  modelviewprojection)

    {


        oPosition  = mul(modelviewprojection,iPosition);
        oTexcoord  = iTexcoord;


    }
```

Figure 3.1. A level using many texture/colour maps.

The fragment program is almost the same as `Phong_frag()`, but we must add

```
float3 iTexcoord : TEXCOORD0,
```

to the parameter list and replace k_d with:

```
float3 kd = tex2D(texMapName,texcoord);
```

Using One-Dimensional Texture Maps

In this section, we look at the use of a one-dimensional (1D) texture map that facilitates cartoon rendering as shown, for example, in Figure 3.2.

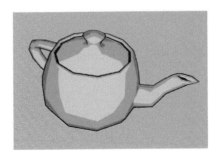

Figure 3.2. Cartoon-style rendering using a 1D texture map.

As we can see from the image, there are three 'cartoon' colours and an emphasised silhouette edge. To achieve this effect, we first render the object in black, with front face culling enabled, using the vertex program (Listing 1.7) to inflate it slightly. The object is then drawn normally with back face culling enabled. In this vertex process the v texture coordinate is set to zero and the u is set to $\mathbf{N} \cdot \mathbf{L}$. The u part of the texture coordinate samples a 1D texture map containing three colours only.

For a dynamic game object, this stylization is very effective in giving a user a feel for the interaction between the object and the lights it is interacting with. The underlying polygonal resolution is apparent in the figure, not only along the silhouette edge but on the border between colours, and this emphasises again that if a vertex program is used on its own for rendering, then the mesh must be of a reasonably high resolution.

Note that the rendering process is multipass in the application. The application program must execute two passes each time using different shaders. The first pass, which inflates and renders in black, uses the (inflate) vertex program and a pass-through fragment program. The second pass uses a pass-through vertex program and the cartoon-render fragment program (Listing 3.2).

Listing 3.2.

Cartoon shader
(second pass).

```
struct app2vert
{
  float4 pos : POSITION;
  float4 color : DIFFUSE;
  float3 normal : NORMAL;
};


struct vert2frag
{
  float4 hpos : POSITION;
  float4 color : COLOR0;
  float2 texcoord : TEXCOORD0;
};


vert2frag main_vert_cartoon(
  app2vert IN,
  uniform float3 lightpos) // in object space
{
```

```
vert2frag OUT;

float3 viewdir = normalize(lightpos-IN.pos.xyz);

OUT.hpos = mul(glstate.matrix.mvp,IN.pos);
OUT.texcoord = max(0,dot(viewdir,IN.normal));
OUT.color = IN.color;

return OUT;
}
```

There is an additional practical problem in this particular example concerning the action of hardware texture filtering. We require texture filtering to apply to all of the game objects which are not cartoon rendered. However, texture filtering should not diminish the hard edge stylization of cartoon-rendered objects, and we still want the colour transition edges to be anti-aliased. This can be achieved by ensuring that the 1D texture map is large (say 256 texels) and blending from region to region over a few texels (Figure 3.3). To prevent texture filtering between the first and last texture pixels, we need to set texture clamp to the 1D texture map.

Combining Texture Maps in a Fragment Program

The development of GPUs has enabled far easier and faster ways of combining texture maps to provide effects in games. Before the advent of GPUs, the term "shader" usually implied a multi-pass program that produced an effect by changing state settings in the pipeline to operate on and blend texture maps. Effects, animated and static, were built up by blending together a number of texture maps. The rationale for this method was that many and varied effects could be implemented by such combinations and artists could create and experiment with the texture combinations in simple editors.

Rather than use a multipass structure to combine maps, we can use a fragment program to access different texture maps and then use normal arithmetic operations to combine and animate them. However, there are hardware restrictions that limit the number of textures and texture accesses from within a shader. If our application exceeds these resources, then we have to revert to a multipass approach.

Figure 3.3. A (256x1)-texel texture map used in the cartoon rendering.

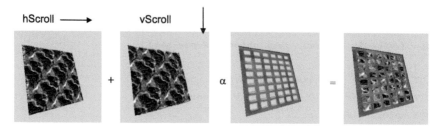

Figure 3.4. Combining texture maps.

Of course, there has to be a reason for combining texture maps in real time otherwise we could model the combination off-line. A common reason is the implementation of (cheap) animation effects. Figure 3.4 shows an animated 'water' effect viewed through a grating. The final texture application consists of the addition of a horizontally scrolling texture, a vertically scrolling texture and a map consisting of a (shaded) grating. The scroll variables are incremented/frame in the application, and we include this simple set of assignments in the fragment program:

```
kd1  = tex2D(water, hScroll);
kd2  = tex2D(water, vScroll);
kd3  = tex2D(grating, texCoord);

kd = (kd1 + kd2)*kd3.alpha + kd3*(1-kd3.alpha);
```

Bump Mapping

Bump mapping, like colour mapping, is used to add interest, as Figure 3.5 demonstrates. It is a mapping technique that has served the graphics community well since its advent in 1978 [BLIN78]. The technique simulates depressions (bumps) in a surface by perturbing the surface normal used in the shading equation according to information stored in the bump map. Thus, the geometry of the surface looks as if it possesses a physical texture. Its enduring popularity over colour mapping is precisely because it gives an effect that looks like real texture—as we interpret in real life—rather than colour mapping where the surface is always locally planar.

The traditional way of implementing bump mapping is to represent the information required to perturb surface normal as a height field. This is the bump map. Then for each fragment the information from the bump map undergoes a

Figure 3.5. A games level rendered with and without bump mapping.

series of mathematical operations to extract the perturbation for the surface normal. Until fairly recently bump mapping in real time was not possible.

The visual efficacy of the technique is such that it has survived for a quarter of a century despite having a number of well-known disadvantages. Principal amongst these is that since we are not perturbing the geometry, the effect is absent along silhouette edges by definition. In a standard implementation, no self-shadows are produced by the bumps.

A variation of the original technique, which is easy to implement in a shader and which nowadays is perhaps the most popular way of implementing the technique, involves storing the new or perturbed normals for the surface as the bump map. Thus, the desired perturbations are precalculated rather than computed at run time from the bump map. Then in the mapping process, instead of interpolating the vertex normals and applying the perturbation derived from the bump map to the interpolated normal, we interpolate the light direction vector **L**, and for each fragment we can fetch the new normal from the bump map and use this together with **L** in our shading equation.

There are two complications involved in this technique. First, we have to range compress and subsequently decompress the normal vector. We store the normals in a conventional RGB texture map whose components are constrained to the range [0,1]. However, the normals, which are normalised, are in the range [-1,1]. And we use a scale and bias to compress these into the range [0,1]. This also enables us to use hardware texture filtering when accessing the normal map. To compress the normal vector, we use

```
Nc   =   0.5  *   N   +   0.5;
```

and to expand

$$N = 2 * Nc - 1.0;$$

Second, the light direction vector **L** and the new normal have to be in the same coordinate space—a point covered in the next section.

Finally, there is a precision issue. Because the normals are stored in 8-bit per channel RGB texture maps and we are using linear texture filtering (and optionally mip-mapping, which is also a linear process), the expanded normal will not be as precise as the original uncompressed version. This can be ameliorated by renormalizing the expanded vector in the fragment program.

Bump Mapping and Tangent (TBN) Space

We choose TBN space (also known as texture tangent space or tangent space) as the common space because a normal map is defined in this space. The normal map needs to be defined in a surface-oriented space, otherwise, if it were defined in world space, the map would have to be recalculated every time the receiving object is rotated. We could use object space, and rotations would not require recalculation of the normal map, but this would not suffice for deformable objects such as an animated character, and so the best solution is to always use tangent space.

In a polygon mesh, we have vertex normals of different orientation at each vertex, and we can define a local coordinate system per vertex. **L** then needs to be defined in the coordinate system of each vertex as shown in Figure 3.6.

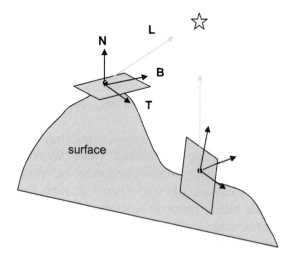

Figure 3.6. TBN or Tangent space is unique to each vertex. **L** is transformed into each System.

Thus, we need to calculate an orthonormal basis at each vertex **TBN**, where

T   is the tangent vector,
B   is the so-called binormal, and
$N = B \times T$ is the normal.

Then the light vector is transformed into this space, also known as surface local space,[2] by:

$$\mathbf{L} = \begin{bmatrix} T_x & B_x & N_x \\ T_y & B_y & N_y \\ T_z & B_z & N_z \end{bmatrix}$$

which can be implemented by the vertex program given as Listing 3.3.

Listing 3.3

Transforming **L** into tangent space.

```
void  bump_vertex (
  float3 position   :   POSITION;

  float3 normal     :   NORMAL;

  float3 tangent    :   TEXCOORD1;

  float3 texCoord   :   TEXCOORD0;


  out float4  oPosition   :   POSITION;

  out float4  bumpUV      :   TEXCOORD0;

  out float4  L           :   TEXCOORD1;


  uniform float3   lightPosition;

  uniform float3   eyePosition;

  uniform float4x4 modelViewProj)
{
    oPosition = mul (modelViewProj, float4 (position,1));
    L = lightPosition - position;

    float3  binormal  = cross (tangent, normal);
    float3x3 rotation = float3x3 (tangent,binormal,normal);
    L = mul (rotation,L);
    bumpUV = texcoord;
}
```

Alternatively we could have used:

```
L = (dot (T,L) ,dot (B,L) ,dot (N,L));
```

....

[2] This space is also known as tangent space or texture tangent space.

If we require a specular contribution, then **H** has to be calculated and also transformed. **L** is then interpolated and all we need in the fragment program to calculate a per-fragment $(\mathbf{N} \cdot \mathbf{L})$ is

```
N = (tex2D(bumpMap,bumpUV).xyz)*2-1;
```

An important efficiency point concerning the operations in this approach is that the only per-fragment operations required in the fragment program is a texture sample **tex2D**(bumpMap,bumpUV) and a dot product $\mathbf{N} \cdot \mathbf{L}$. If, for example, we were to perform the per-vertex calculation in global space, we would have to transform the normal from the normal map using the TBN matrix. However, note that the interpolation of **L**, which is based in a coordinate system that is unique for each vertex, is not correct. It is an approximation that works providing the object tessellation is high, and we must renormalise **L** for every fragment.

Per-Fragment L and H Computation

The above method, although simple, is unsatisfactory and produces artefacts as a function of the object tessellation. It is not correct to linear interpolate **L** and **H** across triangle; we need an accurate **L** and **H** per fragment. The price for this is a more complex fragment program and a simpler vertex program. This a is cost versus quality trade-off, and we would of course prefer complexity to be invested in the vertex program rather than in the fragment program.

However, the choice of per-fragment lighting strategy depends on the object tessellation. If the tessellation is high and regular (like a player character), we can use the complex vertex/simple fragment program approach. But for geometry such as large polygon floors and walls with very low tessellation, we should use the simple vertex/complex fragment strategy.

The Listing 3.4 computes **L** and **H** perfragment thus generating a higher quality lighting for any geometry tesselation.

Listing 3.4

Bump mapping: per-fragment L and H computation.

```
float4 normal_map(
v2f IN,
uniform sampler2D texmap,
uniform sampler2D normalmap) : COLOR
{
float4 normal=tex2D(normalmap,IN.txcoord*tile);
normal.xyz=normal.xyz*2.0-1.0; // transform to [-1,1] range
```

```
// transform normal to world space
normal.xyz=normalize(normal.x*IN.tangent-normal.y*IN.
binormal+normal.z*IN.normal);

// color map
float4 color=tex2D(texmap,IN.txcoord*tile);

// view and light directions
float3 v = normalize(IN.vpos);
float3 l = normalize(IN.lightpos.xyz-IN.vpos);

// compute diffuse and specular terms
float diff=saturate(dot(l,normal.xyz));
float spec=saturate(dot(normalize(l-v),normal.xyz));

// geometry self-shadows
float att = dot(l,IN.normal.xyz)<0?0:1;

// compute final color
float4 finalcolor;
finalcolor.xyz=ambient*color.xyz+
att*(color.xyz*diffuse.xyz*diff+specular.xyz*pow(spec,shine));
finalcolor.w=1.0;

return finalcolor;
}
```

Figure 3.7 shows an example generated by the above fragment program.

Figure 3.7. Per-fragment lighting in bump mapping.

Self Shadows in Bump Mapping

Finally we consider self-shadows in bump mapping.[3] The only difference between the normal implementation of self-shadowing we gave in Chapter 2 (clamping the diffuse component to zero and zeroising the specular component if the diffuse is zero) is that we must also consider the perturbed normal. If either the perturbed normal or the unperturbed normal face away from the light source, the surface is in self-shadow. We consider that the unperturbed normal represents large scale-surface orientation, and the perturbed normal small scale surface orientation and use the test:

```
diffuse = L.z > 0?   max(dot(N,L),0)  : 0;
```

Here **N** is the perturbed normal and **max**(**dot**(N, L), 0) controls small-scale self-shadowing. Large-scale self-shadowing is implemented by testing the z component of the light direction vector. As we are in TBN space, if this component is negative then the surface orientation must face away from the light source. For the specular component, we can use

```
specular = dot(N,L) > 0 && L.z > 0 ? max(dot(N,H),0 : 0;
```

There is, however, a slight problem with this simple approach which may manifest itself visually. The boundary between the dark and lit areas can appear as a sharp transition. This is because the perturbed normal may be larger than the unbumped normal for the same position.

Figure 3.8 shows this problem and an approximate fix for it. We could multiply together the two dot products from light direction with original and perturbed normals to get a smooth transition in boundary region as:

```
diffuse = max(L.z,0)*max(dot(N,L),0);
```

The difference achieved is shown in the figure.

Figure 3.8. Visible self-shadow transition and a cheap cure.

....

[3] The term "self shadow" is something of an established misuse and tends to confuse two separate phenomena: (1) an area of the object which cannot see the light because of its orientation, and (2) an area of a non-convex (or bumped surface) which cannot see the light due to the obstruction of *another part* of the object.

Tangent Space and Triangle Meshes

The remaining question is how do we derive TBN space per vertex for a polygonal object? First, consider that a normal is an implicit representation of the tangent space at a point on a surface. In the case of a curve, a tangent is a line, and for a surface, a tangent is a plane. We specify this plane with two basis vectors, $\mathbf{T}$ and $\mathbf{B}$ and the normal $\mathbf{N}$ is perpendicular to this plane. Consider a single triangle (P_0, P_1, P_2). In world space we can define the tangent plane with the two vectors:

$$\mathbf{T}_1 = P_1 - P_0 \quad \text{and} \quad \mathbf{T}_2 = P_2 - P_0$$

which both lie in the plane of the triangle; but which are not necessarily orthogonal. We require a pair of basis vectors in 3D texture space, rather than world space, and these are given by

$$\mathbf{T} = (u_2 - u_0)\,(P_2 - P_0) + (u_1 - u_0)\,(P_1 - P_0)$$
$$\mathbf{B} = (v_2 - v_0)\,(P_2 - P_0) + (v_2 - v_1)\,(P_1 - P_0)$$
$$\mathbf{N} = \mathbf{B} \times \mathbf{T}$$

where (u_i, v_i) are the texture coordinates for P_i. All we have done so far is defined a TBN system for a single triangle which remains identical over the entire triangle. What we require is a TBN system per vertex which, for a single triangle, will give a unique TBN system at each of the three vertices.

To find the TBN system for every vertex in a polygonal object, we proceed as follows:

for each vertex
    for each triangle that contributes to the vertex
        calculate and sum the $\mathbf{T}$, $\mathbf{B}$ and $\mathbf{N}$ vectors
    normalise each sum

This simple structure should be elaborated by weighting the contributions to the sum. We do this by considering the dot product of the angle that the two triangle edges make at the vertices and using this as a weighting factor in the sum. Consider a cube, for example. At each vertex there are three faces, but as each face is made up of two triangles we may have three, four, five or six triangles at a vertex. Thus an unweighted sum would result in a contribution from each face of either one or two face normals, making the average wrong.

This is almost the same as evaluating vertex normals, except that we now have the normals in a coordinate system that is unique to each vertex. However, note

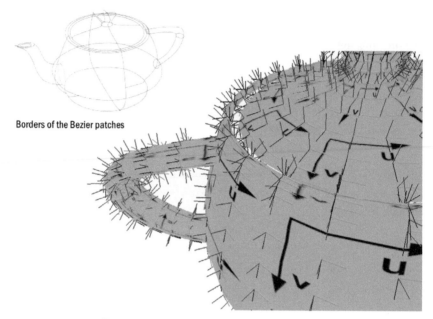

Borders of the Bezier patches

Figure 3.9. Tangent space of the Utah Teapot.

that the averaged **T**,**B** vectors are not necessarily orthogonal. This can be ignored, or we can rotate one of the vectors in the **T,B** until they are orthogonal.

Tangent Space and Bicubic Parametric Objects

That classic icon of computer graphic–the Utah teapot–is actually made up of bicubic Bezier patches and to calculate tangent space, we can either convert it into a polygon mesh, which we have to do to render it, or we can calculate the tangents directly from the patch description (Appendix A7.1). Figure 3.9 shows the **T** (green), **B** (blue) and **N** (red) vectors for each vertex in the Utah teapot. Notice that the tangent direction corresponds to the u texture space direction, and the binormal, to the v.

Some background: the University of Utah was the centre of research into rendering algorithms in the early 1970s and is the home of Gouraud and Phong shading amongst many other computer graphics algorithms still in common usage.

In 1975, M. Newell modeled the Utah Teapot, which has become a much-loved object in computer graphics and one which we use regularly in this text. The original was modelled by sketching the profile of the teapot to estimate suitable control points for bicubic Bezier Patches. The lid, rim and body were then treated as solids of revolution, and the spout and handle were modelled as ducted solids.

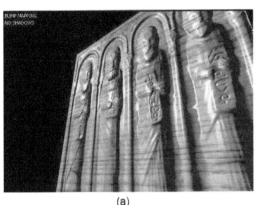

(a)   (b)

Figure 3.10. Showing the visual inadequacy of bump mapping. (a) Bump mapping. (b) The same object using an alternative mapping given in Chapter 5.

This resulted in a total of 32 patches. The boundaries of the patches are shown in the figure. More detail on Bezier patches is given in Appendix A7.1.

Anti-Aliasing Bump Maps

Anti-aliasing is mandatory when using bump maps, and we can use mip-maps for that. When mip-mapping normal maps, we must take care with the averaging of normals for lower mip-map levels. When we add four normals together to compute the lower mip-map pixel value (using (N1+N2+N3+N4) for example) we will need to renormalize the result after the averaging so that all mip-map levels will have the normals with unit size.

A Comparison

Even using a 'good' normal map, bump mapping still exhibits visual inadequacies as Figure 3.10 demonstrates. This shows the same bas relief object rendered using bump mapping compared to the clearly superior relief texture mapping–a topic that we explore in Chapter 5.

Normal Maps

Nowadays, normal maps are used in many applications. As we have seen, we can use them in a simple implementation of bump mapping. But they can, of course, be used in conventional rendering. In general, they can be used to capture the geometry of a high-resolution model in a map. This is sometimes called detail recovery because we render a low-resolution surface and recover the detail during rendering from the normal map. In fact there is no difference between using normal maps in bump mapping and using them in normal rendering; it's just two different ways of categorising what is effectively the same technique.

This raises the question of how normal maps are generated—the topic of this section.

There are many different ways of generating a normal map. The choice of the method depends to some extent on the nature of the geometry being represented, and in this section, we categorise three methods according to the type of model. In increasing order of difficulty, these are as follows:

1. Model is a height map.
2. Model is a bas relief object.
3. Model is a conventional 3D mesh.

The easiest method is the first and involves a simple transformation of a height field, or equivalently a depth map, into a normal map. The source data is texture map $H(u,v)$, a map parameterized using texture map coordinates. This method is sometimes called texture-space bump mapping (or tangent-space bump mapping). A height map is used because it is straightforward to create using a software tool. The steps required to generate a per-texel normal $\mathbf{N_b}$ are as follows:

for each texel in $H(u,v)$
$\quad$ // calculate difference vector in u and v

$\quad$ $\mathbf{V}du = (1,0,\Delta Hu); \quad \mathbf{V}dv = (0,1, \Delta Hv);$
$\quad$ $\mathbf{N}b = \text{normalise}(\text{cross}(\mathbf{V}du,\mathbf{V}dv);$

$\quad$ // the required normal is the normalised cross product of the
$\quad$ // difference vectors

The definitions used in this pseudocode are shown diagrammatically in Figure 3.11.

However, this simple method suffers from a number of disadvantages. It is only really suitable for irregular surface features—such as fissures in rocks—where there is no expectation of a particular regular form. There are artefacts that emerge from calculation inaccuracy and from the fact that we are processing a byte range depth map for which we do not know the range in screen space. The (0–255) range in the depth map transforms to some value unknown at the processing time and an arbitrary scaling factor has to be used. Figure 3.11 shows a depth map and the

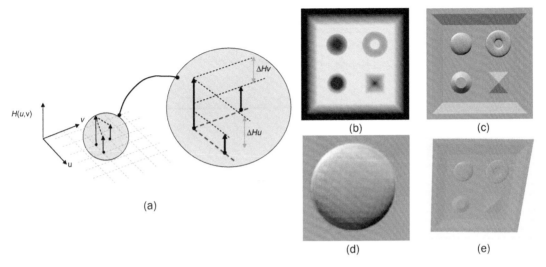

Figure 3.11. Bump mapping using a normal map derived from a dept map by formula. (a) The method; (b) Depth map; (c) Normal map generated from depth map; (d) Detail of normal map exhibiting noise and coherences; (e) Object rendered using the derived normal map as a bump map.

corresponding normal map generated in the manner just described. This should be compared with Figure 3.12 which derives a true normal map.

A bas relief object such as that shown in Figure 3.12 can be considered to be an object which will only ever be viewed from some viewpoint on the surface of a hemisphere lying in the plane of the object. In this case, rather than deriving a normal map by differentiation, we can implement a parallel ray cast as shown in Figure 3.12. Here, a ray is generated from each texel in the normal map and intersects the surface. We can then calculate the surface normal at the point of intersection from the surrounding vertices.

Results using this method for the same object as used in Figure 3.11 are shown in the figure. Easily seen is the difference in visual quality of the rendered object.

The final method is the most general (dealing with any 3D mesh) and produces a very accurate normal map. This method, or variations of it, has been reported by [KRIS96], [COHE98] and [TARI03]. It is the method to which the term "detail recovery" best applies and involves a low resolution polygon mesh model, together with a good texture parameterisation, and a high-resolution model from which the low-resolution mesh is derived.

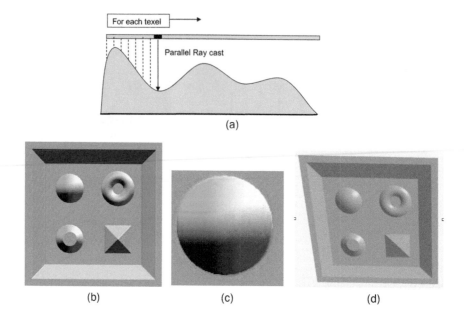

(a)

(b)   (c)   (d)

Figure 3.12. Deriving a normal map from a bas relief type object using a parallel ray cast. (a) The method; (b) The derived normal map; (c) Detail; (c.f. Figure 3.11); (d) The rendered object.

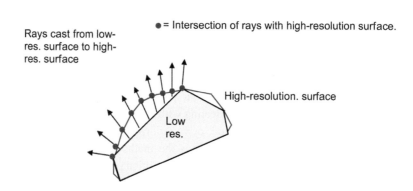

Figure 3.13. Deriving a normal map from a high- resolution 3D mesh.

The method requires a texture coordinate parameterisation. A visualisation of the process is shown in Figure 3.13 and the steps in the processing algorithm are:

for each texel mapped onto the low-resolution surface
    Cast a ray to intersect the high-resolution surface
    Calculate the surface normal of the high resolution surface at this point and assign this to the texel.

We need to determine a direction for the rays cast, and, as we have tried to illustrate in the figure, we can use the direction of the normal of the low-resolution surface. We would normally cast multiple rays per texel to ensure accuracy. There are other possibilities for finding a point on the high-resolution surface, corresponding to the mapped texel on the low-resolution surface. For example, we could pick that point which is closest based on Euclidean distance.

Figure 3.14 shows an illustration of this technique, and it is immediately obvious that the alternative name of this method—detail recovery—is apt. We begin with the high-resolution bunny at 68000 triangles (Figure 3.14(a)). The program then derives a normal map (Figure 3.13(b)) shown in object space. Also shown in Figure 3.14(b) is the wireframe of the low-resolution model. A low-resolution version of the object (500 triangles) is rendered using the normal map (Figure 3.14(c)). For comparison in Figure 3.14d) we show a convention rendering of the low-resolution mesh.

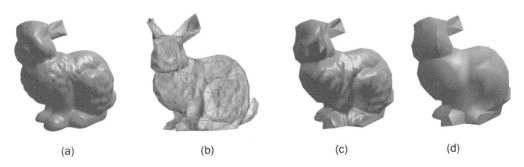

(a)   (b)   (c)   (d)

Figure 3.14. Deriving a normal map from a 3D object using a high and low-resolution mesh. (a) High resolution mesh rendered (approximately 68000 triangles). (b) Low-resolution mesh in wireframe (approximately 500 triangles) with normal map in object space. (c) Low-resolution mesh rendered using the derived normal map. (d) Low resolution mesh rendered conventionally. *Examples created using NVIDIA's Melody Tool.*

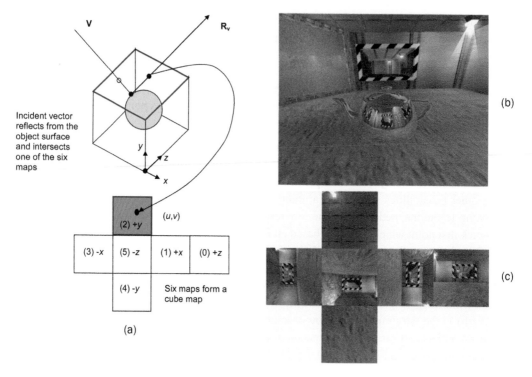

Figure 3.15. Environment or cube mapping. (a) The view vector V is reflected from the surface of the object. (b) A shiny object reflecting a game level. (c) The cube map corresponding to (b).

Environment Mapping

Cube Mapping

Environment mapping means rendering, in the surface of a shiny object, reflections of the environment in which the object is immersed. One of the most popular ways of implementing environment mapping is to use a cube map. The environment map is in fact six maps that we can consider as folding up to form a cube. The reason for the enduring popularity of this approach is that the maps can be easily constructed using a conventional render. For example, if we want to capture the walls of a room, we can set a viewpoint at the centre of a room and render in six directions.

To render the object we reflect the view vector **V** and use the direction of the reflected view vector to index into the cube map face (Figure 3.15).

To calculate the vector $\mathbf{R}_v$, we can use the formula

$$\mathbf{R}_v = \mathbf{V} - 2\mathbf{N}(\mathbf{V} \cdot \mathbf{N})$$

where $\mathbf{N}$ is the surface normal at the point of intersection. But as always, it is better to use a library function if one is available. In this case:

```
reflect(V,N)
```

To calculate the per-vertex reflection vector, we use Listing 3.5. We first note that cube maps are stored in world space and so the vertex position and vertex normal must be transformed into world space using the modelling transform.

Listing 3.5

```
void  Cube_map_vertex(float4 position : POSITION,
                      float2 texCoord : TEXCOORD0,
                      float3 N        : NORMAL,

                  out float4 oPosition  : POSITION,
                  out float2 oTexCoord  : TEXCOORD0,
                  out float3 R          : TEXCOORD1,

              uniform float3    eyePosition,
              uniform float4x4 modelviewProj,
              uniform float4x4 modelWorld)
{
  oPosition = mul(modelviewProj, position);
  oTexCoord = texCoord;

  // Transform position and normal into world space
  float3 wPosition = mul(modelWorld, position).xyz;
  float3 Nw = mul((float3x3)modelWorld, N);


  // Compute the incident and reflected vectors
  float3 V = wPosition - eyePosition;
  R = reflect(V, Nw);
}
```

Cube map vertex shader.

R is output from the vertex program as a (three-component) texture coordinate which is as usual interpolated and used in the fragment program to sample the cube map. The fragment program is Listing 3.6.

Listing 3.6.

Cube map
fragment.

```
void Cube_map_frag(
      float2 texCoord : TEXCOORD0,
      float3 R        : TEXCOORD1,
      out float4 colour   : COLOR,
      uniform samplerCUBE cubeMap)
{
    colour = texCUBE(cubeMap, R);
}
```

Note the new texture sampler **texCUBE()**. The second parameter is understood to be a direction, and the function performs the necessary calculations to find the (u,v) coordinate and the map component. For example, if z is the largest component and negative, face 5 is selected (Figure 3.15(a)) and (u,v) is given by:

$$(u,v) = (x/z, \ y/z)$$

The inaccuracies inherent in this technique are well known. The method is only completely correct if the object is very small and approaches the ideal of a point. Alternatively, we can say that we assume that the objects captured in the environment map are very far from the object being rendered. A more accurate approach would be to have a separate map for each object and also to recalculate the map every time an object moved.

Thus, it is slow to use a cube map in a game for dynamic objects, but we can economise by constructing a new map at a lower frequency than the frame rate, or only constructing a new map if the object has moved by more than a threshold amount.

Another consequence of cube maps is that an object cannot reflect itself and so they are only suitable for convex objects.

Normalisation using Cube Maps

Cube maps can be used as an alternative to using **normalize()**. This may be faster in fragment programs, even for advanced fragment profiles. A normalization cube map is constructed such that the texel intersected by a vector **V**, as in

```
texCUBE(normalisationCube,V);
```

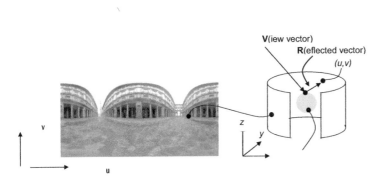

V(iew vector)
R(eflected vector)
(u,v)

Figure 3.16. Environment mapping using a cylindrical map.

contains the normalized value of that vector. The normalized vectors are stored as signed texture components (or alternatively as range-compressed vectors).

Cylindrical Map

A simple alternative to a cube map (which requires six maps) is to use a single cylindrical map sometimes called an angular map. The cost of this simplification is the degradation of the sampling distribution compared to the cube map (which itself suffers from a poor distribution). Also, since there is no library support for this type of map all calculations have to be incorporated in the shader; however, these are straightforward.

This technique has an interesting history. It was first proposed by Bier and Sloan in 1986 [BIER86] as a method for mapping a texture onto a polygonal mesh. That is a mesh without texture coordinates. This preceded the present common practice of authoring texture coordinates where an artist 'pre-fits' a texture map onto an object using interactive software.

Its use as an environment map is convenient because cheap technology exists to create a panoramic image from reality. This takes the form of a camera rotating in a plane parallel to the ground which produces a number of images that are subsequently 'stitched' into a panorama. Such a map is shown in Figure 3.16.

Here, all we need to do is to map the 3D reflected view vector into the 2D map. This mapping is given by

$$d = \frac{1}{2\pi} \frac{\cos^{-1}(y)}{\sqrt{(x^2 + z^2)}}$$

$$u = 0.5 + xd$$

$$v = 0.5 + zd$$

Code for the complete shader is given in Listing 3.7.

Listing 3.7

Cylindrical
mapping.

```
struct appdata
{
        float4 pos : POSITION;
        float3 normal : NORMAL;
        float3 diffuse : DIFFUSE;
        float4 tex : TEXCOORD0;
};

struct vfconn
{
        float4 hpos : POSITION;
        float4 col0 : COLOR0;
        float4 tex0 : TEX0;
};

float4 angular_map(float3 dir)
{
        float d=sqrt(dir.x*dir.x+dir.z*dir.z);
        d=0.159155*acos(dir.y)/d;
        return float4(0.5+dir.x*d,0.5+dir.z*d,1,1);
}

vfconn reflect_angularmap(appdata IN,
                  uniform float4x4 modelviewproj,
                  uniform float3 lightpos,
                  uniform float3 camerapos)
{
   vfconn OUT;

   OUT.hpos = mul(modelviewproj, IN.pos);

   float3 camdir = normalize(IN.pos.xyz-camerapos);
   float3 reflectdir = reflect(camdir,IN.normal);
   OUT.tex0 = angular_map(reflectdir);

   float3 l = normalize(IN.pos.xyz-lightpos);
   float3 h = reflect(l,IN.normal);

   float ndotl = dot(IN.normal,-l);
   float vdoth = dot(camdir,-h);

   float4 illum = lit(ndotl,vdoth,20);
```

```
OUT.col0.xyz = IN.diffuse*(illum.y+illum.zzz+0.5);
OUT.col0.w = 1;

return OUT;
}
```

Texture Shading and Factorising Shading Equations

This technique precalculates the results of the application of a particular lighting model and stores the results in one or more texture maps. At run time, the lighting is turned off, and per-vertex lighting calculations are replaced by one or more texture coordinate calculations. The technique is most powerful when used to implement very complex shading functions. Its utility will obviously diminish as GPUs become more and more powerful. We introduce the principle of the method by looking at a simple example (Phong shading) which demonstrates the principle–as we know Phong shading is efficiently implementable on modern GPUs.

Consider first Phong shading. We recall that if we make the approximation that **L** and **V** are constant then the equation becomes a function of **N** only–in particular a function of the terms $(\mathbf{N} \cdot \mathbf{L})$ and $(\mathbf{N} \cdot \mathbf{H})$. Thus we can write the equation as a bi-variate function and compute a texture map $T(u,v)$ as

$$T(u,v) \; = \; I \; = \; k_a I_a \; + \; I_i\big(k_d(u) \; + \; k_s(v)^n\big)$$

$$\text{where} \quad u = (\mathbf{N} \cdot \mathbf{L}) \; \text{ and } \; v = (\mathbf{N} \cdot \mathbf{H})$$

Calculation at run time reduces to calculating (u,v). Figure 3.17 shows the idea; the object on the right has been rendered from the texture map on the left.

The disadvantage of this method, of course, is that the diffuse color, specular color and specular exponent are constant and a new texture will be required for each different material property.

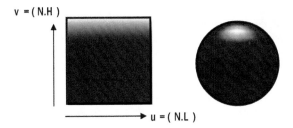

Figure 3.17. Phong shading using a texture map.

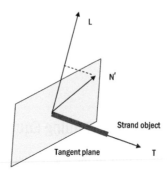

Figure 3.18. Vectors in the strand shading model.

The key to extending this approach to more complex models is factorisation as we demonstrated in the simple case of the Phong model. Many complex lighting models, which, for instance, exhibit anisotropy, can be factorised into independent components that depend on only one or two surface frame coordinates. These separate factors can be stored in texture maps and combined during rendering.

A good example of a model that can be factorised in this way is the Banks model [BANK94], which can be used to render common strand objects like hair and grass. The geometry of the model used in this case is shown in Figure 3.18.

The effect of the model is shown in Figure 3.19. The sphere is an object like a Christmas tree ball which is wrapped in satin cord and clearly shows the anisotropic nature of the model. The bunny shows the model applied to hair or fur strands.

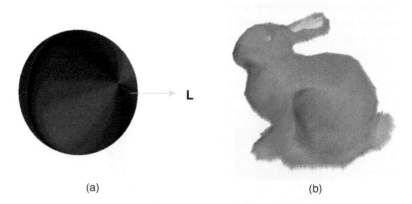

(a)   (b)

Figure 3.19. (a) The Banks anisotropic shading model for a sphere. Sphere image generated using a program written by Heidrich (at http://www9.informatik.uni-erlangen.de/eng/research/rendering/anisotropic/) (b) A similar anisotropic model used to render fur. *Bunny image courtesy of Gary Sheppard, University of Sheffield, UK.*

We define $\mathbf{T}$ the tangent vector to lie in the strand and this defines a tangent plane which will contain the normal. For a cylindrical strand we can choose any direction for the normal, and we choose that normal $\mathbf{N'}$ which is coincident with the projection of $\mathbf{L}$ in the tangent plane, arguing that the most significant light reflection is based on a normal that makes the maximum dot product with $\mathbf{L} \cdot \mathbf{N'}$ is then used in the conventional Phong model (see Chapter 2):

$$I = k_a I_a + I_i\big(k_d(\mathbf{L} \cdot \mathbf{N'}) + k_s(\mathbf{R'} \cdot \mathbf{V})^n\big)$$

$$\text{where} \quad \mathbf{R'} = 2\mathbf{N'}(\mathbf{N'} \cdot \mathbf{V}) - \mathbf{V}$$

Banks showed that the $\mathbf{L} \cdot \mathbf{N'}$ and the $\mathbf{R'} \cdot \mathbf{V}$ terms could be expressed respectively as:

$$\mathbf{L} \cdot \mathbf{N'} = \sqrt{1 - (\mathbf{L} \cdot \mathbf{T})^2}$$

$$\mathbf{R'} \cdot \mathbf{V} = \sqrt{1 - (\mathbf{L} \cdot \mathbf{T})^2}\sqrt{1 - (\mathbf{V} \cdot \mathbf{T})^2} - (\mathbf{L} \cdot \mathbf{T})(\mathbf{V} \cdot \mathbf{T})$$

Enabling the factorisation

$$T(u,v) = T\big(f(\mathbf{L} \cdot \mathbf{N'}), f(\mathbf{V} \cdot \mathbf{T})\big)$$

$$= k_a I_a + I_i\Big(k_d\sqrt{1 - u^2} + k_s\big(\sqrt{1 - u^2}\sqrt{1 - v^2} - \mathbf{u} \cdot \mathbf{v}\big)^n\Big)$$

A per-pixel shader that uses this method needs a tangent vector per fragment. One way to enable this, for surfaces like the sphere in Figure 3.19, is to cache tangents in an anisotropy map. Similar in principle to a bump map, this stores the tangent vectors in a conventional texture map which can be generated procedurally or by pre-processing the object. As with normal mapping the tangents are in TBN space. All we have to do in the shader is to transform $\mathbf{L}$ and $\mathbf{V}$ into tangent space.

Texture Maps as Control Maps

In [FERN03] the authors suggest a useful extension to Listing 3.6—the concept of a control map. Just as we used a texture map to control the nature of the material over a surface, we can easily use a texture to control the value of a reflection parameter over a surface. Listing 3.7 simulates an object which is a perfect mirror. We can use a conventional colour map and a control map that modulates the reflectivity over the surface of the object.

```
void Cube_map_frag(
    float2 texCoord : TEXCOORD0,
    float3 R        : TEXCOORD1,

    out float4 colour   : COLOR,

    uniform samplerCUBE cubeMap,
    uniform sampler2D colMap,
    uniform sampler2D reflectMap)
{
    float4 envColour = texCUBE(cubeMap, R);
    float4 texCol =   tex2D(colMap, texCoord);
    float4 reflect = tex2D(reflectMap, texCoord);

    colour = lerp(texCol,envColour,reflect);
}
```

The parameter `reflect` takes a value between 0 and 1, and the function **lerp()** linearly interpolates between the reflected colour and the colour stored in the texture map according to

```
result = (1 - weight)vectorₐ  +  weight vectorᵦ
```

where the parameters are defined as

```
lerp(vectorA,vectorB,weight);
```

Vertex Shaders and Texture Mapping

Per-Vertex Displacement Mapping

Recent hardware enables vertex programs to access texture maps, and this immediately enables displacement mapping, previously an offline technique, to be implemented in real time. The purpose of a displacement shader is to impose small variations on the vertices of an object to simulate variations in the surface of the object. It enables small detail to be impressed on the surface with little cost (see Figure 3.20. It is the same goal as bump mapping, but the surface is *actually* perturbed (in bump mapping we perturb the normal to make it look as if the surface were perturbed). We can access the texture map to obtain a scalar displacement per vertex and move the vertex along the vertex normal.

Figure 3.20. Dinosaur head with and without per-vertex displacement mapping. *Courtesy NVIDIA Corporation.*

However, this technique has some problems. Unless the perturbations are small, which they mostly are, then the surface tessellation may no longer be valid for rendering. A connected problem is that whenever we move the vertices the surface normals are no longer correct. This is easily seen by considering a planar surface where all the surface normals are $(0,0,1)$. After moving vertices along such normals, they become invalid–they still represent a planar surface. If standard lighting is applied to the surface it will render as a plane despite the vertex perturbations. We cannot recalculate the surface normals in the vertex shader by definition, and thus a normal map which contains the updated normals must also be used.

Appendix 3.1: Texture Map Functions

Portions copyright (c) NVIDIA Corporation, 2001-2005. Reprinted with permission.

Texture Map Functions	
Function	**Description**
`tex1D(sampler1D tex, float s)`	1D nonprojective
`tex1D(sampler1D tex, float s, float dsdx, float dsdy)`	1D nonprojective with derivatives
`tex1D(sampler1D tex, float2 sz)`	1D nonprojective depth compare
`tex1D(sampler1D tex, float2 sz, float dsdx, float dsdy)`	1D nonprojective depth compare with derivatives
`tex1Dproj(sampler1D tex, float2 sq)`	1D projective
`tex1Dproj(sampler1D tex, float3 szq)`	1D projective depth compare
`tex2D(sampler2D tex, float2 s)`	2D nonprojective
`tex2D(sampler2D tex, float2 s, float2 dsdx, float2 dsdy)`	2D nonprojective with derivatives
`tex2D(sampler2D tex, float3 sz)`	2D nonprojective depth compare

Texture Map Functions

Function	Description
tex2D(sampler2D *tex*, float3 *sz*, float2 *dsdx*, float2 *dsdy*)	
	2D nonprojective depth compare with derivatives
tex2Dproj(**sampler2D** *tex*, float3 *sq*)	
	2D projective
tex2Dproj(**sampler2D** *tex*, float4 *szq*)	
	2D projective depth compare
texRECT(**samplerRECT** *tex*, float2 *s*)	
	2D RECT nonprojective
texRECT(**samplerRECT** *tex*, float2 *s*, float2 *dsdx*, float2 *dsdy*)	
	2D RECT nonprojective with derivatives
texRECT(**samplerRECT** *tex*, float3 *sz*)	
	2D RECT nonprojective depth compare
texRECT(**samplerRECT** *tex*, float3 *sz*, float2 *dsdx*, float2 *dsdy*)	
	2D RECT nonprojective depth compare with derivatives
texRECTproj(**samplerRECT** *tex*, float3 *sq*)	
	2D RECT projective
texRECTproj(**samplerRECT** *tex*, float3 *szq*)	
	2D RECT projective depth compare
tex3D(sampler3D *tex*, float3 *s*)	
	3D nonprojective
tex3D(sampler3D *tex*, float3 *s*, float3 *dsdx*, float3 *dsdy*)	
	3D nonprojective with derivatives
tex3Dproj(**sampler3D** *tex*, float4 *szq*)	
	3D projective depth compare

Texture Map Functions	
Function	**Description**
`texCUBE(samplerCUBE tex, float3 s)`	
	Cubemap nonprojective
`texCUBE(samplerCUBE tex, float3 s, float3 dsdx, float3 dsdy)`	
	Cubemap nonprojective with derivatives
`texCUBEproj(samplerCUBE tex, float4 sq)`	
	Cubemap projective

Chapter Four

Rendering Shadows

Introduction

Shadows are an important element in achieving high quality rendering. And as far as human visual perception is concerned, they impart important clues that inform us of the relative positions of objects and light sources. For example, if we render an object on a planar surface without shadows, then we cannot tell from the image if the object is resting on the planar surface or floating above it. The ideal requirements of shadow methods, which can now be achieved with GPUs, are:

- We should be able to cast shadows from all objects onto all other objects.
- Shadows should be 'soft'—hard-edged shadows are unusual in most lit environments.
- Shadow calculation should operate efficiently in real time.

The two popular algorithms that achieve these goals on hardware are stencil shadow volumes and shadow maps.

Stencil Shadow Volumes

The basic shadow volume method was first introduced by Frank Crow in 1977 [CROW77]. The original idea was difficult to implement, although simple in concept.

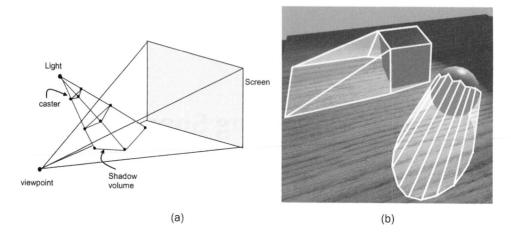

(a)   (b)

Figure 4.1. (a) The shadow volume for a triangle intersecting a view frustum. (b) The shadow volume for a sphere and a box. *Image courtesy Gilliard Lopes and Francisco Fonseca, Paralelo.com.*

Figure 4.1(a) shows the idea. The shadow caster, in this case a triangle, sweeps out an infinite frustum from a point light source, and any objects contained therein are in shadow. We make the frustum finite by considering its intersection with the view frustum, and this intersection is called a shadow volume. Figure 4.1(b) is a visualisation of the shadow volumes for a sphere and a box superimposed on a rendered scene. The silhouette edge of the sphere object with respect to the light source is formed from edges of the triangles that make up the sphere.

The original algorithm used the silhouette of the object as the shadow caster and constructed a shadow polygon object from the polygons that made up the volume. In our illustration, we have used each triangle as a caster, and this will result in a shadow volume object of two triangles and three quadrilaterals. A distinction is made between front-facing shadow polygons (with respect to the viewpoint) and back-facing polygons, and a point is deemed to be in shadow if it is behind a front-facing polygon and in front of a back-facing one (Figure 4.2).

The problem with this classic method and hardware is the determination of the silhouette edge of the caster object. If implemented on the CPU, then it prevents such operations as skinning being implemented as vertex programs. However, solutions to this problem have continued to evolve (see, for example, [MCGU03]).

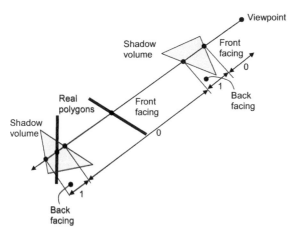

Figure 4.2. Front-and back-facing shadow volumes and the shadow counter value.

In the past, the algorithm was implemented on the CPU by integrating it with a depth-priority hidden surface removal algorithm. For each pixel, we consider a vector or ray from the viewpoint to the pixel and look at the relationship between object polygons and shadow polygons along this line. To do this, a pixel counter is maintained. This is initialised to 1 if the viewpoint is already in shadow, 0 otherwise. As we descend the depth-sorted polygons list of polygons, the counter is incremented when a front-facing polygon is passed and decremented when a back-facing polygon is passed. The value of the counter tells us if we are in shadow when we encounter an object polygon.

With the advent of graphics hardware and in particular stencil buffers, it became possible to implement a shadow volume algorithm in real time. The stencil buffer functions as a per-fragment counter, and the shadow determination pass of the algorithm sets the stencil buffer to zero for illuminated fragments and to a nonzero integer for fragments in shadow. Effectively, we build up a binary mask in the stencil buffer that will represent the influence of the shadow volume at the next pass when the scene is rendered.

For each fragment P (Figure 4.3) in the shadow volume, the method effectively considers the line passing through P and the viewpoint. We need to in effect count the intersections between P and V, the viewpoint. his is effected by rasterising the shadow faces using z-pass. The stencil is set to increment when a front face is rasterized and decrement when a back face is rasterized. If we consider moving along the line in the opposite direction, we would use z-fail.

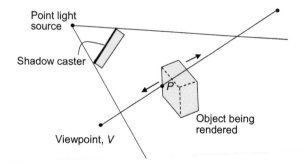

Figure 4.3. A shadow volume for a single polygon.

A generic shadow volume algorithm will have the following simplified structure:

1. Render scene using ambient lighting, writing to the depth buffer.
2. Clear the stencil buffer, calculate the shadow volume for each object and render it (to the stencil buffer) using depth pass or depth fail.
3. Render the scene, darkening pixels that correspond to non-zero stencil values.

The difficulty here is determining the shadow volume for an object, and two common ways of doing this are to construct a shadow volume for each triangle (very inefficient but simple to implement) or construct a shadow volume by extruding edges that form part of the silhouette edge of the object as suggested in the original algorithm. We now detail these two approaches.

Per-Triangle Stencil Shadow Volumes

The brute force way to overcome the silhouette problem is to ignore it and implement a per-triangle approach. That is, we render the silhouette edge of *each* triangle exactly as shown in Figure 4.1(a). Alternatively, we can find the silhouette by using a vertex program (see the next section). The per-triangle technique is straightforward to implement but suffers from high geometry overload and also high fill rate overload. The idea here is to construct a shadow volume per triangle front facing the light. As Figure 4.1(a) shows, the shadow volume then consists of three quads for the sides and two triangles known as caps. This adds up to eight triangles for each triangle extruded.

The algorithm starts by clearing the stencil buffer and masking out the colour and depth buffer writing as we will only be modifying the stencil buffer at this stage.

```
glStencilMask(~0);
glEnable(GL_STENCIL_TEST);
glEnable(GL_STENCIL);
glColorMask(GL_FALSE,GL_FALSE,GL_FALSE,GL_FALSE);
glDepthMask(GL_FALSE);
glClear(GL_STENCIL_BUFFER_BIT);
```

We then draw all shadow volumes so that the back faces decrement the stencil buffer and the front faces increment it. This can be done in two passes as follows:

```
glStencilFunc(GL_ALWAYS,0,~0);


glStencilOp(GL_KEEP,GL_INCR_WRAP_EXT,GL_KEEP);
glCullFace(GL_FRONT);
obj->draw_shadows(l->pos);


glStencilOp(GL_KEEP,GL_DECR_WRAP_EXT,GL_KEEP);
glCullFace(GL_BACK);
obj->draw_shadows(l->pos);
```

Alternatively, we can use an extension called two-sided stencil (also called separate stencil) where you can specify the stencil operation for front faces and back faces. In this way, we can draw the shadow volumes in a single pass.

Using two-sided stencil, we would write

```
glDisable(GL_CULL_FACE);
glEnable(GL_STENCIL_TEST_TWO_SIDE_EXT);


glActiveStencilFaceEXT(GL_BACK);
glStencilFunc(GL_ALWAYS,0,~0);
glStencilOp(GL_KEEP,GL_INCR_WRAP_EXT,GL_KEEP);


glActiveStencilFaceEXT(GL_FRONT);
glStencilOp(GL_KEEP,GL_DECR_WRAP_EXT,GL_KEEP);
glStencilFunc(GL_ALWAYS,0,~0);


obj->draw_shadows(l->pos);
```

```
glDisable(GL_STENCIL_TEST_TWO_SIDE_EXT);
```

and using separate stencil

```
glDisable(GL_CULL_FACE);
glStencilFuncSeparateATI(GL_ALWAYS,GL_ALWAYS,0,~0);
glStencilOpSeparateATI(GL_BACK,GL_KEEP,GL_INCR_WRAP_EXT,GL_KEEP);
glStencilOpSeparateATI(GL_FRONT,GL_KEEP,GL_DECR_WRAP_EXT,GL_KEEP);
obj->draw_shadows(l->pos);
```

When rendering the lighting pass, we set up stencil testing so that only fragments where stencil is set to 0 will receive lighting. This is done as follows:

```
glStencilMask(0);
glColorMask(GL_TRUE,GL_TRUE,GL_TRUE,GL_TRUE);
glStencilOp(GL_KEEP,GL_KEEP,GL_KEEP);
glStencilFunc(GL_EQUAL,0,~0);
```

We can use a vertex shader to extrude the triangle vertices in the light direction which is otherwise an expensive process if implemented on the CPU (Listing 4.1). We send with each vertex extra information indicating whether the vertex should be extruded or not. This is done by passing a fourth component to the vertex position as 0 or 1.

Listing 4.1

Extrudes the triangle vertices in the light direction.

```
struct app2vert
{
        float4 pos : POSITION;
};
struct vert2frag
{
        float4 hpos : POSITION;
};


vert2frag main_vert_shadow(
    app2vert IN,
    uniform float4x4 modelviewproj,
    uniform float4 lightposs)
{
        vert2frag OUT;
```

```
float3 lightdir = normalize(IN.pos.xyz-lightpos.xyz);

float dist = IN.pos.w>0.5 ? lightpos.w : 0.1;

float4 pos = IN.pos;
pos.xyz += lightdir*dist;
pos.w = 1;

OUT.hpos = mul(modelviewproj, pos);
return OUT;
}
```

The geometry processing cost of this method per triangle is two triangles and three quads—a total of eight shadow volume triangles per object triangles—an extremely high cost which motivates the next method. Figure 4.4 shows a scene rendered in this way. This fulfils the first of our original goals (we should be able to cast shadows from all objects onto all other objects), but it is extremely inefficient for complex objects, and it produces hard-edged shadows.

Figure 4.4. A scene rendered using the per-triangle shadow volume method. *Courtesy Gilliard Lopes and Francisco Fonseca.*

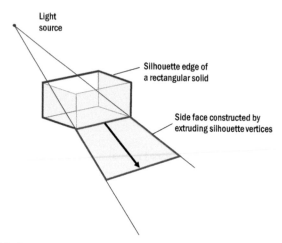

Figure 4.5. Side faces in the shadow volume are formed by extruding components of the silhouette edge.

Per-Edge Stencil Shadow Volumes

The solution to creating shadow volumes more efficiently is to reduce the number of volumes to an absolute minimum. We can do this by finding the silhouette edge of the object and extruding this (Figure 4.5), and this was the original idea used in early implementations as we described above. A hardware implementation for this approach is possible and is a good example of the efficiency of hardware approaches to a 'traditional problem'. Searching through the mesh in the CPU to find a set of silhouette loops is hopelessly inefficient.

The shadow volume for an object is made up of caps and sides. The number of polygons in the shadow volume is no longer fixed at eight triangles but is a function of the number of edges in the silhouette edge. We call the faces of the shadow volume facing the light the 'light cap'. The 'dark cap' comprises back-facing polygons. We now have three component faces in the shadow volume.

- The light cap is constructed from front-facing polygons ($N \cdot L > 0$) and closes the top of the shadow volume.

- The sides (quads) are formed by extruding vertices that are contained by the silhouette edge by a constant distance along the light ray.

- The dark cap is composed of back-facing polygons.

The vertex program checks, for each vertex, the dot product of the vertex normal and light direction vector of each vertex. If this is negative, the vertex is back facing the light and is extruded. In order to generate the shadow volumes, we draw the caps followed by the sides in two passes.

To draw the caps, we render the mesh as in flat shading where each of the three vertices of a triangle possesses the face normal. A back-facing (the light) triangle will be extruded and it will generate the bottom cap. Similarly front-facing triangles will generate the top cap.

For the sides, we draw all edges of the mesh, and for each edge, we draw four vertices. Each edge is defined by two vertices (v_1,v_2) and shared by two faces with different normals $(\mathbf{N_1},\mathbf{N_2})$. The edge is rendered as a quad with the following sequence of vertices and normals:

$$v_1, \mathbf{N}_1$$

$$v_2, \mathbf{N}_1$$

$$v_2, \mathbf{N}_2$$

$$v_1, \mathbf{N}_2$$

Figure 4.6(a) shows an edge which is not a silhouette edge considered as a degenerate quad; Figure 4.6(b) shows an extruded edge. Thus, edges contained in the silhouette will have two of their vertices extruded, generating a valid quad. Edges not on the silhouette edge either have all of their four vertices extruded or none, thus generating degenerate polygons which are discarded by the rasterisation process. With this approach, the geometry draw is reduced to one pass that draws all triangles in the mesh and one pass that draws all the edges in the mesh. The geometry processing will be almost the same as for the previous technique, but the fill rate savings are enormous. Listing 4.2 is the shader or edge extrusion.

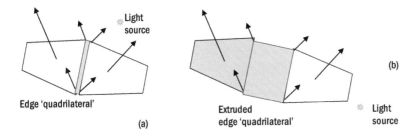

Figure 4.6. Extruding edge 'quadrilaterals'.

Listing 4.2

Shadow volume using
edge extrusion.

```
struct app2vert
{
        float4 pos : POSITION;
        float4 normal : NORMAL;
};


struct vert2frag
{
        float4 hpos : POSITION;
};


vert2frag main_vert_shadow(
        app2vert IN,
        uniform float4x4 modelviewproj,
        uniform float4 lightposs)
{

        vert2frag OUT;

        float3 lightdir=normalize(IN.pos.xyz-lightpos.xyz);

        float dist=dot(lightdir,IN.normal)<0?lightpos.w:0.1;

        float4 pos=IN.pos;

        pos.xyz+=lightdir*dist;
        pos.w=1;

        OUT.hpos = mul(modelviewproj, pos);
        return OUT;
}
```

Efficiency and Shadow Volumes

A visualisation of the efficacy of the per-edge approach is shown in Figure 4.7 which compares the per-edge algorithm with the per-triangles algorithm. The whiteness of the rendered shadow volumes is an indication of their volume density. The per-edge sphere generates a single shadow volume, whereas the per-

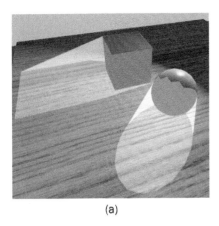 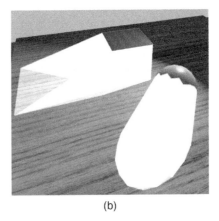

(a)   (b)

Figure 4.7. A visualisation of shadow volume density using (a) per-edge algorithm and (b) per-triangle algorithm. Increasing whiteness equals higher spatial density of shadow volumes. *Courtesy Gilliard Lopes and Francisco Fonseca.*

one triangle will generate a number equal to the number of triangles in the object. Each of these volumes has to be rendered.

Fill rate and geometry cost are the biggest problem with shadow volumes, and this is due to the fact that small casters near a point light source can generate very large shadow volume polygons that occupy a significant area of the current screen image. In practice, for a 10^6 pixel resolution image of some complexity, the fill rate can be 10^9 pixels per frame. High geometry costs originate from scene complexity, and we can say that this algorithm does not scale well for increasing scene complexity.

Apart from scene complexity, the other source of the fill rate problem is the position of the dark cap or the extrusion distance for silhouette edges.

Shadow volumes should be constructed by extruding by the smallest possible distance in order to save on fill rate. Normally, we would use the light influence radius to clip the shadow volume, but this is problematic as shown in Figure 4.8, where we can see that this approach will always leave a lit region whose volume is a function of the distance of the polygon to be extruded. The alternative is to calculate the exact extrusion distance required, but this means passing more information into the shader (polygon plane parameters of four floats). A reasonable compromise is to use a constant distance.

The normal lighting optimisation—comparing the bounding box of an object against the light sphere or bounding box—can also be applied to shadows. If a

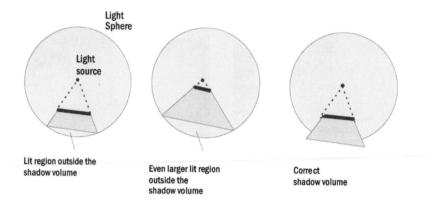

Figure 4.8. Intersecting the light radius and the dark face.

fragment is not within the influence of a light, then it cannot be in the shadow of that light.

This is most conveniently carried out in hardware in two phases. First, we can use a scissor test in *xy* to eliminate shadow volume fragments that are outside a rectangle bounding the light sources range of influence.

```
glEnable(GL_SCISSOR_TEST);
glScissor(left,top,width,height);
```

This test can be used not only to eliminate shadow volume fragments, but also during the lighting pass to discard fragments neither in shadow nor within the range of the light.

Second, we can perform a similar scissoring operation on the light range in *z* by using:

```
glEnable(GL_DEPTH_BOUNDS_EXT);
glDEpthBoundsEXT(zMin,zMax);
```

This implies that we pre-calculate the (zMin, zMax) for each light source prior to its light pass. If a fragment is outside this range it cannot be eliminated.

Shadow Volume Advantages

We now consider some of the advantages of shadow volumes. There are absolutely no restrictions on the nature of the scene—every object can shadow all other objects. It can deal with point sources—the most common type of light source,

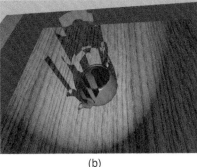

(a)   (b)

Figure 4.9. Shadow 'leaks': (a) per-triangle algorithm and (b) per-edge algorithm. *Courtesy Gilliard Lopes and Francisco Fonseca, Paralelo.com.*

and one that the next technique (shadow maps) has difficulty with. Its accuracy is one pixel, or greater if super-sampling is used. This means that it does not produce the same aliasing artefacts as shadow maps. One of our ideals is not met, however. That is, it produces hard-edged shadows.

Finally, we note that there is a restriction on the nature of the object. If we are using the per-edge approach, then objects must be closed (two manifolds) or shadows 'leak'. This means that we cannot have any edges with only one adjacent face. The teapot is an example of such an object and Figure 4.9 shows the errors produced by the per-edge algorithm. This is avoided by the per-triangle algorithm, but at the cost of efficiency, as we have already discussed.

Projective Texture Mapping and Shadow mapping

Projective mapping is, exactly as the name suggests, equivalent to showing a slide (or a film) through a projector. Figure 4.10 shows a movie playing in a game level. The animation frames are precalculated, and the shader simply has to calculate the texture coordinates for the current frame.

Projective texture differs from normal texture mapping in an important aspect. In conventional texture mapping, a shader will use coordinates (u,v) which are usually determined semi-automatically when a texture map is authored. An artist will use software interactively when the map is authored to fix the mapping of the texture onto the object.

Projective texture, on the other hand, calculates the texture coordinates (u,v) for an object. As the illustration shows, the method is exactly analogous to a slide

Figure 4.10. Projective texture—a movie in a games level.

projector, where the slide is the texture map, forming an image on the surface of an object.

Apart from its occasional use as a virtual projector, the main use of projective texture mapping is to render shadows using a shadow map. Shadow maps compete with shadow volumes for popularity of usage and possess certain advantages over the shadow volume approach as we shall see. The technique was first proposed by L. Williams [WILL78]. The shadow map is a depth map rendered from the point of view of the light source that is being considered.

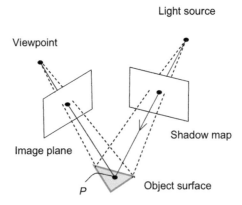

Figure 4.11. Projective texture for shadow mapping. The shadow map is effectively projected onto the object surface.

During rendering, we can consider that the depth map is projected onto the object. For fragment P (Figure 4.11), we compare its depth with the depth stored in the shadow map. If the depth of P is greater than the shadow map depth then there is an object closer to the light source, and P is in shadow.

Of course, we do not physically project the depth map onto the scene, rather we use P to calculate the (u,v) coordinate required to access the shadow map. Thus we need to transform the object geometry from world space, say, into the light source space. We do this as follows:

$$\text{texProjCoord} = \begin{bmatrix} u \\ v \\ z \\ q \end{bmatrix} = \begin{bmatrix} 0.5 & & & 0.5 \\ & 0.5 & & 0.5 \\ & & 0.5 & 0.5 \\ & & & 1 \end{bmatrix} \begin{bmatrix} & & \\ & Light \\ & Space \\ Transformation \end{bmatrix} \begin{bmatrix} x_0 \\ y_0 \\ z_0 \\ w_0 \end{bmatrix}$$

The first matrix multiplication results in values in the range -1 to 1, which are subsequently scaled to the range 0 to 1 required for texture coordinates. The depth comparison is implemented by the sampler function:

```
float4 shadow = tex2Dproj(shadowMap,texProjCoord);
```

This function first divides the u and v coordinates by the q coordinate, then performs the depth comparison between the shadow map value and the value of z/q. It returns a four component vector of the format $(f,f,f,1)$ where f is 0 or 1 depending on whether the fragment is in shadow or not. This value can then be used to modulate the diffuse lighting component.

The vertex and fragment program for shadow mapping is Listing 4.3. Figure 4.12 shows the rendered scene.

Listing 4.3
Vertex and fragment program for shadow mapping.

```
void ShadowMap_vertex(
    float4 position : POSITION,
    float3 normal   : NORMAL,

    out float4 oPosition     : POSITION,
    out float4 texCoordProj  : TEXCOORD0,
    out float4 diffuse       : TEXCOORD1,

    uniform float4x4 modelViewProj,
    uniform float3   lightPos,
```

```
    uniform float4x4 textureMatrix)
{

    oPosition = mul(modelViewProj, position);
    float3 lightDir = normalize(lightPos - position.xyz);
    diffuse = dot(lightDir, normal);

    // Compute texture coordinates/vertex
    texCoordProj = mul(textureMatrix, position);
}

void shadowMap_frag(
    float4 texCoordProj       : TEXCOORD0,
    float4 diffuse            : TEXCOORD1,
    out float4 colour         : COLOR,
    uniform sampler2D shadowMap)
{

    float4 colour = tex2Dproj(shadowMap, texCoordProj);
    colour = colour * diffuse;
}
```

Despite being a very straightforward technique to implement, there are many and varied problems with shadow mapping. Aliasing is the main problem and arises from inaccuracies in the representation of depth and also the classical cause of aliasing—point sampling. Aliasing in shadow mapping manifests as jagged shadow edge borders. Figure 4.13(a) illustrates the point sampling problem where the projection of a pixel onto the object surface and into the shadow map produces a 'footprint' in the shadow map which may include many texels. The area of this footprint is a function of the transformation and the inclination of the surface. Figure 4.13(b) compares a zoom of our shadow test scene rendered with shadow volumes and a shadow map, which clearly demonstrates the problem.

We could, of course, increase the resolution of the shadow maps, but this has an obvious limit. Alternatively, we can adopt an adaptive approach [FERN01] by detecting under-sampled areas in the shadow map and redrawing these at higher resolution, but such an approach is CPU intensive.

To make a correct in-shadow/not in-shadow decision we need to integrate the information over the footprint. Point sampling the depth map will lead to visible errors. You cannot simply average shadow map texels—this would simply result

Figure 4.12. Scene rendered using the shadow map method. *Courtesy Gilliard Lopes and Francisco Fonseca, Paralelo.com.*

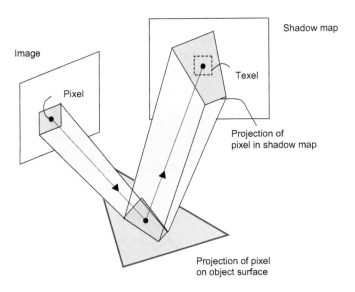

Figure 4.13. Aliasing problems in shadow mapping. (a) Point sampling in shadow mapping. (b) Shadow volume (left) and shadow mapping (right).

1	1	1	0
1	1	1	0
1	1	0	0
1	1	0	0

Figure 4.14. Hardware samples 2 x 2 texels centred on current texel.

in wrong depth values. Integrating the information over an area means averaging the results of the Boolean comparisons in some way. A way to do this is to fetch the surrounding texels. The binary comparison is made for each texel, which results in an array of 1s and 0s. Depth values at each texel are then compared to the current pixel depth from the light. If the value from the shadow map is smaller, then the pixel is in shadow and the lighting amount for this texel is 0. This can be reduced to a single diminution factor by bilinear interpolation.

We return to consider **tex2Dproj** which returns a four component vector of the format $(f, f, f, 1)$. This can perform rudimentary anti-aliasing as follows (Figure 4.14). If bilinear texture filtering is enabled, f is returned in the range 0 to 1. In this case, four depth comparisons are made and the results averaged, resulting in a returned value of 0, 0.25, 0.5, 0.75, or 1. The case in the illustration would yield a value of 0.75. This is called "percentage closer filtering".

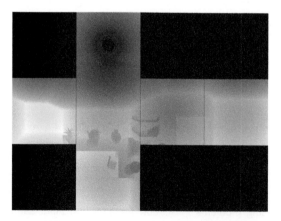

Figure 4.15. Shadow map of a room rendered from an omnidirectional point.

Figure 4.16. Shadow maps in a game level (rotating fan).

Figure 4.17. Shadow maps in a game level (grid).

A second problem is that the method as described is effectively limited to spotlights. It can only capture information within the frustum of the light source. If an omnidirectional source is to be used, we need to construct a shadow map in the form of an environment map—say a cube map—as shown in Figure 4.15. Details on how to implement this technique in hardware are given in [KING04]and [GERA04]. Generating six images per omni-light per frame is costly and currently no extension is available to render directly to a cube map (copy depth map needs to be used instead).

Finally, we look at how shadow maps can be used effectively in games. Figure 4.16 shows shadows generated in a game level from a rotating fan. Shadows from fan blades appear both on the floor and on the fan casing. Figure 4.17 shows shadows from a grid (an alpha texture) enabling shadows cast by the grid to appear on the floor.

Shadow Map Advantages

Although shadow maps alias badly, they are efficient and do not have the object type disadvantage of shadow volumes. To render only requires two passes, and there is no extra geometry to draw. In this respect, they enable large scenes to have shadows, and for this reason alone, they are the preferred option in many games

Because the two principal algorithms—shadow maps and shadow volumes—exhibit mutually exclusive advantages a suggested strategy is to combine them into a hybrid algorithm.

Combining Shadow Maps and Volumes

In this approach, researchers have tried to combine the strengths of each algorithm and at the same time eliminate their weaknesses. In other words, they try to construct a method that efficiently produces accurate (hard) shadows with low fill rate. The first hybrid algorithm was suggested by M. McCool [MCCO00] and was named "Shadow Volume Reconstruction". The key to hybrid algorithms is that the edges visible in the conventional shadow map are projections of the silhouette edge of the object, and we can use image processing technology to detect these edges. McCool used such detected edges to reconstruct the shadow volume for an object (instead of using the above methods).

Methods that use image processing of the shadow maps have to rely on *successful* edge detection of the silhouette edge. Detecting an edge which is not on a silhouette (false positive) does not cause any problems, but not detecting part of a silhouette edge (false negative) will result in a visible error.

To render a silhouette edge we note that the shadow map is in light space and each point $z(x,y)$ is a vertex of an object in this space. We can transform this object into world space (using the inverse of the shadow map projection) and render it.

A more recent hybrid algorithm that exploits current hardware is due to E. Chan *et al.* [CHAN04]. They do this by using the shadow map to quickly find the pixels at the hard edge of the shadows then apply the shadow volume algorithm, rasterizing and updating the stencil buffer only at those pixels that lie on a silhouette edge.

Perspective Shadow Mapping

An increasingly popular variation of shadow maps is perspective shadow map. So far we have discussed shadow volumes, which work in object space, and shadow maps, which work in image space. Perspective shadow maps work in post-projective space, that is, after the perspective transform. The motivation here is that they engender a reduction of the shadow map aliasing problem at virtually zero cost. Figure 4.18 (from [STMI02]) shows a partial scene with shadows rendered by using a conventional shadow map and a perspective shadow map.

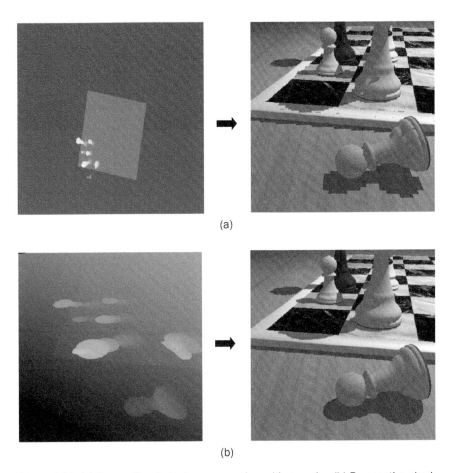

(a)

(b)

Figure 4.18. (a) Conventional shadow map and resulting render. (b) Perspective shadow map and resulting render. *Courtesy Marc Stamminger and George Drettakis.*

With large scenes, the aliasing problem in shadow maps is exacerbated—shadows near to the viewpoint need a higher resolution than shadows far away. And so aliasing is more visible near to the viewpoint. Perspective shadow maps address this problem by enabling a high resolution nearby and a decreased resolution at distances far from the viewpoint as can be seen by comparing Figure 4.18 (a) and (b). By calculating the shadow map in the camera's post-perspective space, we effectively distort the geometry so that objects close to the camera are enlarged while those far away are shrunk—the consequence of the perspective divide. This means that when we calculate the perspective shadow map, objects

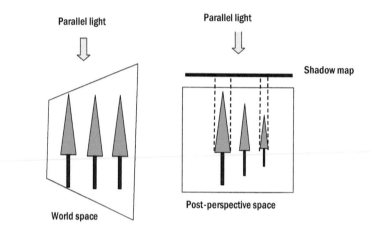

Figure 4.19. Showing the concept of perspective shadow maps: objects of same size but nearer the viewpoint have larger projections in the shadow map. *Adapted from an illustration in [STMI02].*

near the viewpoint will in general project into larger areas in the perspective shadow map which implies a more accurate projection and more accurate shadow edges. The idea is shown in principle in Figure 4.19.

Although a simple concept, perspective shadow maps involve some difficulties. First, consider the case shown in Figure 4.20. Here we show an object outside the view frustum but inside the light frustum. Even although this object cannot be seen by the viewer, it can still cast shadows on the viewed scene. To take this case into account, Stamminger *et al.* suggested using a virtual camera, moving the viewpoint until it includes all objects casting shadows and placing the light in front of the (new) viewpoint.

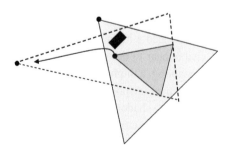

Figure 4.20. Showing an object outside the view frustum but inside the light frustum.

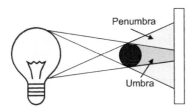

Figure 4.21. Umbra and penumbra.

However, S. Kozlov points out in [KOZL04] that there are problems with this cure. He shows that even a small shift in the viewpoint causes degradation in the shadow quality because it effectively decreases the resolution of the shadow map. Another not insignificant problem is the calculation of the viewpoint shift, which would involve volume intersection calculations on the CPU. These issues, and a new solution, are discussed in depth in [KOZL04].

Soft Shadows

In this final section, we deal with the remaining goal—shadows should have soft edges. Hard-edged shadows created by an ideal point light source are rare in real life, though common in computer graphics because they simplify rendering. Because of the visual importance of this, the effect of using a point light is much more deleterious in shadow generation than it is in Phong shading.

We expect to see the soft-edged shadows due to an area light source. An area or distributed light source will be made up of an umbra and penumbra (Figure 4.21) which merge into each other to produce a gradient towards the edge of the shadow. The relative size of these regions is determined by the size of the distributed light and its distance from the object.

The umbra (darker region) is that area of the shadowed object that is completely cut off from the light, and the penumbra is that part of the surface that receives some light.

With soft shadows in computer graphics we tend to mean softening of the shadow edge or boundary rather than accurately calculating the graduation of light intensity over the entire extent of the shadow. We have already introduced a technique that does just that—percentage closer filtering—the motivation of which was to reduce the jagged shadow edge effect. We can use the same utility to further soften the shadows by increasing the sampling area.

M. Bunell [BUNE04] calls this a brute force method and suggests applying the hardware filter shown in Figure 4.22 sixteen times over an area centred on the reference

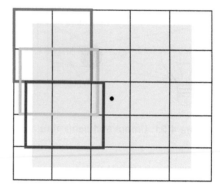

Figure 4.22. 5 x 5 texels being sampled 16 times by `tex2DProj`.

pixel, making an effective total of 64 samples. Effectively, we are convolving the 2 x 2 percentage closer hardware filter over this larger area. Three of the 16 hardware filter positions are shown in the illustration (displaced horizontally for clarity). Each hardware filter is performing the operation illustrated in Figure 4.14.

Shadow Techniques for Relief Texture Mapped Objects

We have included this section in the chapter on shadows for the obvious reason that it is a shadow technique, but it should be read only after reading the next chapter, which details relief mapping.

Integrating shadows to the relief map objects is an important feature in fully integrating the effect into a game scenario. The corrected depth option (see Chapter 5), which ensures that the depth values stored in Z-buffer include the displaced depth from the relief map, makes it possible to implement correct shadow effects for such objects. We consider the use of stencil shadows and shadow maps in this context. We can implement three types of shadows: shadows from relief object to the world, from the world to relief object and from relief object to itself (self-shadows).

Let us first consider what can be achieved using stencil volume shadows. When generating the shadow volumes, we can only use the polygons from the original mesh to generate the volume. This means that the shadows from relief objects to the world will not show the displaced geometry of the relief texture, but will reflect the shape of the original triangle mesh without the displaced pixels (Figure 4.23).

However, as we have the corrected depth stored in Z-buffer when rendering the lighting pass we can have shadows volumes from the world projected onto the relief objects correctly, and they will follow the displaced geometry properly. Self-shadows (relief object to itself) are not possible with stencil shadows.

Figure 4.23. A relief mapped object cannot produce correct object to world shadows using shadow volumes.

Thus, using relief maps in conjunction with shadow volumes, we have the following:

- Relief object to world: correct silhouette or displacement visible in shadows is not possible.

- World to relief object: shadows can project on displaced pixels correctly.

- Relief object to relief object: not possible.

Relief mapped objects integrate much better into shadow map algorithms. Using a shadow map, we can resolve all three cases; as for any other object, we render the relief mapped object into the shadow map. As the shadow map only needs depth values, the shader, used when rendering the object to the shadow map, does not need to calculate lighting. Also if no self-shadows are desired, we could simplify the ray intersect function to invoke only the linear search (as in this case we only need to know if a pixel has an intersection and we do not need the exact intersection point). The shader used when rendering relief objects to a shadow map is given in Listing 4.4, and an example is shown in Figure 4.24.

To project shadows from the world to the relief map objects, we need to pass the shadow map texture and light matrix (light frustum view/projection/bias multiplied by inverse camera view matrix). Then, just before calculating the final colour in the shader we project the displaced pixel position into the light space and compare the depth map at that position to the pixel depth in light space.

113

Figure 4.24. Using relief mapped objects in conjunction with shadow maps. Shadows from relief object to world.

```
#ifdef RM_SHADOWS
        // transform pixel position to shadow map space
        sm=mul(viewinverse_lightviewprojbias,position);
        sm/=sm.w;
        if (sm.z>f1tex2D(shadowmap,sm.xy))
                att=0;  // set attenuation to 0
#endif
```

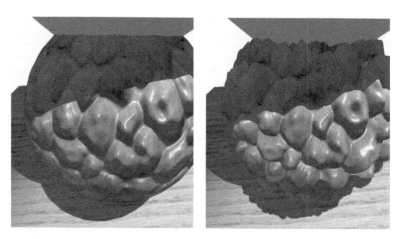

Figure 4.25. Shadows from world to relief objects. Left image shows normal mapping, and right image, relief mapping (notice how the shadow boundary follows the displaced relief correctly).

An example of this approach is shown in Figure 4.25. This is compared with a conventional render using a normal map in conjunction with a shadow map.

Thus, using relief maps in conjunction with shadow maps, we can implement the following:

- Relief object to world: good silhouette and displacement visible in shadows.

- World to relief object: Shadows can project on displaced pixels correctly.

- Relief object to relief object: possible if full linear/binary search and depth correct used when rendering to shadow map.

Listing 4.4

Using relief mapped objects in conjunction with shadow maps.

```
float ray_intersect_rm_shadow(
                in sampler2D reliefmap,
                in float2 tx,
                in float3 v,
                in float f,
                in float tmax)
{
   const int linear_search_steps=10;

   float t=0.0;
   float best_t=tmax+0.001;
   float size=best_t/linear_search_steps;

   // search for first point inside object
   for( int i=0;i<linear_search_steps-1;i++ )
   {
                t+=size;
                float3 p=ray_position(t,tx,v,f);
                float4 tex=tex2D(reliefmap,p.xy);
                if (best_t>tmax)
                if (p.z>tex.w)
                        best_t=t;
   }

   return best_t;
}
```

```
f2s main_frag_relief_shadow(
        v2f IN,
        uniform sampler2D rmtex:TEXUNIT0,       // rm texture map
        uniform float4 planes,           // near and far plane info
        uniform float tile,                  // tile factor
        uniform float depth)            // depth factor
    {

        f2s OUT;

        // view vector in eye space
        float3 view=normalize(IN.vpos);

        // view vector in tangent space
        float3 v=normalize(float3(dot(view,IN.tangent.xyz),
                dot(view,IN.binormal.xyz),dot(-view,IN.normal)));

        // mapping scale from object to texture space
        float2 mapping=float2(IN.tangent.w,IN.binormal.w)/tile;

        // quadric coefficients transformed to texture space
        float2 quadric=IN.curvature.xy*mapping.xy*mapping.xy/depth;

        // view vector in texture space
        v.xy/=mapping;
        v.z/=depth;

        // quadric applied to view vector coodinates
        float f=quadric.x*v.x*v.x+quadric.y*v.y*v.y;

        // compute max distance for search min(t(z=0),t(z=1))
        float d=v.z*v.z-4*f;
        float tmax=100;
        if (d>0)                 // t when z=1
                tmax=(-v.z+sqrt(d))/(-2*f);
        d=v.z/f;                 // t when z=0
        if (d>0)
                tmax=min(tmax,d);
```

```
#ifndef RM_DEPTHCORRECT
        // no depth correct, use simple ray_intersect
        float t=ray_intersect_rm_shadow(rmtex,IN.
texcoord*tile,v,f,tmax);
        if (t>tmax)
                discard; // no intesection, discard fragment
#else
        // with depth correct, use full ray_intersect
        float t=ray_intersect_rm(rmtex,IN.texcoord*tile,v,f,tmax);
        if (t>tmax)
                discard; // no intesection, discard fragment

        // compute displaced pixel position in view space
        float3 p=IN.vpos.xyz+view*t;

        // a=-far/(far-near)
        // b=-far*near/(far-near)
        // Z=(a*z+b)/-z
        OUT.depth=((planes.x*p.z+planes.y)/-p.z);
#endif

        return OUT;
}
```

Chapter Five

Advanced Mapping Techniques and Ray Tracing on the GPU

Introduction

In Chapter 3, we described how to implement bump mapping–the popular and long–lived method that enables apparent surface detail to appear on the surface of a rendered object without perturbing the surface geometry. In this chapter, we will look at ways to expand this illusion. We want to do this by retaining the overall advantage of bump mapping–that it is a texture map approach. In particular, we want to be able to map relief textures onto an arbitrary polygonal model.

We will also in the course of this chapter see that we can use GPUs to implement algorithms such as ray tracing. By that we mean GPUs can be used for algorithms other than shading equations and their associated geometric calculations. It is the case that GPUs are beginning to be used for applications that lie outside the rendering field–fluid mechanics is an example [MARK04]. The motivation here is to use the greater power of the hardware (compared to the CPU). This culture has come to be known as GPGPUure or General Purpose computing on a GPU.[1]

The following sections show the evolution of methods that cache detailed surface geometry in texture maps–specifically, height maps (or equivalently depth maps). These are presented in approximate order of complexity and cost. A particular method can be chosen depending on the demands of the application. The series also demonstrates the evolution and refinement of a single idea, which is how much of computer graphics research progresses.

....

[1] See www.gpgpu.org for examples and links to applications.

The methods will demonstrate that, by including depth in textures, we can design methods that result in much higher image quality than is normally achievable with maps. Depth is calculated and stored per texel and this is the main difference between these techniques and conventional texture and bump mapping. The aim of all the described methods is to render small-scale surface geometry using texture maps.

Connected with most of the described procedures are ray tracing methods. Although these are part of the mapping algorithms they can be used in other applications.

Depth and Normal Maps

In the methods that follow, we store the render attributes– colour, normal and depth–in texture maps. Normal and depth map calculations are carried out offline. Figure 5.1 shows the idea. We consider a depth map to be coplanar with a bounding box face of the object and invoke a parallel ray cast to find the depth at each pixel. This is subsequently normalised by the depth of the bounding box and stored in byte format. The normal is calculated at the same time from the surface geometry. This is identical to the normal calculation method used in Chapter 3, except for the addition of the derivation of the normalised depth map.

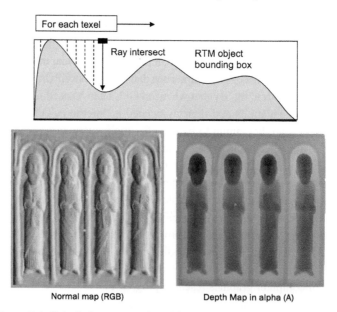

Normal map (RGB)   Depth Map in alpha (A)

Figure 5.1. Calculating a normal and depth map for a 'bas relief' object.

A general problem with the technique, which is obvious from the illustration, is that we can only deal, in this implementation, with convex objects. We can only recover information in the render phase that has been obtained in the precalculation phase. A parallel ray cast will not necessarily detect all concavities. It can only 'see' those that are visible in a viewing direction equal to the ray cast direction.

Having represented the surface detail geometry in this way, we can invoke calculations such as ray tracing in this bounding box space or a transformation of it. Effectively, the depth and normal maps replace the geometry, and we define an object as a texture map (RGBA) where the normal map is stored in RGB and the depth of the surface from the plane of the bounding box is stored in alpha as shown in Figure 5.1.

Parallax Mapping

Parallax mapping also known as offset texture mapping [KANE01], is the simplest of the depth-oriented techniques. The rendering attributes for the object, normal and colour are stored in texture maps. The principle is shown in Figure 5.2 where a view vector is intersecting the surface of an object in tangent space. For any view ray, we need to find the intersection with the surface. The information we have at the fragment is the depth of P, and we use this to find an approximation of the desired intersection P''.

In a fragment program we make two texture accesses, the first one gets the depth information d at the fragments position in texture space. Then we offset the texture coordinates for the fragments by the product of this value and the view vector in tangent space. The normal and colour are now fetched using the offset texture coordinates. Offsetting the coordinates causes the normal and colour at point P' to be used. This is an approximation to the correct point P'' but we hope that P' is closer to P'' than P.

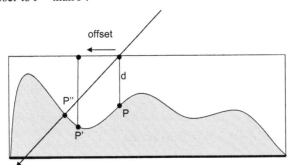

Figure 5.2. Parallax mapping—point P´ is rendered.

The Cg implementation of this technique is given in Listing 5.1.

```
f2s main_frag_parallax(
    v2f IN,
    uniform sampler2D rmtex:TEXUNIT0,      // relief map
    uniform sampler2D colortex:TEXUNIT1, // color map
    uniform float4 ambient, // ambient color
    uniform float4 diffuse, // diffuse color
    uniform float4 specular, // specular color
    uniform float tile)      // tile factor
{

    f2s OUT;

    // view and light directions
    float3 v = normalize(IN.vpos);
    float3 l = normalize(IN.lightpos.xyz - IN.vpos);

    float2 uv = IN.texcoord*tile;

    // parallax code
    float3x3 tbn = float3x3(IN.tangent,IN.binormal,IN.normal);
    float height = tex2D(rmtex,uv).w * 0.06 - 0.03;
    uv += height * mul(tbn,v).xy;

    // normal map
    float4 normal = tex2D(rmtex,uv);
    normal.xyz = normal.xyz*2.0 - 1.0; // trafsform to [-1,1]


    // transform normal to world space
    normal.xyz = normalize(normal.x*IN.tangent +
                normal.y*IN.binormal + normal.z*IN.normal);

    // color map
    float4 color = tex2D(colortex,uv);

    // compute diffuse and specular terms
```

```
float att  = saturate(dot(l,IN.normal.xyz));
float diff = saturate(dot(l,normal.xyz));
float spec = saturate(dot(normalize(l-v),normal.xyz));

// compute final color
float4 finalcolor;
finalcolor.xyz = ambient.xyz*color.xyz +
                 att*(color.xyz*diffuse.xyz*diff +
                 specular.xyz*pow(spec,specular.w));
finalcolor.w = 1.0;

OUT.color = finalcolor;

return OUT;
}
```

An image using this shader is presented in Figure 5.9 where it is compared with a bump or normal map render and an RTM render. Although, as we discuss later, there are artefacts, for the cost of one extra texture access and simple arithmetic, parallax mapping gives a significant visual image improvement over normal or bump mapping. However, because of its inaccuracy it is only suitable for irregular surface detail where the visual effect of the inaccuracies are less noticeable. In the next section, we describe how to use depth-enhanced texture maps in a more accurate manner.

Relief Texture Mapping (RTM)

Basic Algorithm

This method, introduced by M. Oliveira *et al.* [OLIV00], was named Relief Texture Mapping (RTM), and its goal is again the rendering of complex surface 3D detail using a depth-enhanced texture map as rendering data. A fragment program uses the map together with the view direction to generate different views of the object.

Figure 5.3 shows views from different angles generated from a single texture map containing normal and depth data. A single square polygon (a quad) is being drawn, and the program also performs per-fragment lighting calculations with diffuse and specular components.

Figure 5.3. Rendered RTM object.

Now the object shown in the preceding illustrations is effectively a 2½ D object which we wish to view from the front. Thus, a single RTM will suffice in this case. If we want to view a 3D object from any angle then we require five or six RTMs as Figure 5.4 demonstrates.

In this case we never want to view from below so we only have five RTMs. A maximum of three RTMs will be used at any given time in the render.

We now describe the algorithm. The technique as originally reported in [OLIV00] was an offline implementation and used forward mapping. Our implementation is real-time and uses inverse mapping. The difference between forward and inverse mapping in this context will be explained later. To render the RTM, we use an inverse mapping process where, for each pixel, we must compute what RTM texel must be moved to that pixel. (This contrasts with forward mapping, where for each texel in the RTM map, we compute its destination pixel and move the texel there.)

Figure 5.4. An object which can be viewed from front, back, left side, right side and top needs five RTMs.

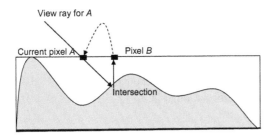

Figure 5.5. RTM algorithm—using the information at pixel B to render A.

Thus for a given pixel (A) in the RTM and a camera view direction, we define a ray (Figure 5.5). This ray produces an intersection point at the surface, and we assign the colour calculated at that hit point from the corresponding RTM texel (B) to A. Inverse mapping is required, because in a fragment shader, each pixel must compute its colour.

The remaining question is: how do we find the intersection point of the view-pixel ray with the object? We will show three ways of solving this which depend on the nature of the object.

RTM—Multi Pass for Planar Objects

In this approach we divide the object's depth information into 'depth slices' or planes parallel to the RTM plane. This produces what is known as a layered depth image, as shown, for example in Figure 5.6. In this example, the view ray through pixel A produces three intersection points on the three slices.

To find the ray slice intersects, we effect as many passes as there are slices. Again, given the current pixel A we ideally need to find the RTM texel C, corresponding

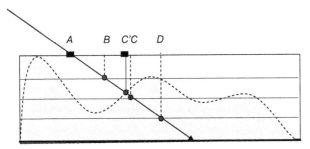

Figure 5.6. Inverse mapping to assign a render colour to the current pixel A. In this example, C is selected incurring an error. The correct pixel is C'.

to the intersection point. In this particular example, the scheme would work as follows:

Pass 1, Slice 1
>Ray intersects plane 1.
>Depth is greater than RTM object depth at D.
>Render using information at D.

Pass 2, Slice 2
>Ray intersects plane 2.
>Depth is greater than RTM object depth at C.
>Render using information at C.

Pass 3, Slice 3
>Ray intersects plane 3.
>Depth is less than RTM object depth at B.
>Discard.

The net result in this case is that A is rendered using the information at C. This incurs an error as the correct pixel is C'. The magnitude of the overall error is a function of the number of slices or passes.

The total number of passes required is thus

$$(\text{number of RTMs used}) \times (\text{number of slices})$$

One of the advantages of depth slicing is that it provides useful options. Since the cost of the pre-warp is a function of the number of passes or slices, we can easily set up a level of detail (LOD) scheme. Figure 5.7 shows four LODs obtained by varying the number of slices.

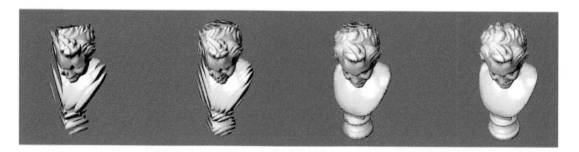

Figure 5.7. Rendering the head from three RTMs using a varying number of depth slices.

Figure 5.8. The image on the left uses RTMs aligned with the bounding box planes. The image on the right has slices normal to the view direction.

As is evident from the illustration, the slices exhibit strong coherence at a low slice resolution. Another option available using this algorithm is to define slices through the depth field that are normal to the view direction. Rendering the head using a view-aligned depth planes approach is compared to the RTM face-aligned depth planes approach in Figure 5.8.

Listing 5.2 is the shader for this multipass depth-slicing algorithm.

Listing 5.2

Multipass depth-slice RTM shader.

```
struct app2vert
{
    float4 pos  : POSITION;
    float4 color : DIFFUSE;
    float4 texcoord: TEXCOORD0;
};


struct vert2frag
{
    float4 hpos  : POSITION;
    float4 color : COLOR0;
    float4 texcoord : TEXCOORD0;
};


struct frag2screen
{
    float4 color : COLOR;
};
```

```
float2 project_uv(float3 p,float4 u,float4 v)
{
    return float2(dot(p,u.xyz)/u.w, dot(p,v.xyz)/v.w);
}


vert2frag main_vert(
    app2vert IN,
    uniform float4x4 modelviewproj)
{
    vert2frag OUT;

    OUT.hpos = mul(modelviewproj, IN.pos);
    OUT.color = IN.color;
    OUT.texcoord = IN.pos;

    return OUT;
}


frag2screen main_frag(
    vert2frag IN,
// texture map front (rgb:normal, alpha:depth)
    uniform sampler2D texdtb1,
// texture map back (rgb:normal, alpha:depth)
    uniform sampler2D texdtb2,
// plane (xyz:normal, w:distance)
    uniform float4 plane,
// base vertex pos (xyz)
    uniform float4 pos,
// base u axis (xyz:normalized, w:length)
    uniform float4 u,
// base v axis (xyz:normalized, w:length)
    uniform float4 v,
// depth related constants
    uniform float4 depth,
// camera position (xyz)
    uniform float4 camerapos,
// lightposition (xyz)
    uniform float4 lightpos,
```

```
// specular color (xyz:rgb, w:exponent)
    uniform float4 specular)
{

    frag2screen OUT;

    float4 c=float4(0,0,0,0);
    float4 t1,t2;
    float3 viewdir,lightdir,p;
    float2 uv;

    // compute view direction
    viewdir = normalize(IN.opos.xyz - camerapos.xyz);

    // transform point into local space
    p = IN.opos.xyz - pos.xyz;

    // intersect depth plane
    p+= depth.w*(-viewdir / dot(plane.xyz, viewdir));

    // compute texcoord
    uv = project_uv(p, u, v);
    // front texture
    t1 = f4tex2D(texdtb1, uv);
    // back texture
    t2 = f4tex2D(texdtb2, float2(1-uv.x,uv.y));
    t2.w = 1.0-t2.w;

    // test is pixel depth is inside range
    if ((depth.x-t1.w)*(depth.x-t2.w) < 0) && t2.w > t1.w)
        c.w = 1;

    // transform point into global space
    p += pos.xyz;

    // expand normal from normal map
    t1.xyz = normalize(t1.xyz*-0.5);

    // compute light direction
```

```
lightdir = normalize(lightpos.xyz - p);

// diffuse+specular lighting
float diff = saturate(dot(lightdir,t1.xyz));
float spec = pow(saturate(
        dot(normalize(lightdir-viewdir), t1.xyz)),
        specular.w);

// compute final color
c.xyz = IN.color.xyz*diff.xxx +
        specular.xyz*spec.xxx;

OUT.color=c;
return OUT;
}
```

RTM—Single-Pass Approach for Planar Objects

This methods uses the same basic approach as in the previous section, but now we make all computations in a single pass with more precision for the intersection and with self-shadows included. The efficacy of these can be seen in Figure 5.9. Also shown in the figure is a comparison with bump mapping again showing the visual superiority of this technique.

The crux of the shader is the use of an efficient ray intersect routine, enabling an exact depth of the intersection along the ray to be returned. The addition of shadows results in more computation (two ray intersect calculations per fragment), and to facilitate this, we incorporate an efficient search algorithm (linear and binary) to calculate the required ray intersections and also whether the point is in shadow or not.

Self-shadows are a useful addition, but general shadowing would be even better. The fact that an accurate depth is calculated means that it would also be possible to use shadow maps or stencil shadows in addition to the self-shadows. However, the current complexity compiles to around 200 (400 with shadows) assembly instructions (compared to around 30 for bump mapping) —a very large increase.

In this example we use a hybrid of a linear and binary chopping search algorithms to drastically speed up the ray intersection calculations required. (This

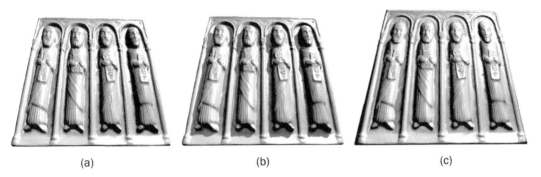

(a) (b) (c)

Figure 5.9. (a) RTM without self-shadows. (b) RTM with self-shadows. (c) The same object rendered using a conventional bump map technique

should be compared with the algorithm used in the previous section that requires up to 256 passes for a good image quality).

The algorithm is easily understood by referring to Figure 5.10. Here A is the pixel currently being rendered. We find the surface intersection point P by calling a ray intersect calculation which takes as input the start and end points of the ray (A) and (B) (see the pseudocode in Figure 5.11). Point P defines depth d_1. An identical procedure is followed with the light ray to find depth d_2. If d_2 is less than d_1 then the point P is in self shadow (the case in the figure) and rendered accordingly; otherwise, standard illumination is applied. The pseudocode for the main algorithm is shown in Figure 5.11.

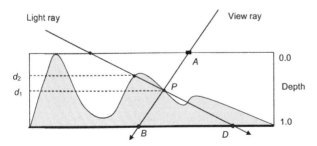

Figure 5.10. Two rays are used to render the RTM object and to determine whether it is in self-shadow.

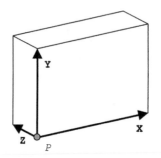

Relief object box defined by point *P* and three vectors (**X, Y, Z**). **X** and **Y** will be the relief texture map axis and **Z** will give the maximum depth.

```
relief_depth = length(Z);
relief_norma l = -Z / relief_depth;
```

Figure 5.11. Pseudocode and conventions for the main algorithm.

```
float4 main_rtm()
{
  A = pixel position in global space passed in texcoord0
  viewdir = normalize( A - camera_pos );
  size = relief_depth / dot( -relief_normal, viewdir);
  B = A + viewdir * size;
  V = B - A;
  d1 = ray_intersect_rtm( A, V );
  P = A + d1 * V;
  lightdir = normalize( P - light_pos );
  size = relief_depth / dot( -relief_normal, lightdir);
  C = P - d1 * size * lightdir;
  D = C + lightdir * size;
  V = D - C;
  d2 = ray_intersect_rtm( C, V );
  if (d2<d1)
        // pixel in shadow
        color = shadow_color()
  else
        // light pixel, apply standard lighting
        color = phong_lighting();
  return color;
}
```

For reasons that will be explained shortly, the ray intersect routine is a coarse-resolution linear search followed by a fine-resolution binary search. First, we examine the binary search. This is a simple binary chop between points A and B if we ignore for a moment the linear search. Starting at a point halfway along the ray, we invoke the test inside or outside the RTM object. If inside, we move backwards otherwise we move forwards, the recursion being implemented as a deterministic loop as follows:

```
float ray_intersect_rtm( float2 P, float2 V )
{
    linear_search_steps = 10;
    binary_search_steps = 6;

    depth = 0.0;
    size = 1.0/linear_search_steps;

    // find first point inside object
    loop from 1 to linear_search_steps
        depth = depth + size;
        d = rtm depth value at pixel (P+V*depth);
        if ( d < depth )
            break loop;

    // recurse with binary search around first
    // point inside object to find best depth
    best_depth = 1.0;
    loop from 1 to binary_search_steps
        size = size*0.5;
        d = rtm depth value at pixel (P+V*depth);
        if ( d < depth )
            // if point is inside object
            // store depth and move backward
            best_depth = depth
            depth = depth - size;
        else
            // else it is outside object
            // move forward
            depth = depth + size

    return best_depth;
}
```

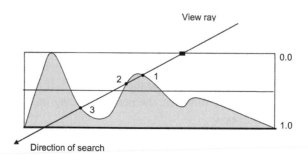

Figure 5.12. A binary search alone will result in point 3 as the intersection.

Now we examine the need for a linear search that precedes the binary search. Figure 5.12 shows what would happen, in this particular case, if we applied only a binary chop.

In the figure there are three ray surface intersections labelled 1, 2 and 3. The first invocation of the chop (intersection of view ray and depth plane $Z=0.5$) is outside and we move forward, ending up at point 3. We note that this error is a consequence of concavities in the surface. If the surface were everywhere convex, then a binary search would suffice.

This is easily corrected by applying a linear search first. Consider an example. Say we choose a resolution for the linear search of 10 (0.1, 0.2, … 1.0). We terminate the linear search when we first enter the object. We then switch to the binary search with a starting resolution of 0.1 at this point. Say the first invocation of the binary search returns "0.3 inside". We then move to 0.25 (0.3 - 0.05) and recurse within the new 0.05 depth interval (each time reducing the interval by half).

But even with this enhancement, there is still a problem. If the linear search encounters a thin object part (less than the search interval of, say, 0.1) it will 'jump over' it. Thus there is a limit to the thinness of object protrusions for a fixed search interval. This problem is exacerbated as the view ray incidence angle approaches being parallel to the surface. These errors are noticeable on shadow edges from the pyramid, (Figure 5.13, where the width of the object at its edges is too small) it looks like the shadows have lower resolution at such points.

We have to reduce the linear search intervals as a function of such surface detail and view/surface angle. To do this correctly, we would need to define an interval that is smaller than the smallest path through any protrusion. This would require a lengthy preprocessing phase that sampled a set of low-incidence view vectors at every texel of the RTM object.

Figure 5.13. Artefacts generated by object parts that are too thin for the linear search.

Texture Filtering and Mip-Mapping

Both texture filtering and mip-mapping work well with this shader. Texture filtering will facilitate good normal interpolation around surface corners, and mip-mapping will speed up the shader considerably (especially when using large tiles where lower mip-map levels are used). Both normal and depth components are mip-mapped to lower resolutions.

Pixel Shader 3.0 Optimizations

The new Pixel Shader version 3.0 allows variable loops and true if/else statements. The relief mapping shader could take advantage of this, especially in the linear search loop. There, we could break out of the loop on the first point found to be inside the object, theoretically saving time of several unneeded loop passes.

Listing 5.3 is the complete Cg code for the shader (main and ray intersection functions):

Listing 5.3

The complete RTM fragment shader.

```
frag2screen main_frag_rm(
    vert2frag IN,
    // rm texture map
    uniform sampler2D rmtex:TEXUNIT0,
    // color texture map
    uniform sampler2D colortex:TEXUNIT1,
    // base vertex pos (xyz)
    uniform float4 axis_pos,
    // base x axis (xyz:normalized, w:length)
```

135

```
    uniform float4 axis_x,
    // base y axis (xyz:normalized, w:length)
    uniform float4 axis_y,
    // base z axis (xyz:normalized, w:length)
    uniform float4 axis_z,
    // camera position (xyz)
    uniform float4 camerapos,
    // lightposition (xyz)
    uniform float4 lightpos,
    // specular color (xyz:rgb, w:exponent)
    uniform float4 specular)
{

    frag2screen OUT;

    float4 p;
    float3 v,l,s;
    float2 dp,ds;
    float d,dl;

    const float shadow_threshold=0.02;
    const float shadow_intensity=0.4;

    // ray intersect in view direction
    v  = normalize(IN.opos.xyz - camerapos.xyz);
    p  = IN.opos - axis_pos;
    s  = axis_z.w*v/dot(axis_z.xyz,v);
    dp = project_uv(p.xyz,axis_x,axis_y);
    ds = project_uv(s,axis_x,axis_y);
    d  = ray_intersect_rm(rmtex,dp,ds);

    // get rm and color texture points
    float2 uv = dp + ds*d;
    float4 t = f4tex2D(rmtex,uv);
    float3 color = IN.color.xyz*f3tex2D(colortex,uv);

    // expand normal from normal map in local polygon space
    t.xy = t.xy*2.0 - 1.0;
    t.z = sqrt(1.0 - dot(t.xy,t.xy));
```

```
    t.xyz = normalize(t.x*axis_x.xyz +
              t.y*axis_y.xyz - t.z*axis_z.xyz);

    // compute light direction
    p.xyz + =axis_pos.xyz + s*d;
    l = normalize(p.xyz - lightpos.xyz);

    // compute diffuse and specular terms
    float diff = saturate(dot(-l,t.xyz));
    float spec = saturate(dot(normalize(-l-v),t.xyz));

#ifdef RM_SHADOWS
    // ray intersect in light direction
    s  = axis_z.w*l/dot(axis_z.xyz,l);
    p.xyz -= d*s + axis_pos.xyz;
    dp = project_uv(p.xyz, axis_x, axis_y);
    ds = project_uv(s, axis_x, axis_y);
    dl = ray_intersect_rm(rmtex, dp, ds);
    // if pixel in shadow
    if (dl < d-shadow_threshold)
    {
        color *= shadow_intensity;
        specular = 0;
    }
#endif

    // compute final color
    OUT.color.xyz = color*diff +
            specular.xyz*pow(spec,specular.w);
    OUT.color.w = (d<0.996 ? 1.0 : 0.0);

    return OUT;
}

float ray_intersect_rm(
    in sampler2D rmtex,
    in float2 dp,
    in float2 ds)
```

```
{
    const int linear_search_steps = 10;
    const int binary_search_steps = 5;
    float depth_step = 1.0/linear_search_steps;

    // current size of search window
    float size = depth_step;
    // current depth position
    float depth = 0.0;
    // best match found (starts with last position 1.0)
    float best_depth = 1.0;

    // search front to back for first point inside object
    for( int i=0;i<linear_search_steps-1;i++ )
    {
        depth += size;
        float4 t = f4tex2D(rmtex, dp + ds*depth);

        if (best_depth > 0.996)          // if no depth found yet
        if (depth >= t.w)
#ifdef RM_DOUBLEDEPTH
        if (depth <= t.z)
#endif
            best_depth = depth;          // store best depth
    }
    depth = best_depth;

    // recurse around first point (depth) for closest match
    for( int i=0;i<binary_search_steps;i++ )
    {
        size*=0.5;
        float4 t = f4tex2D(rmtex, dp + ds*depth);
        if (depth >= t.w)
#ifdef RM_DOUBLEDEPTH
        if (depth <= t.z)
#endif
        {
            best_depth = depth;
```

```
        depth -= 2*size;
    }
    depth += size;
}
return best_depth;
}
```

Single RTM with Double Depth Values (Restricted 3D Objects)

This extension gives an effect that approximates the five map method we used to produce Figure 5.4. The significant advantage of the method is that it only uses a single map rather than five or six. It represents closed objects whose geometry can be captured using two depth maps. It means that the complete geometry of a certain type of 3D object can be represented by a single map. The right-hand column of Figure 5.14 shows two results achieved using this method. The left column shows the RTM rendered using the unenhanced method (that is from a single depth RTM). Here the expected extruded effect is visible where bundles of parallel lines emerge along the z direction.

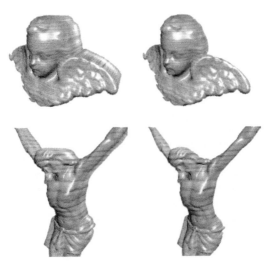

Figure 5.14. Angel and Christ relief maps using double depth. Conventional single depth RTM used to render left images; double depth was used to render the right column (back of figures are capped by back depth map).

Figure 5.15. Double depth relief maps (Angel and Christ). Front and back depth maps encoded in blue and alpha channels.

This is a simple enhancement and involves adding a second depth map to the blue channel that will hold the depth values looking from the back of the object as shown in Figure 5.15. This means now we will have the normal x and y components encoded only in red and green and two depth maps (back and front) encoded in blue and alpha. However, since the normal vector is normalized, the z component can be retrieved in the fragment shader from:

$$z = \sqrt{1 - x^2 - y^2}$$

In this method we consider a point to be inside the object if its depth is bigger than the front depth map and smaller than the back depth map.

Comparing the two columns in Figure 5.14 you can see the 'capping' effect of using the back depth map. In the left-hand column, the rendering extends to maximum depth. The capping occurs in the following way. If the search returns a depth of 1.0, then this means that the ray has missed the object and may be going through a region of space rendered as the extrusion region in the left-hand imagery in the figure. Thus, all the shader has to do to effect a capping operation is to set alpha to 0.0 if the depth is 1.0:

```
OUT.color.w = (d<1.0 ? 1.0 : 0.0)
```

The double-depth option is included in the ray intersection function from Listing 5.3 in the form of an extra if statement comparing the back depth value both in linear and binary search steps.

Relief Texture Mapping—for 3D objects

We now present the final variation of the RTM technique that can be applied to any object geometry. Here, we effectively have two geometries—the geometry of the RTM and the geometry of the object. (In the previous sections the RTM was

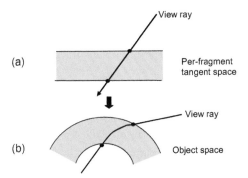

Figure 5.16. Working in per-fragment tangent space is analogous to 'bent' ray tracing.

the object.) Consider the graphical representation of the algorithm in the previous technique with the geometry of the RTM represented as a slab (Figure 5.16(a)). Now consider removing the planar constraint so that we can deal with arbitrary shaped objects by bending the relief volume. We end up with Figure 5.16(b). If we maintain the same simple ray intersection code, we will be effectively bending the ray through the relief volume. We can effect this process by working in the per-fragment tangent space of the object. We can consider the object to be locally planar and use the same algorithm.

Thus, for each fragment the method remains effectively the same, and we only have to calculate the ray intersection start point and its direction in the fragment tangent space. We do this by transforming the view ray into the tangent space of the fragment.

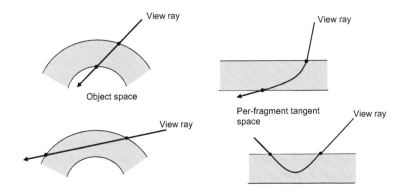

Figure 5.17. Ray events as a function of incidence angle, relief depth and curvature of object.

Figure 5.18. RTM for arbitrary polygonal objects.

Bending the intersection ray—a consequence of considering the surface to be planar at every fragment—is not without its problems. Consider Figure 5.17(a) which shows a bent ray entering and exiting the surface. This ray will intersect with the surface of the RTM. Figure 5.17(b) shows a bent ray that will enter the top surface bounding volume of the RTM and then exit through the same surface. This ray may intersect the surface or it may not. Such ray events will occur near silhouette edges. These ray events are a consequence of the angle of incidence, the relief depth and the curvature of the receiving surface. We deal with this problem in the next section.

Two images using this approach are shown in Figure 5.18, was produced using the shader in Listing 5.4. There are two problems with this enhancement: silhouette edges are smooth, and the shadow calculation is more complex. Silhouette edges are smooth because we use the same ray intersection function as the previous approach and this considers the object locally planar per fragment. We will deal with this problem shortly.

We now consider self shadow in RTM objects. (Shadows cast by RTM objects and shadows cast onto RTM objects are dealt with in Chapter 4.) Self-shadows need to be evaluated in tangent space. We effectively invoke the algorithm (for planar surfaces) for each fragment in each fragment's tangent space. Referring to Figure 5.19, the process begins at point p_1 in tangent space which is the fragment texture coordinate. We then transform the view vector into tangent space to find the ray intersection direction $\mathbf{V}$. Calling the ray intersection function will return

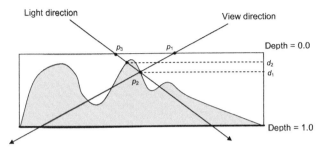

Figure 5.19. Per-fragment tangent space.

the intersection depth d_1. We can then calculate the intersection point p_2:

$$p_2 = p_1 + d_1 \times \mathbf{V}$$

We can now calculate the light direction vector $\mathbf{V}$ from light position to p_2. But we need the light vector entry point in order to call the ray intersection function from the light direction. This is given by

$$p_3 = p_2 - d_1 \times \mathbf{L}$$

Calling the ray intersection function with p_3 (entry point) and $\mathbf{L}$ (direction) will return the intersection depth d_2 along the light direction. If d_2 is smaller than d_1 it means we are in shadow.

·· Listing 5.4

```
struct v2f
{
        float4 hpos : POSITION;
        float4 color : COLOR0;
        float3 vpos : TEXCOORD0;
        float2 texcoord : TEXCOORD1;
        float3 normal : TEXCOORD2;
        float3 tangent : TEXCOORD3;
        float3 binormal : TEXCOORD4;
};


struct f2s
{
        float4 color : COLOR;
};
```

RTM shader for arbitrary polygonal objects.

```
// use linear and binary search
float ray_intersect_rm(
        in sampler2D reliefmap,
        in float2 dp,
        in float2 ds)
{
    const int linear_search_steps=10;

    // current size of search window
    float size=1.0/linear_search_steps;
    // current depth position
    float depth=0.0;

    // search for first point inside object
    for( int i=0;i<linear_search_steps-1;i++ )
    {
        float4 t=tex2D(reliefmap,dp+ds*depth);

        if (depth<t.w)
            depth+=size;
    }

    const int binary_search_steps=6;

    // recurse around first point for closest match
    for( int i=0;i<binary_search_steps;i++ )
    {
        size*=0.5;
        float4 t=tex2D(reliefmap,dp+ds*depth);
        if (depth<t.w)
            depth+=2*size;
        depth-=size;
    }

    return depth;
}
```

```
f2s main_frag_relief(
    v2f IN,
    // rm texture map
    uniform sampler2D rmtex:TEXUNIT0,
    // color texture map
    uniform sampler2D colortex:TEXUNIT1,
    // camera position
    uniform float4 camerapos,
    // light position
    uniform float4 lightpos,
    // ambient color
    uniform float4 ambient,
    // diffuse color
    uniform float4 diffuse,
    // specular color
    uniform float4 specular,
    // tile factor
    uniform float tile,
    // depth factor
    uniform float depth)
{
    f2s OUT;

    float4 t,c;
    float3 p,v,l,s;
    float2 dp,ds,uv;
    float d,a;

    // ray intersect in view direction
    p  = IN.vpos;
    v  = normalize(p);
    a  = dot(IN.normal,-v);
    s  = float3(dot(v,IN.tangent.xyz), dot(v,IN.binormal.xyz), a);
    s  *= depth/a;
    ds = s.xy;
    dp = IN.texcoord*tile;
    d  = ray_intersect_rm(rmtex,dp,ds);
```

```
// get rm and color texture points
uv = dp+ds*d;
t  = tex2D(rmtex,uv);
c  = tex2D(colortex,uv);

// expand normal from normal map in local polygon space
t.xyz -= 0.5;
t.xyz = normalize(t.x*IN.tangent.xyz +
        t.y*IN.binormal.xyz + t.z*IN.normal);

// compute light direction
p += v*d/(a*depth);
l  = normalize(p-lightpos.xyz);

// compute diffuse and specular terms
float att  = saturate(dot(-l,IN.normal));
float diff = saturate(dot(-l,t.xyz));
float spec = saturate(dot(normalize(-l-v),t.xyz));

float4 finalcolor = ambient*c;

// compute final color
finalcolor.xyz += att*(c.xyz*diffuse.xyz*diff +
        specular.xyz*pow(spec,specular.w));
finalcolor.w = 1.0;

OUT.color = finalcolor;
return OUT;


}
```

Depth Correction

We can update each fragment's depth value to reflect the newly generated relief surface. These values are required to integrate RTM objects into scenes—for example, to generate correct shadows. To find the corrected depth value to output from the shader, we use the fragment depth (z component of its position in view space). Then we transform the fragment depth into the current Z-buffer range, defined by the near and far plane distances, with the following formula:

$$z_{depth} = \frac{\dfrac{far * near}{depth} + far}{far - near}$$

By using corrected depth values we can compose several different relief maps —one for each object represented in this way and they will intersect each other correctly at the fragment level, implementing a 3D compositing operation Also standard triangle based geometry can interpenetrate the relief maps correctly, as shown in Figure 5.20. Another benefit that emerges from corrected depth values in the relief map is that it enables shadows from other objects to project onto the relief map. The projected shadows will follow the displaced relief surface correctly. Both stencil shadows and shadow maps will work with the corrected depth relief map. (Shadows from RTM objects and from other objects onto RTM objects are dealt with in Chapter 4.)

The code for the corrected depth computation is as follows:

```
uniform float2 planes;

...

// a=-far/(far-near)
// b=-far*near/(far-near)
// Z=(a*z+b)/-z
OUT.depth = ((planes.x*p.z + planes.y) / -p.z);
```

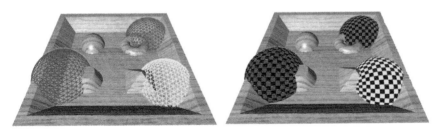

Figure 5.20. Interpenetration of relief-mapped objects at fragment level.

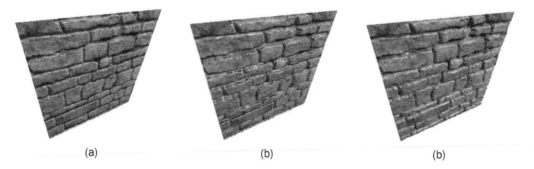

(a)   (b)   (b)

Figure 5.21. Comparing (a) bump mapping, (b) parallax mapping and (c) relief mapping

A Visual Comparison of Three Methods

This section presents a comparison for three of the methods used in Chapters 3 and 5: normal/bump mapping, parallax mapping and relief mapping. An image rendered using the same texture for each of the three methods is shown in Figure 5.21. We have deliberately chosen a 'bad' viewing angle to highlight the differences amongst the methods.

As expected normal mapping exhibits little feel of depth. Parallax mapping is much better in this regard, but there are significant artefacts and distortions. We conclude that the third image (relief mapping) gives the best result.

Silhouette Edges and Relief Texture Mapping

In previous sections, we treated the object as being locally planar at each fragment. In this way the ray travelling through the object was considered a line through tangent space. This planar approach is simple and efficient but lacks the ability to produce the silhouette edge correctly.

An interesting extension to the planar approach is to consider estimating the curvature of the surface receiving the relief map at every fragment. As we shall see, this will enable us to implement a curved ray in texture space and decide whether a ray should be discarded because it misses the surface, or whether it should render the fragment.

An RTM sphere is shown in Figure 5.22 with and without a correct silhouette edge. We will now describe how this enhancement is achieved. Consider Figure 5.23 which shows two view rays. V_A intersects the height field whereas V_B misses. However, the ray intersection procedure will return the coordinates of the intersection of V_B with a tiled version of the texture. All fragments resulting

Figure 5.22. Relief-mapped sphere with and without the silhouette edge enhancement.

from the scan conversion of the object will contribute to an intersection and the silhouette of the object will match the silhouette of the underlying polygonal object, which in the case of the object in Figure 5.22 is a circle. This situation is shown in Figure 5.23(a).

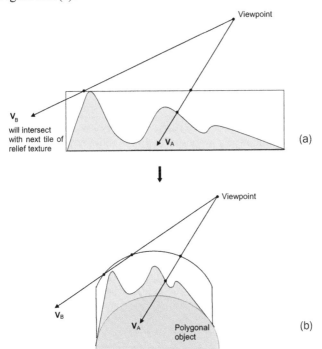

Figure 5.23. (a) V_B will intersect with a relief texture. (b) Relief object is locally deformed to fit the object's surface. V_B can be discarded.

A method that can decide whether ray $\mathbf{V_B}$ should be discarded, so that a correct silhouette can emerge, is to bend the relief texture to fit the curvature of the surface. Figure 5.23(b) shows that $\mathbf{V_B}$ can be discarded. This abstraction can be implemented in texture space. To do this, we need a method of estimating surface curvature. Thus, we now require a method that determines if a ray can be discarded and a method that finds the intersection in the deformed relief object.

Curvature Estimation

In this section, we will use an estimation of the per fragment curvature. To do this, we estimate surface curvature at each vertex and have this information linearly interpolate to the fragments. Curvature will be evaluated in the two tangent space directions (which are aligned with texture space u and v directions at each vertex). In practice, curvature estimation per vertex would be calculated offline and the vertex information passed to the GPU, enhanced with the curvature parameters.

A simple estimation of curvature of a mesh object is given by fitting a quadric to the surface (explained full in the next section). This quadric effectively becomes the upper and lower surfaces of the relief texture's bounding box (Figure 5.23(b)). We use the set of paraboloids (see Figure 5.27) defined by

$$Ax^2 + By^2 + z = 0 \tag{5.1}$$

and estimate A and B at each vertex to quantify the local curvature around that vertex (see the next section for details). This quadric is considered to be aligned with the vertex tangent space, so the vertex is positioned at $(0,0,0)$ in the quadric space, and z is aligned with direction $(0,0,1)$. The quadric will then be used in the pixel shader to bend the ray as it goes through the relief map.

We must clearly differentiate between object space, tangent space and texture space. In object space coordinates are relative to the world origin $(0,0,0)$ and

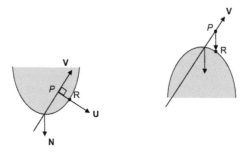

Figure 5.24. Calculating the ray-quadric distance: (a) Positive curvature. (b) Negative curvature.

main axis alignment—(1,0,0), (0,1,0) and (0,0,1). In tangent space (vertex or fragment), the coordinates are relative to the vertex/fragment position and oriented as the vertex/fragment normal and tangent vectors, but the scaling of the tangent space is the same as the scaling in object space (only translation and rotation differ between them).

In texture space, we scale tangent space so that one texture tile (size 1.0 in texture space) maps to some distance in object space. Also, the depth expressed in the range [0.0,1.0] in texture space will map to some depth in object space. Thus it is important to know at each vertex/fragment the size of the mapping (or how big one texture tile is in object space at that position). As mapping a complex object is not a simple task, usually the mapping scale at each point on the object will vary and texture will compress/expand over the object surface (only planar surfaces can have a simple mapping that will have constant mapping scale at every point).

Thus, we end up requiring four new floats at each vertex (curvature in two directions and mapping scale in two directions). These can be calculated offline and stored in the geometry file, as they are constants for a nondeformable mesh. For the mapping scale, all we need to do is compute the texture space positions (0,0), (1,0) and (0,1) in object space for every triangle in the mesh and then average the length of each u and v texture axis at the vertices. This can be done in the tangent space computation method and stored in the tangent space vector 4th component (scale of tangent vector in object space stored in w). Thus in order to move from tangent space to texture space we divide x and y by the texture scale in each tangent direction and z by the desired relief depth in object space.

Ray-Quadric Distance Calculation

To calculate intersections in texture space, we need the distance along the ray from the quadric. We compute the depth in texture space at point P for a given value of t:

$$P = (\mathbf{V}_{\text{texture\_space}} \times t)$$

Consider the case shown in Figure 5.24(a). $\mathbf{U}$ is a unit vector perpendicular to $\mathbf{V}$ and coplanar to $\mathbf{V}$ and $\mathbf{N}$. R is the point on the quadric reached by moving distance s from P along $\mathbf{U}$. That is:

$$R = P + \mathbf{U}s$$

We obtain s by substituting R into the equation for the quadric (Equation 5.1):

$$A(P_x + \mathbf{U}_x s)^2 + B(P_y + \mathbf{U}_y s)^2 - (P_z + \mathbf{U}_z s) = 0$$

giving the positive value of s as:

$$s = \frac{-b + \sqrt{b^2 - 4ac}}{2a} \tag{5.2}$$

where:

$$a = AU_x^2 + B\,U_y^2$$
$$b = 2AP_x\,\mathbf{U}_x + 2BP_y\,\mathbf{U}_y$$
$$c = AP_x^2 + B\,P_y^2 - P_z$$

If the discriminant of Equation 5.2 is negative, then the situation shown in Figure 5.24(b) pertains and the ray quadric distance is given by

$$d = P_z - (AP_x^2 + BP_y^2) \tag{5.3}$$

which is the difference between the z coordinate of P and the z coordinate of the quadric evaluated at (P_x, P_y).

Computing the discriminant of Equation 5.2 and then evaluating Equation 5.2 or 5.3 is very costly as the procedure is repeated many times per fragment. A simpler approximate solution is to use Equation 5.3 for all cases. This gives a twofold speed-up with barely noticeable visual difference between the approximate and the accurate evaluation.

In the fragment program (see Listing 5.6), we use a linear/binary search approach just like in previous relief mapping implementations. But now we use a `ray_position` function (Listing 5.5) which computes texture space position for a given search parameter t.

Listing 5.5

Ray position function.

```
float3 ray_position(
    // search parameter
    in float t,
    // original pixel texcoord
    in float2 tx,
    // view vector in texture space
    in float3 v,
    // data z constant
    in float dataz)
```

```
{
    float3 r = v*t;
    r.z -= t*t*dataz;
    r.xy += tx;
    return r;
}
```

The `ray_intersect` function (Listing 5.6) now calls the `ray_position` at each search step to evaluate the current bent ray position and compares texture depth to bent ray depth for an intersection.

Listing 5.6

Ray intersect function.

```
float ray_intersect_rm(
    in sampler2D reliefmap,
    in float2 tx,
    in float3 v,
    in float tmax,
    in float dataz)
{
    float t=0.0;
    float size=(tmax+0.001)/linear_search_steps;

    const int linear_search_steps=10;

    // search for first point inside object
    for( int i=0;i<linear_search_steps;i++ )
    {
        float3 p = ray_position(t,tx,v,dataz);
        float4 tex = tex2D(reliefmap,p.xy);
        if (p.z < tex.w)
            t += size;
    }

    const int binary_search_steps=6;
```

```
// recurse around first point for closest match
for( int i=0;i<binary_search_steps;i++ )
{
    size *= 0.5;
    float3 p = ray_position(t,tx,v,dataz);
    float4 tex = tex2D(reliefmap,p.xy);
    if (p.z < tex.w)
        t += 2*size;
    t -= size;
}


    return t;
}
```

We can optimise the search by considering the cases detailed in Figure 5.25 for positive curvature:

- The ray is confined inside the texture space depth range ($d_{max}<1.0$). In this case we may or may not intersect with the relief object; we search until t_{max} at $z = 0$.

- The bent ray crosses the greatest possible depth ($d_{max}>1.0$), the ray must intersect the relief object and cannot be discarded; we search until t_{max} at $z=1$.

For a negative curvature quadric the ray must intersect and cannot be discarded; we search until t_{max} at $z =1$.

To calculate the maximum search parameter (t_{max}) we solve Equation 5.3 for $d=0$ and for $d=1$ and take the smaller of the two solutions. This will distribute the search samples along the minimum distance needed, making the best possible use of the samples.

$$\mathbf{V}_z t - f t^2 = \{ 0 \text{ or } 1 \}$$

where

$$f = A\mathbf{V}_x^2 + B\mathbf{V}_y^2 \text{ (}\mathbf{V} \text{ changes only by fragment).}$$

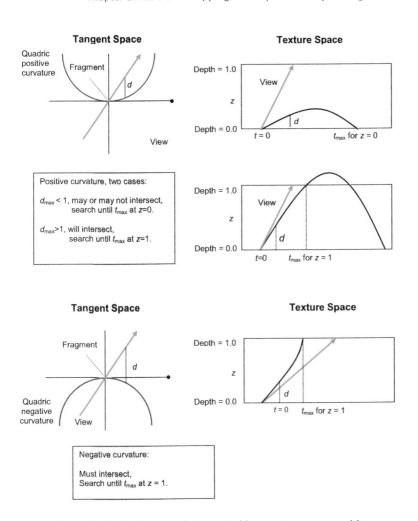

Figure 5.25. Ray tracing a fragment with curvature as a quadric.

for d = 0, the solution is

$$\frac{-\mathbf{V}_z}{f}$$

for d = 1, the solution is

$$\frac{\mathbf{V}_z - \sqrt{\mathbf{V}_z^2 - 4f}}{2f}$$

The main function (Listing 5.7) starts by transforming the quadric and view vector to texture space and then calculates t_{max} (maximum search parameter). Then it calls the ray intersection function, and if no intersection is found, it discards the fragment (fragment outside silhouette edge). If an intersection is found, it uses the normal and colour at the intersected position in a standard lighting computation. The pixel depth is also updated to reflect the displaced position.

```
f2s main_frag_relief(
    v2f IN,
    uniform sampler2D rmtex:TEXUNIT0,
    uniform sampler2D colortex:TEXUNIT1,
    uniform sampler2D shadowmap:TEXUNIT2,
    // light position in view space
    uniform float4 lightpos,
    // ambient color
    uniform float4 ambient,
    // diffuse color
    uniform float4 diffuse,
    // specular color
    uniform float4 specular,
    // near and far plane information
    uniform float2 planes,
    // tile factor
    uniform float tile,
    // depth factor
    uniform float depth,
    // shadow map matrix
    uniform float4x4 viewinv_lightviewprojbias)
{
    f2s OUT;

    // view vector in eye space
```

```
float3 view=normalize(IN.vpos.xyz);

// view vector in tangent space
float3 v=normalize(float3(dot(view,IN.tangent.xyz),
    dot(view,IN.binormal.xyz),dot(-view,IN.normal)));

// vector perpendicular to view closest to (0,0,1)
float3 u=normalize(2*v*v.z-float3(0,0,2));

// mapping scale from object to texture space
float3 mapping=float3(tile/IN.tangent.w,
    tile/IN.binormal.w,1.0/depth);

// quadric constants
float dataz=IN.curvature.x*v.x*v.x+
    IN.curvature.y*v.y*v.y;
dataz=sign(dataz)*max(abs(dataz),0.001);

// compute max distance for search min(t(z=0),t(z=1))
float d=v.z*v.z-4*dataz*depth;
float tmax=50;
if (d>0)        // t when z=1
    tmax=min(tmax,(-v.z+sqrt(d))/(-2*dataz));
d=v.z/dataz;    // t when z=0
if (d>0)
    tmax=min(tmax,d);

// transform view and quadric data to texture space
v*=mapping;
dataz*=mapping.z;

// ray intersect depth map
float t=ray_intersect_rm(rmtex,
```

```
        IN.texcoord*tile,v,tmax,dataz);
    if (t>tmax)
        discard; // no intesection, discard fragment


    // compute intersected position
    float3 p=ray_position(t,IN.texcoord*tile,v,dataz);


    // get normal and color at intersection point
    float4 n=tex2D(rmtex,p.xy);
    float4 c=tex2D(colortex,p.xy);


    // compute displaced pixel position in view space
    p=IN.vpos+view*t;


#ifdef RM_DEPTHCORRECT
    // a=-far/(far-near)
    // b=-far*near/(far-near)
    // Z=(a*z+b)/-z
    OUT.depth=((planes.x*p.z+planes.y)/-p.z);
#endif


    // compute light direction
    float3 l=normalize(p-lightpos.xyz);
    // compute diffuse and specular terms
    float att=saturate(dot(-l,IN.normal));


#ifdef RM_SHADOWS
    // shadow map
    float4 sm=float4(p,1.0);
    sm=mul(viewinv_lightviewprojbias,sm);
    sm/=sm.w;
    if (sm.z>=f1tex2D(shadowmap,sm.xy))
        att=0;
```

```
#endif

    // expand normal from normal map into view space
    n.xyz-=0.5;
    n.xyz=normalize(n.x*IN.tangent.xyz+
        n.y*IN.binormal.xyz+n.z*IN.normal);
    float diff=saturate(dot(-l,n.xyz));
    float spec=saturate(dot(normalize(-l-view),n.xyz));


    // compute final color
    float4 finalcolor=ambient*c;
    finalcolor.xyz+=att*(c.xyz*diffuse.xyz*diff+
        specular.xyz*pow(spec,specular.w));
    finalcolor.w=1.0;


    OUT.color=finalcolor;
    return OUT;
}
```

Examples of this final variation of the RTM approach are shown in Figure 5.26. In the case of the teapot, the rendering polygonal resolution (1600 triangles) is superimposed in red wireframe. This demonstrates the power of the method: high-quality detail rendering, including silhouette edge, using a low polygon count. The sphere demonstrates the use of a high-depth RTM.

Although the shaders are long, the teapot example renders at greater than 100 frames per second. The cost is predominantly a function of the precision of the linear search, which itself is dependent on the size of the smallest detail in the map. Another factor that determines cost is the maximum depth of the relief map, which by definition, requires more search samples.

A not insignificant advantage is that authoring content is straightforward. If you have a tool for creating normal maps, then adding depth is simple. Finally, once the map is created, it requires no extra processing as is the case with a related method [WANG03]—a technique called VDM or View-Dependent Displacement Mapping.

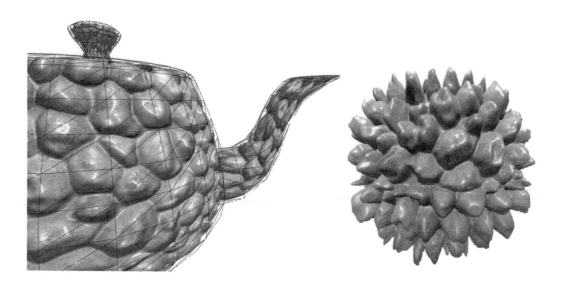

Figure 5.26. The final RTM method. (a) Teapot: wireframe shows rendering resolution. (b) Sphere with high depth RTM.

Per-Vertex Curvature Estimation using Quadrics

In the previous section, we described a method that will allow us to render correctly the geometry of silhouette edges. To do this, we need to calculate the surface curvature at any point on the mesh. Differential geometry gives us a way of measuring the curvature of a surface at a point P. If we consider that for a very small region surrounding P, our surface is locally planar, we can say informally that curvature is related to how rapidly the surface departs from the tangent plane at P. This leads us to say that, for a sufficiently small neighbourhood around P, to a first approximation the curvature is given by a plane. If the surface is twice differentiable, then it can be shown (see, for example [PETI02]) to a second approximation a small neighbourhood around P takes the form of a so-called osculating paraboloid or quadric of one of nine types. One way of measuring curvature therefore is to find the coefficients of the quadric that best fits the surface. We can restrict ourselves, for efficiency in the method, to a subset of four of the nine quadrics without losing too much accuracy. These are the quadrics defined by the simple quadratic equation

$$Ax^2 + By^2 + z = 0$$

where

$A = B = 0$ defines a plane,

A or $B = 0$ defines a parabolic cylinder,

A and B have the same sign defines a paraboloid and

A and B have different signs defines a hyperbolic paraboloid.

We can thus classify the curvature at a point P by calculating the coefficients A and B. These forms are shown in Figure 5.27. If we can calculate A and B for a polygon mesh we can then consider the surface in the vicinity of the vertex to possess one of these four forms.

Having calculated A and B we can pass these parameters into a vertex program and the interpolator will produce values at each fragment. Thus, we have at each fragment a quadric centred at the pixel with orientation aligning with the pixel tangent space. The pixel is always point $(0,0,0)$ in quadric space.

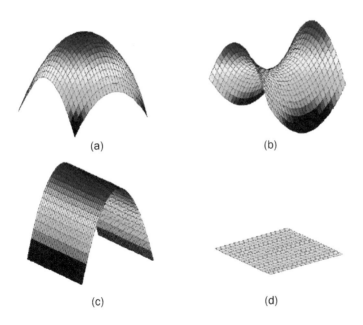

(a)

(b)

(c)

(d)

Figure 5.27. Quadrics defined by the equation $Ax^2 + By^2 + z = 0$. (a) Paraboloid. (b) Hyperbolic paraboloid. (c) Parabolic cylinder. (d) Plane.

In order to find the coefficients A and B for a given vertex we use the vertex ring neighbourhood around it. We simply transform the neighbouring vertices to the tangent space of the vertex tangent space and inject them into the following equation form (for n neighbor vertices):

$$\begin{bmatrix} x_0^2 & y_0^2 \\ x_1^2 & y_1^2 \\ x_2^2 & y_2^2 \\ \cdots & \cdots \\ x_n^2 & y_n^2 \end{bmatrix} \begin{bmatrix} A \\ B \end{bmatrix} = \begin{bmatrix} z_0 \\ z_1 \\ z_2 \\ \cdots \\ z_n \end{bmatrix}$$

This is a simple over determined system we need to solve in order to find A and B. We can use a least squares algorithm to quickly resolve the system. A matrix system in form $Ex=F$ can be solved as follows:

$$Ex = F$$
$$E^T Ex = E^T F$$
$$x = (E^T E)^{-1}(E^T F)$$

In our case, the E matrix with (n x 2) elements have all neighbor vertices x and y positions squared (one line per vertex). The F matrix with (n x 1) elements has all z positions (as the vertex is in tangent space of the centre vertex, this will be the distance to the plane defined by the centre vertex normal).

Thus, all we need to do is to multiply the matrix E with its transpose resulting in a (2 x 2) matrix. Then we multiply E transpose with F resulting in a (2 x 1) matrix. To find our quadric curvature parameters A and B we simply multiply the two previous matrices together resulting in a (2 x 1) matrix with A and B values. The code is given in Listing 5.8.

Listing 5.8

Solves matrix system
Ex = *F* using
least squares.

```
// solve matrix system Ex=F using least squares
// E[n,2] and F[n,1] result stored in (x,Y)
// R = (RT*R)^-1 * (RT*F)
void pMesh::solve_least_squares(
int n, const float *E, const float *E,
float& x,float& y)
{
    x=0;
```

```
y=0;
if (n<3) return;

int i,j,k;

// ET = transpose of E
float *ET = new float[n*2];
for( i=0;i<n;i++ )
{
    ET[i] = E[i*2];
    ET[i+n] = E[i*2+1];
}

// M = ET * E
float M[2][2];
for( j=0;j<2;j++ )
for( i=0;i<2;i++ )
{
    M[j][i] = 0;
    for( k=0;k<n;k++ )
        M[j][i] += ET[j*n+k]*E[k*2+i];
}

// MI = inverse M
float det,MI[2][2];
det = M[0][0]*M[1][1] - M[0][1]*M[1][0];
if (fabs(det)>0.001f)
{
    det=1.0f/det;
    MI[0][0] = M[1][1]*det;
    MI[0][1] =-M[0][1]*det;
    MI[1][0] =-M[1][0]*det;
    MI[1][1] = M[0][0]*det;

    // ETB = ET * F
    float ETF[2]={ 0,0 };
    for( i=0;i<2;i++ )
    for( j=0;j<n;j++ )
```

```
        ETF[i] += ET[i*n+j]*F[j];


    // (x,y) = MI * ETF
    x = MI[0][0]*ETF[0] + MI[0][1]*ETF[1];
    y = MI[1][0]*ETF[0] + MI[1][1]*ETF[1];
  }


  delete ET;
}
```

Figure 5.28 shows results from the method: the curvature for a torus and a teapot (red means positive curvature, blue means negative and green means planar). Left images illustrate curvature for tangent direction, and right images for binormal direction.

Omni-Directional Displacement Maps (ODD)

This final application is useful for caching surface detail that tiles infinitely (a brick wall, for example). Such surfaces are commonly used in computer games levels and architectural applications. The application uses what is effectively a four-dimensional texture map encoded as a 2D map and has very large memory requirements–the reason for restricting it to a tileable surface. It is similar in effect, but very different in detail, to a (periodic) bump map.

Figure 5.28. Colour representing curvature for the teapot and a torus: red = positive curvature, blue = negative curvature and green = planar. Left is tangent direction and right is binormal direction.

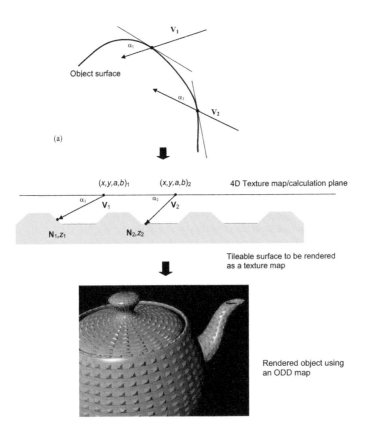

Figure 5.29. Rendering sequence in omni-directional depth mapping (ODD).

We begin by considering the rendering principle since this will enable us to understand the construction of the 4D map better. To render a point on the surface of an object, we calculate a 4D texture coordinate (x,y,a,b). The (x,y) coordinate is the conventional pre-authored mapping and the (a,b) component is calculated. Each (x,y) pixel is a 'super' pixel—an array of 16 x 16 (a,b) pixels. This array contains information associated with 16 x 16 rays which is the surface normal $\mathbf{N}$ at the point intersected by each ray and the distance z of that intersection along the ray.

Figure 5.29 shows the idea in some detail. Rays are cast in a precalculation phase from a plane positioned close to the tileable surface (i.e. h should be small with respect to w as shown in Figure 5.30). For a current view direction $\mathbf{V}$ we calculate the intersection angle α of the view ray with the surface (Figure 5.29(a). The (a,b) coordinate is calculated from α and V and used to index the 16 x 16

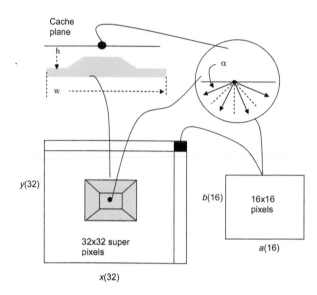

Figure 5.30. 4D texture map (32 x 32 x 16 x 16): for each pixel 16 x 16 rays are cast into a hemisphere positioned on the calculation plane.

array; thus matching the current view ray to the stored directions (Figure 5.29(b)). The texture pixel (N,z) is then used to render in the normal manner. The distance z along the ray enables a more accurate specification of **L**—one which includes the distance from the light.

The vertex/fragment program division is as follows. The vertex program transforms **L** and the tangent space vectors to view space, and the fragment program calculates the 4D texture coordinate.

We now look in some detail at the construction of the 4D texture map, how it caches the information we require and how the 4D coordinates are calculated in the render phase. For each of 32 x 32 (say) super pixels we cast 16 x16 (say) rays into a hemisphere placed on a calculation or cache-surface placed close to the tileable surface. This is shown in Figure 5.30, where 4 rays in 2D space are illustrated. The ray directions are given by

$$R_x = \cos(a)\,\sin(b)$$
$$R_y = \cos(b) \qquad\qquad \text{where } 0 \le a, b \le \pi$$
$$R_z = \sin(a)\,\sin(b)$$

These rays intersect the geometry of the tileable surface, and the surface normal **N** at the point of intersection, together with the distance z to the intersection, is stored in the pixel.

At render time to retrieve the duple (**N**,z) we need to calculate a 2D texture map coordinate (u,v) from the 4D coordinate (x,y,a,b). The (x,y) coordinate is the normal database texture coordinate. The (a,b) coordinate is calculated for a particular (x,y) by finding the pixel that contains the direction closest to the view direction:

$$a = \frac{\cos^{-1}\left(\frac{A}{\sqrt{1-B^2}}\right)}{\delta}$$

$$b = \frac{\cos^{-1}(B)}{\pi}$$

where: $A = \mathbf{T} \cdot \mathbf{V}$, $B = \mathbf{B} \cdot \mathbf{V}$, $\mathbf{V}$ is the view vector, $\mathbf{T}$ is the tangent vector and $\mathbf{B}$ is the binormal.

Now that we have the 4D coordinate (x,y,a,b) we can calculate the 2D (u,v) coordinate to index into the map:

$$u = \frac{\text{floor}(x,32) + a}{32}$$

$$v = \frac{\text{floor}(y,32) + b}{32}$$

We observe that we can order the 4D map in two ways (x,y,a,b) or (a,b,x,y). The relevance of this is that the different orders will exhibit different image structure, which then has ramifications for the anti-aliasing hardware for the texture mapping.

For the pin/pyramid surface used in Figure 5.29 we show in Figure 5.31 the (a,b,x,y) organization. This colour or RGB encoding shows the cached normals. Thus, the centre super pixel of this map is a 32 x 32 array which stores the information gathered by all the vertical arrays. This gives a perfect normal image of a pin or pyramid with four normals together with the floor normal. As we move away from the centre of the map, one or two faces predominate depending on the direction. At the edges of the map, there is spatial or geometric aliasing because the ray sampling density is low and the distance is large.

Finally Figure 5.32 shows an (x,y,a,b) and an (a,b,x,y) organization for a brick surface. Objects rendered using this method are shown in Figure 5.33. The (x,y,a,b) shows the information associated with the 16x16 ray directions for a single (x,y) super pixel. Compared to the pin surface the (a,b,x,y) does not exhibit spatial aliasing. This is because the height of the bricks above the plane on which they are placed is less than the height of the pins.

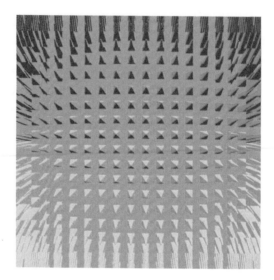

Figure 5.31. An (a,b,x,y) organized 4D texture map for the pin/pyramid surface.

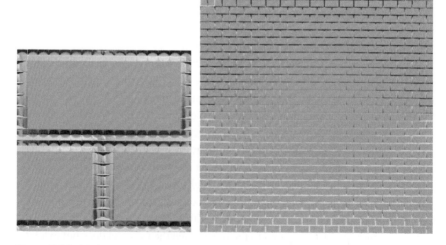

Figure 5.32. (a) An (x,y,a,b) organization for a brick surface. (b) An (a,b,x,y) organization for the same brick surface.

Figure 5.33. Two objects rendered using the brick texture.

Code for the complete shader is given in Listing 5.9.

Listing 5.9.

Vertex and fragment
shader for ODD mapping.

```
v2f displace_map_vert(
    a2v IN,
    uniform float4 lightpos,
    uniform float4x4 view,
    uniform float4x4 modelview,
    uniform float4x4 modelviewproj)
{
    v2f OUT;

    // vertex position in object space
    float4 pos = float4(IN.pos.xyz, 1.0);

    // compute modelview rotation only part
    float3x3 modelviewrot;
    modelviewrot[0] = modelview[0].xyz;
    modelviewrot[1] = modelview[1].xyz;
    modelviewrot[2] = modelview[2].xyz;

    // vertex position in clip space
    OUT.hpos = mul(modelviewproj, pos);
```

169

```
    // vertex position in view space
    // with model transformations
    OUT.vpos = mul(modelview, pos).xyz;


    // light position in view space
    OUT.lightpos = mul(view,float4(lightpos.xyz, 1.0));
    OUT.lightpos.w = lightpos.w; // light radius


    // tangent space vectors in view space
    // with model transformations
    OUT.tangent = mul(modelviewrot, IN.tangent);
    OUT.binormal = mul(modelviewrot, IN.binormal);
    OUT.normal = mul(modelviewrot, IN.normal);


    // copy color and texture coordinates
    OUT.color = IN.color;
    OUT.txcoord = IN.txcoord.xy;


    return OUT;
}


float4 displace_map_frag(
    v2f IN,
    uniform float4 diffuse,
    uniform float4 specular,
    uniform float4 constants,
    uniform float2 tile,
    uniform float depth,
    uniform sampler2D texmap,
    uniform sampler2D dispmap,
    uniform sampler2D dispindxmap) : COLOR
{
    float4 t;
    float3 viewdir,lightdir,halfdir;
    float2 uv,uv1,uv2,uv3;
    float HdotL,NdotL;
```

```
// compute directions
viewdir = normalize(IN.vpos);
lightdir = normalize(IN.lightpos.xyz - IN.vpos);
halfdir = normalize(lightdir - viewdir);


// normalize tangent space
float3 tangent = normalize(IN.tangent);
float3 binormal = normalize(IN.binormal);
float3 normal = normalize(IN.normal);


// project viewdir XY into tangent space (uv1)
uv1.x=dot(viewdir, tangent);
uv1.y=dot(viewdir, binormal);


// displace AB texture coordinate (uv2)
// simple mapping
t = f4tex2D(dispindxmap, uv1.xy*0.5 + 0.5);
uv2 = t.xy+t.zw*0.005;
// full mapping
// uv2=1.0-0.31831*float2(acos(uv1.x/
//     sqrt(1.0-uv1.y*uv1.y)),acos(uv1.y));


// compute displace XY texture coordinate (uv3)
uv3 = fmod(IN.txcoord.xy*tile,1.0);


// compute 4D->2D displace texture coordinate
// (uv2,uv3)->(uv)
uv = (floor(uv2*constants.xy)+uv3.xy)*constants.zw;


// get displace pixel with normal (xyz) and depth (w)
t = f4tex2D(dispmap,uv) - float4(0.5,0.5,0.5,0.0);
if (depth==0) t=float4(0,0,1,0);


// project normal into tangent space
t.xyz = normalize(tangent*t.x +
        binormal*t.y + normal*t.z);


// diffuse texture mapping (using depth as offset)
```

```
    diffuse *= f4tex2D(texmap, uv3 + uv1*t.w*depth);

    // diffuse and specular lighting
    NdotL = saturate(dot(lightdir.xyz, t.xyz));
    HdotL = saturate(dot(halfdir, t.xyz));
    t.xyz = diffuse.xyz*NdotL +
            specular.xyz*pow(HdotL,specular.w);
    t.xyz *= sqrt(saturate(dot(normal, lightdir)));
    t.w = diffuse.w;
    return t;
}
```

Chapter Six

Common Games Effects

Introduction

Modern games are enlivened by effects that go beyond conventional rendering, and these are now firmly established as part of the games culture. In this chapter, we will describe how to implement some of the most common of these. Examples tend to fall into two categories:

- effects implemented by special rendering algorithms, most commonly effects that simulate kinds of blurring phenomena, or
- postprocessing effects where we operate on the rendered image.[1]

Blurring Effects and Distributed Ray Tracing

In a landmark paper published more than two decades ago, R. L. Cook [COOK84] introduced a distributed ray tracing model to the graphics community that unified many of the light object interactions that we see in real life. In particular his model accounted for

- blurred reflections of objects in surfaces due to surface roughness,
- blurred refractions due to impurities in transparent material,
- soft shadows,
- depth of field due to the focal depth of lens, and
- motion blur due to relative motion between the camera and an object.

....

[1] See also Chapter 2 for another example of a postprocessing method—HDR rendering.

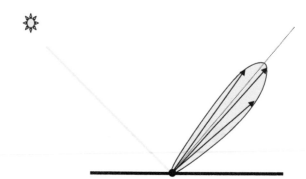

Figure 6.1. Stochastically sampling a reflection lobe by spawning many reflected rays.

Prior to this work, ray tracing models had produced perfect reflection and refraction effects and hard-edged shadows by using infinitesimally thin rays. Cook's technique recognized that, in practice, light incident on a surface was reflected and refracted into lobes. This is due to the fact that partially transparent materials contain impurities which scatter incident light, and reflective surfaces are never in practice perfect mirrors. Figure 6.1 shows the basic idea. A thin beam of incident light striking a surface produces a spread reflection lobe. The technique was called "distributed ray tracing" and involved casting a bundle of 16 rays per pixel, which stochastically sampled reflection and refraction lobes approximating an integral over the reflection/refraction lobe. He also showed how the same technique of stochastic sampling could be used to simulate soft shadows, depth of field and motion blur. Distributing rays over a lens produced depth of field, and distributing over time produced motion blur.

We will now discuss the implementation of two of these effects: depth of field and motion blur. Both of these effects try to overcome the fact that conventional rendering functions as a perfect pinhole camera with an infinitely short exposure time.

Depth of Field

Objects in computer graphics are normally rendered in an image plane using a pinhole camera model. That is to say, no matter how far or how near the objects are from the camera, they are always in sharp focus. Most of the time, this is deemed to be a desirable property. In certain contexts, however, simulating a real camera to achieve depth of field effects may be required. Depth of field means that

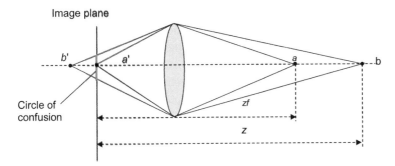

Figure 6.2. Depth of field conventions.

only objects at a certain distance from the camera lens are in sharp focus. Further and nearer objects produce a blurred image on the film plane. Depth of field causes the blurring of all objects that are not near to, or in the focal plane of the lens.

Twenty years after the publication of Cook's paper, it is the case that the best quality depth of field effect is obtained using distributed ray tracing. This is because the method simulates a lens and traces rays through it. However, the method is not suitable for real-time implementation, and we must consider less accurate algorithms.

First we define the geometry of a simple convex lens system. Figure 6.2 shows such a lens. Point a positioned at the focal distance of the lens will be imaged perfectly—the so-called circle of confusion is zero. Point b images at b' and the point is blurred into a circle of confusion in the image plane. The diameter of the circle of confusion is given by

$$d = \alpha \, \frac{|z - z_f|}{z} \qquad\qquad \alpha = \frac{F^2}{n(z_f - F)}$$

where z is the focal distance, F is the focal length of the lens, $n = F/A$ is the aperture number and A is the aperture (lens diameter).

Note that the circle of confusion diameter varies linearly with the absolute value of $(z - z_f)$ The simplest algorithm uses this fact. Other approaches use the circle of confusion more accurately. In a comparative overview of depth of field approaches, J. Demers [DEME04] calls the algorithm reverse-mapped Z-buffer depth of field and suggests that it is the one most likely to be useful for real-time applications.

The algorithm blurs each pixel according to its circle of confusion which, as we have seen, is a function of its depth. This can be achieved by rendering the scene to texture and creating mip-maps. The texture access per fragment uses (a function of) the diameter of the circle of confusion as equal derivative parameters in `texrect()`. The effect of this is to blur the texture across a square-shaped window which approximates the circle of confusion. However, this approach will only suffice for static imagery. Generating mip-maps per frame takes too long.

Motion Blur

As is well known, motion blur occurs in film because of the finite exposure time of the camera when moving objects are being recorded. It is categorised in computer graphics as anti-aliasing in the time domain, and its utility in computer animation is to add smoothness to the animation that might otherwise exhibit some jerkiness. Motion blur, as the name implies, blurs those parts of a rendered image that are in motion. The blurring is not, or should not, be perceived in the animation and can only be seen in individual frames. Just as the computer camera functions as a perfect pinhole device, so also does it function as a camera with an infinitely small exposure time—and this is the reason that animations, without motion blur, can appear to be jerky and/or exhibit strobing effects.

This fact was recognised by early traditional animators who used 'speed-lines' or 'streak-lines' to enhance the illusion of motion. In computer graphics, the traditional spatial anti-aliasing approach—super sampling—is very expensive when used to simulate motion blur. We would have to render a frame at many instances and calculate an 'average' frame effectively filtering in the time domain.

Before the advent of GPUs, most motion blur implementations used an accumulation buffer. By rendering the scene at a sample rate greater than the desired frame rate and accumulating the results, a good motion blur effect can be achieved.

Much of the development of motion blur algorithms was based on the supersampling principle albeit using more efficient versions of the method. We have to remember that motion blur is just one item of work that has to be done in a frame and most of the methods are ways of avoiding rendering the scene many times to implement temporal super-sampling.

An early attempt at computationally viable motion blur is described by M. Potmesil [POTM83] wherein a frame is calculated and blurred by convolving it with the spread function of the camera motion. This is a post-processing operation and is thus not a correct solution. Within the time interval that comprises the virtual camera's exposure or shutter time, the visibility situation may change.

It is easy to see why we cannot correctly simulate motion blur using the information from a single frame. A single object moving against a background will reveal information in the background that may be hidden if a frame is rendered at a particular instant. There can also be problems due to changes in shading. Cook in [COOK84] gives the example of a textured spinning top, where the texture is blurred along with the highlight and shadows. In this particular example, the highlights and shadows should remain unblurred since they remain static unless the light is in motion. These examples hint at the complexity of the problem.

Coming up to date, we now look at a typical GPU implementation for motion blur in [SHIM03]. In this work, the authors calculate the optic flow of the scene and effectively perform a line integral convolution of the rendered scene with the optic flow. The optic flow is a vector field and expresses the motion of each vertex of any moving object. For a moving object, the per-vertex motion vector can be calculated in a vertex program. The vector is determined by the relative motion of the vertex normal and the direction and speed of the motion. So per vertex the vector offset is

$$\mathbf{W} = (\hat{\mathbf{N}} \cdot \hat{\mathbf{V}})\mathbf{V}$$

where $\mathbf{N}$ is the vertex normal and $\mathbf{V}$ is the motion vector of the vertex.

The object and the vertex offsets are rendered to texture (with range adjustment), and a fragment program warps the object based on the vector offset field. This is an iterative process. The warped object is blended with the original object image, and the result is used as the original image in the next iteration. Blending is carried out in the direction of the vector field and in the opposite direction with a lesser scaling factor. This means that the trailing edges of the objects are blurred more than the leading edges, producing the desired effect. The algorithm operates in texture or image space and only adds a single postprocessing step to the scene render.

We will now discuss in some detail a similar algorithm. This appears to have been suggested first by [GREE03] and is called geometry stretching. The algorithm requires two passes because it compares two renders of the scene to evaluate the image space motion then uses this motion to render a blurring between the two renders.

The vertex program uses the previous and current vertex positions to evaluate vertex motion. It then applies a dot product test to determine if the vertex normal is moving in the direction of that motion. If the vertex normal is facing the motion, it remains unaltered, otherwise it is set to its value in the previous frame. This is the basis of the so-called geometry stretching.

To perform this operation, we need to use the current and previous model view matrices:

```
float 4x4 prevModelView    = mul(View,prevModel);
```

where `View` is the current view matrix. Note that we must use the previous vertex position in the current view to account for inter-frame camera motion.

The vertex motion is calculated as

```
float4 P     = mul(modelView, fromApp.coord);
float4 Pprev = mul(prevModelView, fromApp.coord);
float3 motionVector = P.xyz - Pprev.xyz;
```

This is then used to calculate if the vertex normal is front facing or back facing with respect to the motion. The vertex position finalised after the dot product test is multiplied by the projection matrix and passed to the fragment program in the position register. The motion in screen space is then calculated and stored as a texture coordinate. The complete vertex program is Listing 6.1.

Listing 6.1

Vertex program to produce motion blur using geometry stretching.

```
struct appToVertex
{
    float4 coord : POSITION;
    float3 normal : NORMAL;
};


struct v2f
{
    float4 hpos : POSITION;
    float3 velocity : TEXCOORD0;
    float3 winPos : TEXCOORD1;
    float4 color : COLOR;
};


v2f main(appToVertex fromApp,
         uniform float2 halfSceneRes,
         uniform float4x4 modelView,
         uniform float4x4 prevModel,
         uniform float4x4 modelViewProj,
         uniform float4x4 prevProj,
         uniform float4x4 View)
{
    v2f toFrag;
    float4x4 prevModelView = mul(View,prevModel);
    float4x4 prevModelViewProj = mul(prevProj,prevModelView);

    float4 P = mul(modelView, fromApp.coord);
```

```
float4 Pprev = mul(prevModelView, fromApp.coord);

float3 N = mul((float3x3)modelView, fromApp.normal);
float3 motionVector = P.xyz - Pprev.xyz;

P = mul(modelViewProj, fromApp.coord);
Pprev = mul(prevModelViewProj, fromApp.coord);

float flag = dot(motionVector, N) > 0;
float4 Pstretch = flag ? P : Pprev;

toFrag.hpos = Pstretch;
P.xyz = P.xyz / P.w;

Pprev.xyz = Pprev.xyz / Pprev.w;
Pstretch.xy = (((Pstretch.xy / Pstretch.w)*

halfSceneRes) + halfSceneRes);
    toFrag.winPos.xyz = Pstretch.xyz;

    float3 dP = P.xyz - Pprev.xyz;
    toFrag.velocity.xy = dP.xy*halfSceneRes;

    return toFrag;
}
```

The fragment program is now supplied with three textures: the scene rendered from the current and previous frame together with a depth map from current frame. The per fragment motion vector is interpolated from the vertices in a TEXCOORD register. Thus all that the fragment program has to do is to sample the two scene textures each time offsetting by a value based on the motion vector of the fragment:

```
for (i=0; i<samples; i+=1)
{
    float t = i / (samples-1);
    a += texRECT(sceneTex, fromVert.texCoord.xy -
    (fromVert.velocity.xy*t));
    a += texRECT(sceneTex2, fromVert.texCoord.xy +
    (fromVert.velocity.xy*t));
}
```

The final result in a, is a mix of the background and the object, depending on the amount of movement. The complete fragment program is given as Listing 6.2.

Listing 6.2.

Fragment program to produce motion blur using geometry stretching.

```
struct v2f
{
    float3 velocity : TEXCOORD0;
    float3 texCoord : TEXCOORD1;
};


struct f2f
{
    float4 col : COLOR;
};


f2f main(v2f fromVert,
         uniform float4 farnear,
         uniform samplerRECT sceneTex: TEXUNIT0,
         uniform samplerRECT sceneTex2: TEXUNIT1,
         uniform samplerRECT depthTex : TEXUNIT2)
{
    f2f toScreen;

    float depth = texRECT(depthTex, fromVert.texCoord.xy);

    // (far*near/depth+far)/(far-near)
    float depthCalc = ((farnear.x*farnear.y)/
            (-fromVert.texCoord.z)+farnear.x)/
            (farnear.x-farnear.y);

    int i;
    const float samples = 10;
    float4 a = 0; // accumulator
    for( i=0; i<samples; i++ )
    {
        float t = i / (samples-1);
        a += texRECT(sceneTex, fromVert.texCoord.xy -
                fromVert.velocity.xy*t);
```

```
        a += texRECT(sceneTex2, fromVert.texCoord.xy +
                     fromVert.velocity.xy*t);
    }


  toScreen.col = depth < depthCalc ?
          texRECT(sceneTex,fromVert.texCoord.xy)  :
          a/(samples*2);


    return toScreen;
}
```

Figure 6.3 shows a result achieved using this method. This should be compared with the result of a simple accumulator buffer approach which exhibits a ghosting effect trailing behind the direction of motion. This effect was produced by using the accumulation buffer to move a time window of five frames through the sequence. That is, for every frame, we subtract the first frame in the window and add the new frame.

That the method is not perfect can be seen in the noticeable dual image of the interior of the spout. It is, however, superior to the accumulator buffer approach, which produces only a trailing motion, and it is considerably less expensive.

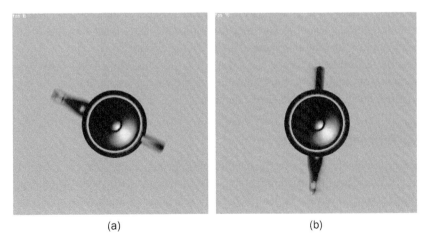

(a)   (b)

Figure 6.3. (a) Teapot rendered using the motion blur algorithm. (b) For comparison, an image rendered using the accumulator buffer approach. *Courtesy Peter Dahl, Technical University of Denmark.*

There are two considerations concerning depth which must be handled. Because the motion-blurred object is being layered on top of an existing render, the depth buffer must be cleared to prevent any z fighting artefacts, and so the fragment program must explicitly test for depth. Also note that the blurring, considered as a layer, must also be depth tested.

Depth testing is achieved by copying the Z-buffer to texture and testing explicitly in the fragment program as

```
toScreen.col = depth < depthCalc ?
         texRECT(sceneTex,fromVert.texCoord.xy) :
         a/(samples*2);
```

which tests if the value in the depth buffer is less than the calculated depth of the blurred layer signifying an occluding surface. If this is the case, the occluding object is rendered. The linear object depth must be converted to Z-buffer depth space using

```
// (far*near/depth+far)/(far-near)
float depthCalc = ((farnear.x * farnear.y) /
        (-fromVert.texCoord.z) + farnear.x) /
        (farnear.x - farnear.y);
```

A well-known problem with this method, and many other similar methods, is shown in Figure 6.4. Here (hopefully) you can see that the object occluding the motion-blurred teapot is bleeding its colour into that object—an inevitable consequence of the sampling method used in the program.

Finally, the limitations of the method are fairly obvious. First, it only deals with motion in a straight line and secondly, due to the way in which the stretching is calculated, it can only handle closed objects.

Post-Processing Effects

Postprocessing effects generally operate, as the name suggests, on rendered imagery. These are 2D image processing operations, commonly such phenomena as glow, glare and refraction due to hot regions in space. Some games effects try to imitate what we perceive in reality. Others, like the scene ripple example, are 'fantasy' effects. The following generic algorithm structure is usual:

1. Render the scene to memory buffer.
2. Process this image according to the desired effect.
3. Blend it to the original image.

Figure 6.4. Colour bleeding in the motion blur algorithm. *Courtesy Peter Dahl, Technical University of Denmark.*

In practice, the memory buffer, usually called P-buffer, is effectively equivalent to a frame buffer and consequently supports all the standard frame buffer options such as depth, stencil and double buffering. It can be used as a texture map directly after rendering to it without any copy penalties.

We now describe some examples using the approach.

Scene Ripple Effect

This effect is used to distort the entire rendered image as if space itself were deformed. This is an animated effect, and its efficacy is difficult to illustrate with static imagery. The effect is such that the object appears to be immersed in a perturbed, viscous and transparent fluid (Figure 6.5). In this example, the distortion function causes the deformation to emanate from a single point, and the effect persists for a short period (say 0.5 sececonds). The distortion fades in and out so that no abrupt transitions are visible.

When the effect is active, we render the entire scene to a texture (P-buffer) instead of rendering to the frame buffer and then draw this texture as a full screen aligned quad using a shader to deform the image. We can use either a vertex program or a fragment program to deform the image. (Both a vertex and a fragment program are given in Listing 6.3.) The vertex program sets up a regular

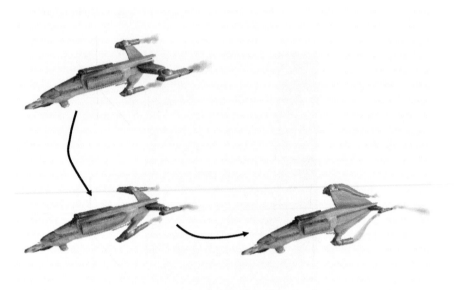

Figure 6.5. Scene ripple.

grid to sample the deformation function. This uses the full screen aligned quad which is tessellated to a sufficiently high resolution so that the space between the vertices of the grid is small enough to capture the deformation effect. The fragment program version works in the same way but uses a single quad because the deformation function is sampled for each fragment.

Listing 6.3

Scene ripple shaders
(vertex and fragment
program).

```
struct app2vert
{
        float4 pos : POSITION;
        float4 color : DIFFUSE;
        float4 texcoord : TEXCOORD0;
};


struct vert2frag
{
        float4 hpos : POSITION;
        float4 color : COLOR0;
```

184

```
        float4 texcoord : TEXCOORD0;
};


struct frag2screen
{
        float4 color : COLOR;
};


vert2frag main_ripple_vert(
        app2vert IN,
        uniform float4x4 modelviewproj,
        uniform float4 point)
{
        vert2frag OUT;

        OUT.hpos = mul(modelviewproj,IN.pos);
        OUT.color = IN.color;

        float2 vec = IN.pos.xy-point.xy;

        float dist = length(vec);
        if (dist > 0.0)
                vec /= dist;

        float w=0.0;
        if (dist < point.z)
                w = 1.0 - dist/point.z;

        w *= point.w*cos(w*7.853981634);

        OUT.texcoord.xy = IN.pos.xy+vec*w;

        return OUT;
}


frag2screen main_ripple_frag(
        vert2frag IN,
        uniform sampler2D texture:TEXUNIT0,
```

```
        uniform float4 point)
{
        frag2screen OUT;

        float2 vec = IN.texcoord.xy - point.xy;

        float dist = length(vec);
        if (dist > 0.0)
                vec /= dist;

        float w = 0.0;
        if (dist < point.z)
                w = 1.0-dist/point.z;

        w *= point.w*cos(w*7.853981634);

        OUT.color.xyz = f3tex2D(texture,
                        IN.texcoord.xy+vec*w);

        OUT.color.w=1.0;

        return OUT;
}
```

The deformation function is 1.25 cycles of a radial cosine function modulated by a linear fall-off. This is applied to a single point in the image and spreads out from this point as the radius r is incremented per frame (Figure 6.6). The function modulates the coordinates of the texture prior to sampling the texture, and the image is thus distorted in the required manner.

There is degradation in the deformed image because the resolution of the texture is lower than the screen resolution as textures must be a power of two in size,[2] but this is not too noticeable because the effect is animated and only lasts for a short time.

Glow Effect

Figure 6.7 shows a scene without and with glow. The glow effect is applied only to objects with self-illumination (in this case the sun), and the result is that colour

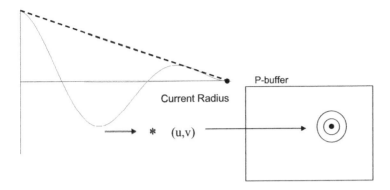

Figure 6.6. Texture coordinate modulation in the scene ripple shader.

from the glowing object bleeds into nearby objects. This effect is achieved by the following algorithm:

1. Render the scene as normal to the frame buffer.
2. Render scene into glow texture. That is, render objects without self-illumination as black, and render glow objects with their self-illumination colour.
3. Blur glow texture horizontally and vertically using a two-pass approach.
4. Blend glow texture into scene using additive blending.

Figure 6.7. Glow effect.

. . . .

[2] Some newer hardware supports textures that are not power of two.

There is an important efficiency point concerning the blurring step of this algorithm. Standard 2D blurring requires per-fragment texture access to neighboring fragments. For example, a standard 7 x 7 blur kernel would require 49 texture accesses per fragment. But this can be reduced by using a two-pass approach where we blur horizontally and then vertically, reducing it to only 14 (7 + 7) texture accesses per fragment[3]. The shader is given in Listing 6.4.

```
struct vert2frag
{
        float4 hpos : POSITION;
        float4 color : COLOR0;
        float2 texcoord : TEXCOORD0;
};
struct frag2screen
{
        float4 color : COLOR;
};


#define NUMPOINTS 7


frag2screen main_blur(
        vert2frag IN,
        uniform sampler2D texture:TEXUNIT0,
        uniform float3 dispuv[NUMPOINTS])
{
        frag2screen OUT;

        float3 tex = float3(0.0,0.0,0.0);
        for( int i=0;i<NUMPOINTS;i++ )
            tex += dispuv[i].z * f3tex2D(texture,
                    IN.texcoord.xy + dispuv[i].xy);

        OUT.color.xyz = tex;
        OUT.color.w = 1.0;

        return OUT;
}
```

......

[3] That these two approaches are equivalent is a standard result in image processing theory.

Chapter Seven

Recorded Animation:
Interpolation and Management

Introduction

Broadly speaking, computer animation can be identified as belonging to one of three categories:

- **Offline animation for film production**. This genre, pioneered by Pixar, uses a combination of high-quality rendering tools (for example, RenderMan) and cinematographic techniques for lighting and camera work to produce full-length (90 minutes.) animation features. An interesting fact concerning such films is that the production time is more or less exactly the same as for manually produced animations of the same length—approximately four years—emphasising perhaps that there are no computer shortcuts as far as the art is concerned.

- **Precalculated animation 'played' in real time**. This is the mainstream genre in computer games. The animation is either created using Motion Capture (MoCap) or created by an artist in software. The results of this precalculation, or recording, are then stored in some form and the real-time phase involves fetching the sequence, decoding it and playing it in real time. This type of animation is the topic of this chapter.

- **Real-time animation.** The animation sequence is calculated in real time—a common games example being particle systems. Another example is rigid body simulation where classical dynamics is used to animate the behaviour of an object in real time. Real-time animation in games has benefited from the same increase in rendering quality enjoyed by static objects due to hardware advances, and this is particularly true in character animation.

It is, of course, the latter two that are predominant in games, and it is these that we will discuss in Chapters 8 and 9.

Animation, Rendering and Computer Games

The computer games industry tends to look upon rendering as a solved problem, and this area is now artist dominated, whereas a decade ago it was programmer dominated. Animation, however, is definitely not a solved problem and determines, along with rendering, the believability of a game. The three predominant factors that determine the believability of a computer game can be loosely categorised as

- *rendering quality* meaning all the factors that contribute to the overall look of the game including the art creation;

- *motion quality* meaning the quality of the animation of whatever type;

- *artificial Intelligence* a very loose categorisation meaning the overall game concept, interaction with player and whatever other factors that do not fall into the first two categories.

In this chapter, we will be dealing with the second factor. We begin with an observation on the interaction of the first two factors—rendering quality and motion quality. Two of the most common animation requirements in a game are body motion and facial motion. For body motion the current *de facto* standard in the games industry is MoCap. The quality of MoCap is very high and can be perceived to be such on fairly crude models—we believe the motion—whatever the render quality and/or complexity of the character is. MoCap controlling the two structures in Figure 7.1 is recognisably human whether applied to the stick figure on the left or the skeleton on the right.

On the other hand, for human character facial animation, believability is much more difficult to achieve (Figure 7.2). We need very high render quality and very high motion quality. MoCap for facial expressions is difficult, particularly when we need to implement small-scale deformations (wrinkling). Because of the difficulties in capturing skin wrinkling, this genre is currently artist dominated where it is deemed that the most powerful approach is to build animation from authored static key poses. (The wrinkling expressions shown in Figure 7.2 were *not* captured using MoCap technology, as we explain in Chapter 10.)

When we consider convincing visual speech and integrating this with appropriate facial expressions, 'automatically' generated animation is very much a research issue.

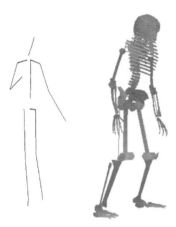

Figure 7.1. High quality MoCap motion can be perceived whatever the quality of the character.

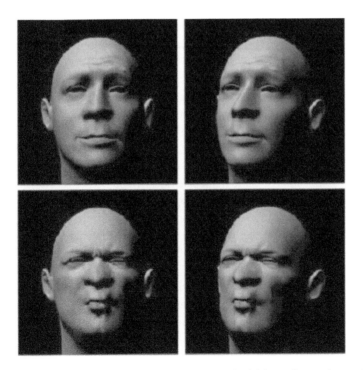

Figure 7.2. Facial expressions and visual speech require high-quality motion and high-quality rendering. *Courtesy M. Sanchez, University of Sheffield.*

Keyframing and its Management

The most common form of creating animation in real time is to interpolate keyframes. Keyframe animation is the most basic method of producing real-time animation sequences and has a long history going back to cel animation in the 1930s. Conventional wisdom has it that it was developed by Walt Disney to manage workflow in the production of his full-length cartoon films. Keyframe artists, many of whom became famous in their own right, produced keys—important facial and body poses that carried the essence of the character and its motion—and in-between artists produced a series of frames that interpolated the keyframes. In-between artists were paid much less than keyframe artists. Beneath the in-between artists were the cel painters—who presumably were paid even less. Thus, keyframe animation became a mass production process of the film industry.

The computer imitation of this technique was initially applied to the position of moving rigid bodies but was quickly generalised to allow for any parameter that controls the motion of an object, in particular rotation. Note that "keyframe" is something of a misnomer in computer animation because we never interpolate frame images, as the original in-betweeners did, but we interpolate parameters controlling the motion.

Nowadays, dealing with rotation, in the form of joint angles, for a skeletal model is probably the commonest form of animation in the games industry. Another games context in which we commonly use rotations is in controlling the orientation of a third-person camera determined by a look-at point (see Chapter 11). When we are interpolating rotational motion, quaternions are used to overcome the inherent disadvantages of other forms of representing rotation, such as Euler angles. Interpolation of keyframes representing rotational angles is routinely used with MoCap data . This is because, at the moment, MoCap data may be below the required game frame rate (ideally 100 frames/second). Thus we can regard MoCap samples as keys and apply quaternion interpolation.

Joint angle control may also originate from authoring software where an animator builds a skeleton, then creates static key poses by interacting with the virtual skeleton. Alternatively, a physical version of this approach, known as a Digital Input Device,[1] can be used.

Successful and flexible keyframe animation is a matter of good data management which results in a compact representation and is thus fast to access. We do not, for example, need to store keys with equal time intervals between them. Action in the animation may be busy or still depending on the time in the sequence, and we can store more keyframes where needed.

. . . .

[1] Originally called a Dinosaur Input Device because of its usage in the film Jurassic Park, a DID is a skeletal armature, with digital encoders at the joints which measure joint angles. The armature matches the skeletal structure of the character to be animated. To set up a key pose, an animator poses the armature, and all the joint angles for that key pose are input to software. Many contemporary devices are available depending on the character to be animated. A significant advantage over MoCap is that there are no restrictions on animating nonhuman characters.

A keyframe animation is a collection of keys. A single key will contain a time and its associated key data as shown in Table 7.1, which shows the options available per entity type and the memory requirements. For example, we could use scalar animation to control light radius and camera angles, vector animation for position and colour, and quaternion animation for rotations.

Entity	Linear	Nonlinear	Output
Scalar	1 float	3 floats (Bézier)	1 float
Vector	3 floats	9 floats (Bézier)	3 floats
Quaternion	4 floats (slerp)	12 floats (squad)	4 floats

Table 7.1

Entity types in keyframe animation.

In order to access this data to fetch the value for any given time t, we start by finding the two keyframes around this time value ($t_1 < t < t_2$). We then normalize the time values for the interpolation. The nature of the interpolation we use for keys is a function of the data representation. This process is represented in Figure 7.3 where at time t, we have in general to interpolate between many pairs of adjacent keys. Note that the keys need not be evenly spaced, an animator may have spaced the keys unevenly to control speed.

Linear Interpolation for Scalars and Vectors

We have included basic linear interpolation for completeness, but it is rarely used to animate entities such as rigid bodies. Even if we had a set of vertices, for say a rigid body, at key positions in the scene, then using linear interpolation would produce a function which would be piecewise linear with discontinuities at the keys. The animation would thus be jerky. Jerkiness in animation due to discontinuities in the interpolated function of the control parameter is very noticeable and is to be avoided at all costs, but simple linear interpolation does have its uses. It can

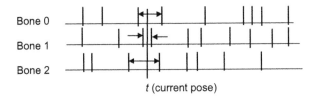

Figure 7.3. Keyframes and intervals.

be used in the animation of parameters, such as colour and size, in game objects. Here, we generally only have two keys and so linear interpolation is fine.

To calculate in-betweens using linear interpolation is straightforward:

$$u = \frac{(t - t_1)}{(t_2 - t_1)}$$

$$k = k_1(1 - u) + k_2 u$$

where u is a parameter $(0 < u \leq 1)$, t is the time of the required interpolation, t_1 and t_2 are the times for the keyframes and k_1 and k_2 are the data for the keyframes.

We can use the function `lerp` to perform the interpolation in a shader as

```
float3  position = lerp(k1,k2,u);
```

Bézier Curves for Scalars and Vectors

This is an extremely popular method of playing animation in a game which is derived from a pre-designed animation sequence. It is *not* strictly speaking a keyframe method in the sense that we use interpolation, but rather it is a pre-authored interpolant in the form of a curve. Animation software such as 3D Studio MAX enables animators to design a Bézier curve interpolant through static keys. (See Appendix A7.1 for more details on Bézier curves.) This is done by adjusting the tangent vector of the curves which can be used to control motion through the keys. Unlike using a piecewise linear interpolant, this can result in smooth motion. In this way, the artists' design is encoded in the set of control points, and this is what we decode in real time. To construct the in-between values in real time, all we need to do is to evaluate the Bézier curve.

An entire multisegment Bézier curve is represented by $4n - (n\text{-}1)$ control points. Figure A7.1.4 shows a four-segment curve represented by 13 control points, 5 of which are end points. For each segment, the two end control points are interpolating, and the two middle control points are noninterpolating (only end control points are shown in the figure). Thus, we choose to use the endpoints of individual segments as the keys, and given a pair of keys, we need to fetch the other two (noninterpolating) control points to evaluate the curve. A way to organise this is for each key to store its value (x,y,z) and its previous and next endpoints. So for a segment k_i, k_{i+1} we fetch ki<next> and k_{i+1} <previous> giving the 4 control points k_i, k_i<next>, k_{i+1}<previous>, k_{i+1}. This explains the requirement for nine floats per key in Table 7.1.

Given the 4 control points, we generate the Bézier curve for as many frames as we require as follows:

$$Q(u) = \sum_{i=0}^{3} P_i B_i(u)$$

where

$$u = \frac{(t - t_1)}{(t_2 - t_1)}$$

The code to evaluate a Bézier curve is given as Listing 7.1.

Listing 7.1

Evaluating a Bézier curve.

```
void pAnimation::evaluate_Bezier(
        // key values in sequence
        const float *p,
        // key size (1-scalar, 3-vector)
        int n,
        // value of u for current sample (0-1)
        float u,
        // output
        float *o)
{
        float u2=1.0f-u;

        float B[4];
        B[0]=u2*u2*u2;
        B[1]=3.0f*u*u2*u2;
        B[2]=3.0f*u*u*u2;
        B[3]=u*u*u;

        int a,b,c;
        for( a=0;a<n;a++ )
                o[a]=0;

        c=0;
        for( a=0;a<4;a++ )
                for( b=0;b<n;b++ )
                        o[b]+=p[c++]*B[a];
}
```

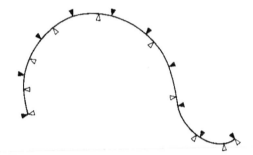

Figure 7.4. Intervals of equal parametric length (white) do not correspond to equal intervals in arclength (black).

However, this is only an approximate method because we are sampling the curve at equal intervals in the parameter u. As Figure 7.4 demonstrates, equal parametric intervals do not correspond to equal distances along the curve. In reconstructing the desired effect, we need to step along the curve in equal increments replacing u with a new parameter called the arclength.

If we do not do this then we will not reproduce the motion that the animator created interactively, providing that the software sampled the curve by arclength during the creation phase. This can be done at some cost by a method we can call "accumulating chord length" (Figure 7.5).

To do this for a curve we evaluate $Q(u)$ for small increments in u (say 0.01) and calculate the chord length $u_{i+1} - u_i$ adding the accumulated total each time into the table. We now have a piecewise linear version of the curve at a high resolution and can step along it in approximate equal arclength units. The cost of this for each curve is one order of magnitude more Bézier evaluations (for $u = 0.01$ and 10 samples).

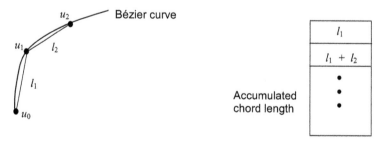

Figure 7.5. Equal arclength evaluation of a Bézier curve.

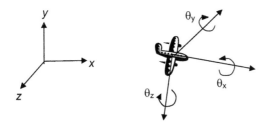

Figure 7.6. Euler angles.

Representing and Interpolating Rotation

Whilst it is clear how to interpolate position, such is not the case for rotation. There are many ways in which rotation can be represented. The most familiar is probably Euler angle representation (Figure 7.6). Here, the current orientation of an object is specified by three rotational angles about the axes of its local coordinate system.

Euler angles are intuitive and can be used to create an intuitive interface for defining rotational angles, but they suffer from certain disadvantages when they are used to represent key orientations and we try to interpolate between them. We will look at one particular case to demonstrate the problem; for a fuller discussion and a description of the notorious gimbal lock problem—another problem with Euler angles—see [WATT92].

The main problem with Euler angles can easily be demonstrated using a simple illustration. Figure 7.7 shows two paths of a character rotating about the local

Figure 7.7. Two different paths between the same keys result from the interpolation choice of Euler angles.

origin between two keys. Using Euler angles, the first image interpolates an x rotation or roll to achieve the in-betweens:

$$R(0,0,0)\ldots,R(\pi t,0,0),\ldots R(\pi,0,0) \qquad\qquad 0 < t < 1$$

The second interpolates both a y and z rotation:

$$R(0,0,0)\ldots,R(0,\pi t,\pi t),\ldots R(0,\pi,\pi) \qquad\qquad 0 < t < 1$$

The resulting in between sequences are completely different—the first producing a direct rotation between the keys, and the second, a twisting and rotating motion. In other words, the order in which the angles are specified determines the path of the rotation between the keys.

There are, in fact, an infinity of paths between the two keys and although the second animation may be the one desired, generally we require an 'intuitive' path to result from the interpolation—the shortest path. Thus the question is: how is an animator to specify a desired path between two keys given that any such path has to be specified as three Euler angles in a particular order? Yet another problem with Euler interpolation is that it tends to exhibit jerkiness, something we cannot tolerate in modern games.

We can avoid such difficulties by using quaternions to represent rotation. Quaternions are 'four vectors'

$$q = s + x\mathbf{i} + y\mathbf{j} + z\mathbf{k} = (s,\mathbf{v})$$

and can be considered as a generalisation of complex numbers with s as the real part and x,y,z as the imaginary part. (Basic quaternion maths is given in Appendix 7.2.)

We can regard a quaternion as an entity which specifies the change in orientation from a previous orientation (just like Euler angles). The information that we need to specify this rotation is just four floats. This is due to a famous theorem by Euler who proposed that one orientation can reach another by a single rotation about an axis. And so any orientation change can be represented by a vector $\mathbf{n}$ and an angle θ.

We can construct a physical intuition for a quaternion as follows (Figure 7.8):

1. (x,y,z) is a point in 3D space;
2. Construct an axis $\mathbf{n}$ from the origin to the point (x, y, z);
3. Consider a rotation about that axis, following the right-hand rule;
4. A quaternion is an entity that transform $\mathbf{r}$ to $R\mathbf{r}$.

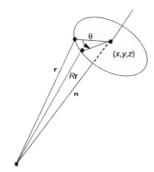

Figure 7.8. A quaternion is an entity that transforms r to *Rr*.

Now we return to our example (Figure 7.7) and see what quaternion interpolation gives us. We can represent (Appendix A7.1) the first single x-roll of π by the quaternion

$$(\cos(\tfrac{\pi}{2}), \sin(\tfrac{\pi}{2})\,(1,0,0)) = (0,(1,0,0))$$

Similarly a y-roll of π and a z-roll of π are given by $(0,(0,1,0))$ and $(0,(0,0,1))$ respectively. Now the effect of a y-roll of π followed by a z-roll of π can be represented by the single quaternion formed by multiplying these two quaternions together:

$$(0,(0,1,0))\,(0,(0,0,1)) = (0,(0,1,0) \times (0,0,1))$$

$$= (0,(1,0,0))$$

which is identically the single x-roll of π. We conclude that representing rotations using quaternions will give us a smooth change in orientation between two keys along a 'good' path.

Interpolating Quaternions

Given the superiority of quaternion parameterization over Euler angle parameterization, this section covers the issue of interpolating rotation in quaternion space. Consider an animator sitting at a workstation and interactively setting up a sequence of key orientations by whatever method is appropriate. This is usually done with the principal rotation operations, but now the restrictions that were placed on the animator when using Euler angles, namely using a fixed number of principal rotations in a fixed order for each key, can be removed. In general, each key will be represented as a single rotation matrix. This sequence of matrices will then be converted into a sequence of quaternions. Interpolation between key quaternions is performed, and this produces a sequence of in-between quaternions, which are then converted back into rotation matrices. The matrices are then applied to the object. The fact that a quaternion interpolation is being used can be transparent to the animator.

Moving in and out of Quaternion Space

The implementation of such a scheme requires us to move into and out of quaternion space, that is, to go from a general rotation matrix to a quaternion and vice versa. Now, to rotate a vector $\mathbf{p}$ with the quaternion q we use the operation

$$q(0,\mathbf{p})q^{-1}$$

where q is the quaternion:

$$\left(\cos\left(\tfrac{\theta}{2}\right),\ \sin\left(\tfrac{\theta}{2}\right),\ n\right) = (s,(x,y,z))$$

It can be shown that this is exactly equivalent to applying the following rotation matrix to the vector:

$$M = \begin{bmatrix} 1 - 2(y^2 + z^2) & 2xy - 2sz & 2sy + 2xz & 0 \\ 2xy + 2sz & 1 - 2(x^2 + z^2) & -2sx + 2yz & 0 \\ -2sy + 2xz & -2sx + 2yz & 1 - 2(x^2 + y^2) & 0 \\ 0 & 0 & 0 & 1 \end{bmatrix}$$

By these means, then, we can move from quaternion space to rotation matrices. The inverse mapping, from a rotation matrix to a quaternion, is as follows. All that is required is to convert a general rotation matrix:

$$\begin{bmatrix} M_{00} & M_{01} & M_{02} & M_{03} \\ M_{10} & M_{11} & M_{12} & M_{13} \\ M_{20} & M_{21} & M_{22} & M_{23} \\ M_{30} & M_{31} & M_{32} & M_{33} \end{bmatrix}$$

where $M_{03} = M_{13} = M_{23} = M_{30} = M_{31} = M_{32} = 0$ and $M_{33} = 1$, into the matrix format directly above. Given a general rotation matrix the first thing to do is to examine the sum of its diagonal components M_{ii} which is:

$$4 - 4(x^2 + y^2 + z^2)$$

since the quaternion corresponding to the rotation matrix is of unit magnitude we have:

$$s^2 + x^2 + y^2 + z^2 = 1$$

and:

$$4 - 4(x^2 + y^2 + z^2) = 4 - 4(1 - s^2) = 4s^2$$

Thus, for a 4 x 4 homogeneous matrix we have:

$$s = \pm \frac{1}{2}\sqrt{M_{00} + M_{11} + M_{22} + M_{33}}$$

and

$$x = \frac{M_{21} - M_{12}}{4s}$$

$$y = \frac{M_{02} - M_{20}}{4s}$$

$$z = \frac{M_{10} - M_{01}}{4s}$$

Spherical Linear Interpolation (slerp)

We now discuss how to interpolate in quaternion space. Since a rotation maps onto a quaternion of unit magnitude, the entire group of rotations maps onto the surface of the 4D unit hypersphere in quaternion space. Curves interpolating through key orientations should therefore lie on the surface of this sphere.

However, we cannot visualise 4D, but consider instead a visualisation in 3D— a unit sphere. Since we will always be using unit quaternions, the interpolated quaternions will also be unit quaternions. Bearing in mind that the rotation takes place about a fixed point, we can visualise the 'motion' of a quaternion as it moves from one key to another as a point on the surface of the unit sphere.

Consider the simplest case of interpolating between just two key quaternions. A naive, straightforward linear interpolation between the two keys results in a motion that speeds up in the middle. An analogy of this process in a 2D plane is shown in Figure 7.9 which shows that the path on the surface of the sphere yielded by linear interpolation gives unequal angles and causes a speed-up in angular velocity.

This is because we are not moving along the surface of the hypersphere but cutting across it. In order to ensure a steady rotation, we must employ spherical linear interpolation (or slerp), where we move along an arc of the geodesic that passes through the two keys.

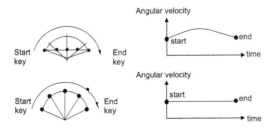

Figure 7.9. A 2D analogy showing the difference between linear interpolation and simple spherical linear interpolation (slerp).

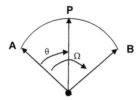

Figure 7.10. Spherical linear interpolation.

The formula for spherical linear interpolation is easy to derive geometrically. Consider the 2D case of two vectors **A** and **B** separated by angle Ω and vector **P** which makes an angle θ with **A** as shown in Figure 7.10 . **P** is derived from spherical interpolation between **A** and **B,** and we write

$$\mathbf{P} = \alpha\mathbf{A} + \beta\mathbf{B}$$

Trivially we can solve for α and given

$$|\mathbf{P}| = 1$$

$$\mathbf{A} \cdot \mathbf{B} = \cos \Omega$$

$$\mathbf{A} \cdot \mathbf{P} = \cos \theta$$

to give

$$\mathbf{P} = \mathbf{A}\,\frac{\sin(\Omega - \theta)}{\sin \Omega} + \mathbf{B}\,\frac{\sin \theta}{\sin \Omega}$$

Spherical linear interpolation between two unit quaternions q_1 and q_2, where

$$q_1 q_2 = \cos \Omega$$

is obtained by generalising the above to four dimensions and replacing θ by Ω where $u \in [0,1]$. We write

$$\text{slerp}(q_1, q_2, u) = q_1\frac{\sin(1 - u)\Omega}{\sin \Omega} + q_2\,\frac{\sin \Omega u}{\sin \Omega}$$

Now, given any two key quaternions, p and q, there exist two possible arcs along which one can move, corresponding to alternative starting directions on the geodesic that connects them. One of them goes around the long way, and this is the one that we wish to avoid. Naively one might assume that this reduces to either spherically interpolating between p and q by the angle Ω, where

$$pq = \cos \Omega$$

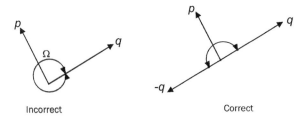

Figure 7.11. Shortest arc determination on quaternion hypersphere.

or interpolating in the opposite direction by the angle $2\pi - \Omega$. This however will not produce the desired effect. The reason for this is that the topology of the hypersphere of orientation is not just a straightforward extension of the 3D Euclidean sphere. To appreciate this, it is sufficient to consider the fact that every rotation has two representations in quaternion space, namely q and $-q$; that is the effect of q and $-q$ is the same. That this is so is due to the fact that algebraically the operator $q()q^{-1}$ has exactly the same effect as $(-q)()(-q)^{-1}$. Thus points diametrically opposed represent the same rotation. Because of this topological oddity, care must be taken when determining the shortest arc. A strategy that works is to choose either interpolating between the quaternion pairs p and q or the pair p and $-q$. Given two key orientations p and q, find the magnitude of their difference, that is $(p-q)(p-q)$, and compare this to the magnitude of the difference when the second key is negated, that is $(p+q)(p+q)$. If the former is smaller then we are already moving along the smallest arc and nothing needs to be done. If, however, the second is smallest, then we replace q by $-q$ and proceed. These considerations are shown schematically in Figure 7.11.

So far, we have described the spherical equivalent of linear interpolation between two key orientations, and, just as was the case for linear interpolation, spherical linear interpolation between more than two key orientations will produce jerky, sharply changing motion across the keys.

The situation is summarised in Figure 7.12 as a 3D analogy which shows that the curve on the surface of the sphere is not continuous through the keys. Also shown in this figure is the angular velocity, which is constant between keys and discontinuous at the keys. The angular velocity can be made constant across all frames by assigning to each interval between keys a number of frames proportional to the magnitude of the interval. That is, we calculate the magnitude of the angle θ between a pair of keys q_t and q_{t+1} as:

$$\cos \theta = q_i \cdot q_{i+1}$$

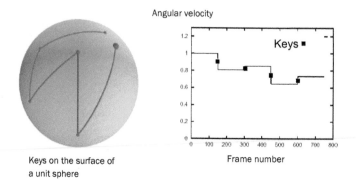

Angular velocity

Keys ■

Keys on the surface of
a unit sphere

Frame number

Figure 7.12. Slerp through six keys. *Courtesy E. Dam, M. Koch and M. Lillholm University of Copenhagen.*

where the inner product of two quaternions $q = (s,v)$ and $q' = (s',v')$ is defined as:

$$qq' = ss' + vv'$$

Curing the path continuity is more difficult. What is required for higher order continuity is the spherical equivalent of the cubic spline. Unfortunately because we are now working on the surface of a 4D hypersphere, the problem is far more complex than constructing splines in 3D Euclidean space. K. Shoemake [SHOE87] has tackled this problem. A visualisation of one of the solutions is shown in Figure 7.13.

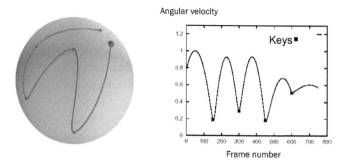

Angular velocity

Keys■

Frame number

Figure 7.13. Squad through six keys (compare with Figure 7.12). *Courtesy E. Dam, M. Koch and M.Lillholm, University of Copenhagen.*

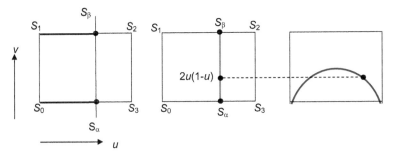

Figure 7.14. Constructing a parabola using a quad.

Comparing this figure with Figure 7.12 we can see that now the interpolation curve is continuous through the keys and the angular velocity is continuous with local minima at the keys. The name of the technique is squad which is now explained.

We start by considering four points (S_0, S_1, S_2, S_3) at the corners of a quad shown in Figure 7.14 We linearly interpolate by an amount $u \in [0,1]$, along the horizontal edges to get the intermediate points S_α, S_β, where

$$S_\alpha = S_0(1 - u) + S_3 u$$

$$S_\beta = S_1(1 - u) + S_2 u$$

Now we perform a vertical linear interpolation by an amount

$$v = 2u(1 - u)$$

to get the point

$$p = S_\alpha (1 - v) + S_\beta v$$

As u varies from 0 to 1, the locus of p will trace out a parabola. This process of bilinear interpolation, where the second interpolation is thus restricted, is called parabolic blending.

Note that we can write the above algorithmically as

$$p = \text{lin}(\text{lin}(S_0, S_3, u), \text{lin}(S_1, S_2, u), 2u(1 - u))$$

where lin() is defined as $S_i (1 - u) + S_j u$.

W. Boehm [BOEHM82] shows how, given a Bézier curve segment with control points (b_0, b_1, b_2, b_3) one can derive the quadrangle points (b_0, S_1, S_2, b_3) corresponding to the above construction. This has the geometric significance of enabling us to visualise the cubic as a parabola whose quadrangle points are not necessarily parallel or coplanar. The cubic can be thought of as a warped parabola. This enables us to think of a cubic spline as a series of three linear interpolations.

The mathematical significance of this construction is that it shows how to construct a cubic as a series of three linear interpolations of the quadrangle points. In [SHOE87] this construction is taken onto the surface of the 4D hypersphere by constructing a spherical curve, using three spherical linear interpolations of a quadrangle of unit quaternions. This is defined as squad(), where

$$\text{squad}(b_0, S_1, S_2, b_3, ut) \ = \ \text{slerp}(\text{slerp}(b_0, b_3, ut), \text{slerp}(S_1, S_2, ut), 2u(1 - u)).$$

Given a series of quaternion keys, we can construct a cubic segment across keys q_i and q_{i+1} by constructing a quadrangle of quaternions (q_i, a_i, b_{i+1}, q_{i+1}) where a_i, b_{i+1} have to be determined. These inner quadrangle points are chosen in such a way to ensure that continuity of tangents across adjacent cubic segments is guaranteed. The derivation for the inner quadrangle points is difficult involving as it does the calculus and exponentiation of quaternions, and we will just quote the results, referring the interested reader to [SHOE87].

$$a_i = b_i = q_i \exp\left(- \frac{\ln\left(q_i^{-1}, q_{i+1}\right) + \ln\left(q_i^{-1}, q_{i+1}\right)}{4}\right)$$

where, for the unit quaternion

$$q \ = \ (\cos \theta, \text{cin } \theta, \mathbf{v})$$

$$|\mathbf{v}| \ = \ 1$$

$$\ln(c) \ = \ (0, \theta\mathbf{v})$$

and, inversely, for the pure quaternion (zero scalar part)

$$q \ = \ (0, \theta, \mathbf{v})$$

$$\exp(q) \ = \ (\cos \theta, \sin \theta, \mathbf{v})$$

Finally, we mention a potential difficulty when applying quaternions. Quaternion interpolation is indiscriminate in that it does not prefer any one direction to any other. Interpolating between two keys produces a move that depends on the orientations of the keys and nothing else. This is inconvenient when choreographing the virtual camera. Normally when moving a camera the film plane is always required to be upright—this is usually specified by an 'up' vector. By its very nature, the notion of a preferred direction cannot easily be built into the quaternion representation, and if it is used in this context, the camera up vector may have to be reset or some other fix employed. (Roll of the camera is, of course, used in certain contexts.)

Appendix 7.1: Bézier Curves and Patches

Bézier Curves

Bézier curves (and surface patches) have found usage in computer graphics for decades, particularly in the Computer Aided Design (CAD) industry. We tend to use a cubic form because it gives the best compromise between the generality of the curve or surface patch—its ability to represent a desired shape—and its cost.

A Bézier curve traces a path or trajectory through 3D space and is often called a space curve. It is defined as a parametric function which means that the space curve $Q(u)$ is defined in terms of a parameter u ($0 <= u <= 1$). As u varies from 0 to 1 we arrive at values for the position (x,y,z) of a point on $Q(u)$ by scaling or blending so-called control points, P_i. That is each point on the curve is determined by scaling each control point by a cubic polynomial known as a basis or blending function. Two of the control points—the end points—are interpolating and two are non-interpolating. The entire curve is then defined by the position of P_i in 3D space (together with the basis functions which are constant curves). The curve is then given by:

$$Q(u) = \sum_{i=0}^{3} P_i B_i(u) \qquad \text{(A7.1.1)}$$

and in the case of a Bézier curve the basis or blending functions are the Bernstein cubic polynomials:

$$B_0(u) = (1-u)^3$$
$$B_1(u) = 3u(1-u)^2$$
$$B_2(u) = 3u^2(1-u)$$
$$B_3(u) = u^3$$

Figure A7.1.1 shows these polynomials and a Bézier curve (projected into the 2D space of the diagram).

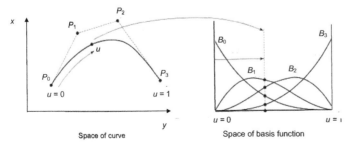

Figure A7.1.1. The construction of a Bézier curve from basis functions.

A useful intuitive notion is the following. As we move physically along the curve from $u = 0$ to $u = 1$ we simultaneously move a vertical line in the basis function space that defines four values for the basis functions. Weighting each basis function by the control points and summing, we obtain the corresponding point in the space of the curve. We note that for any value of u (except $u = 0$ and $u = 1$) all the functions are non-zero. This means that the position of all the control points contribute to every point on the curve (except at the end points). At $u=0$ only B_0 is non-zero. Therefore;

$$Q(0) = P_0$$

and similarly,

$$Q(1) = P_3$$

We also note that:

$$B_0(u) = B_1(u) + B_2(u) + B_3(u) = 1$$

Joining the four control points together gives the so-called control polygon, and moving the control points around produces new curves. Moving a single control point of the curve distorts its shape in an intuitive manner.

This is demonstrated in Figure A7.1.2. The effect of moving the end-points is obvious. When we move the inner control points P_1 and P_2 we change the orientation of the tangent vectors to the curves at the end points - again obvious. Less obvious is that the positions of P_1 and P_2 also control the magnitude of the tangent vectors at the end-points and it can be shown that:

$$Q_u(0) = 3(P_1 - P_0)$$
$$Q_u(1) = 3(P_2 - P_3)$$

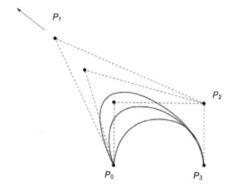

Figure A7.1.2. Moving a control point of a Bézier curve.

where Q_u is the tangent vector to the curve (first derivative) at the end-point. It can be seen that the curve is pulled towards the tangent vector with greater magnitude, which is controlled by the position of the control points.

At this point, it is useful to consider all the ramifications of representing a curve with control points. The most important property, as far as interaction is concerned, is that moving the control points gives an intuitive change in curve shape. Another way of putting it is to say that the curve mimics the shape of the control polygon.

Now consider transforming curves. Because the curves are defined as linear combinations of the control points, the curve is transformed by any affine transformation (rotation, scaling, translation etc.) in 3D space by applying the appropriate transformations to the set of control points. Thus, to transform a curve, we transform the control points then compute the points on the curve. In this context, note that it is not easy to transform a curve by computing the points then transforming (as we might do with an implicit description). For example, it is not clear in scaling how many points need to ensure smoothness when the curve has been magnified. Note here that perspective transformations are non-affine, so we cannot map control points to screen space and compute the curve there.

Finally, a useful alternative notation to the summation form is the following. First we expand Equation A7.1.1 to give:

$$Q(u) = P_0(1-u)^3 + P_1 3u(1-u)^2 + P_2(1-u) + P_3 u^3$$

This can then be written in matrix notation as

$$Q(u) = UB_z P$$

$$= [u^3 \ u^2 \ u \ 1] \begin{bmatrix} -1 & 3 & -3 & 1 \\ 3 & -6 & 3 & 0 \\ -3 & 3 & 0 & 0 \\ 1 & 0 & 0 & 0 \end{bmatrix} \begin{bmatrix} P_0 \\ P_1 \\ P_2 \\ P_3 \end{bmatrix}$$

Joining Bézier Curve Segments

Curve segments, defined by a set of four control points, can be joined to make up more complex curves than that obtainable from a single segment. This results in a so-called piecewise polynomial curve. An alternative method of representing more complex curves is to increase the degree of the polynomial, but this has computational and mathematical disadvantages, and it is generally considered easier to split the curve into cubic segments. Connecting curve segments implies that constraints must apply at the joins. The default constraint is positional continuity; the next best is first-order (or tangential) . The difference between positional and first-order continuity for a Bézier curve is shown in Figure A7.1.3.

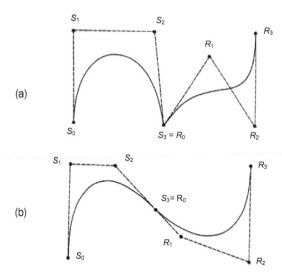

(a)

(b)

Figure A7.1.3. Joining two Bézier segments. (a) Positional continuity. (b) Tangential continuity.

Positional continuity means that the end-point of the first segment is coincident with the start-point of the second. First-order, or tangential, continuity means that the edges of the characteristic polygon are collinear, as shown in the figure. This means that the tangent vectors, at the end of one curve and the start of the other, match to within a constant. In shaded surfaces, maintaining only positional continuity would possibly result in the joins being visible in the final rendered object.

If the control points of the two segments are S_i and R_i then first-order continuity is maintained if:

$$(S_3 - S_2) = k(R_1 - R_0)$$

Using this condition, a composite Bézier curve is easily built up by adding a single segment at a time.

Figure A7.1.4 is an example of a multisegment Bézier curve. In this case, four curves are joined, and first-order continuity is maintained between them.

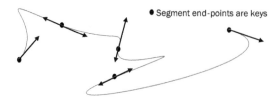

• Segment end-points are keys

Figure A7.1.4. Four Bézier curves joined with tangential continuity.

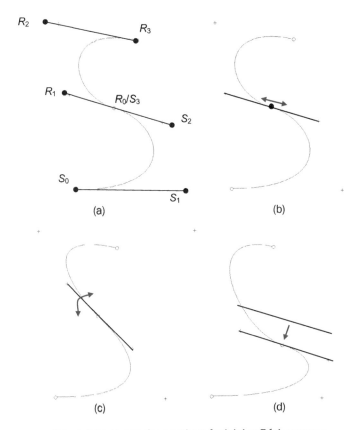

Figure A7.1.5. Interface options for joining Bézier curves.

It is useful to consider the ramifications for an interface through which a user can edit multisegment curves and maintain continuity. Figure A7.1.5 shows some possibilities. The illustration assumes that the user has already constructed a two segment curve whose shape is to be altered around the area of the join point S_3/R_0.

To maintain continuity we must operate simultaneously on R_1, R_0/S_3 and S_2. We can do this by:

- maintaining the orientation of the line R_1,S_2 and moving the join point up and down this line (Figure A7.1.5(a)),

- maintaining the position of the join point and rotating the line R_1,S_2 about this point (Figure A7.1.5(b)) and

- moving all three control points as a locked unit (Figure A7.1.5(c)).

These three editing possibilities or constraints will enable the user to change the shape of curves made up of any number of segments while at the same time maintaining first-order continuity between the curve segments. It is precisely tools like this that are used in animation authoring software.

Bézier Patches

The treatment of parametric cubic curve segments given above is easily generalised to bi-parametric cubic surface patches. A point on the surface patch is given by a bi-parametric function and a set of blending or basis functions is used for each parameter. A cubic Bézier patch is defined as

$$Q(u,v) = \sum_{i=0}^{3} \sum_{j=0}^{3} P_{ij} B_i(u) B_j(v) \qquad (A7.1.2)$$

Mathematically, the 3D surfaces are said to be generated from the Cartesian product of two curves. A Bézier patch and its control points are shown in Figure A7.1.6 where the patch is displayed using iso-parametric lines.

The 16 control points form a characteristic polyhedron and this bears a relationship to the shape of the surface, in the same way that the lines joining the control points in a curve relate to the curve segment.

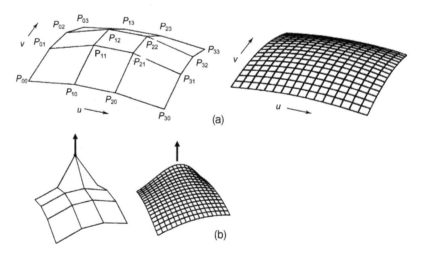

Figure A7.1.6. Bézier Patch. (a) Sixteen control points and patch as isoparametric curves. (b) moving one of the control points deforms the curve.

It can be seen intuitively that 12 of the control points are associated with the boundary edges of the patch (4 of them specifying the end-points). Only the corner vertices lie in the surface. In fact, if we consider the control points to form a matrix of 4 x 4 points, then the four groups of 4 points forming the edges of the matrix are the control points for the boundary curves of the patch. Thus, the edges of the patch are made up of four Bézier curves, as indeed are the isoparametric curves in the figure. We can now see that the remaining 4 control points must specify the shape of the surface contained between the boundary edges.

The properties of the Bézier curve formulation are extended into the surface domain. Figure A7.1.6(b) shows a patch being deformed by 'pulling up' a single control point. The intuitive feel for the surface through its control points and the ability to ensure first-order continuity are maintained.

The way in which the control points work can be seen by analogy with the cubic curve.

The matrix convention for Equation A7.1.2 is

$$Q(u,v) = [u^3 \ u^2 \ u \ 1] [B \ \boldsymbol{P} \ B^{\mathrm{T}}] \begin{bmatrix} v^3 \\ v^2 \\ v \\ 1 \end{bmatrix}$$

where

$$B = \begin{bmatrix} -1 & 3 & -3 & 1 \\ 3 & -6 & 3 & 0 \\ -3 & 3 & 0 & 0 \\ 1 & 0 & 0 & 0 \end{bmatrix}$$

$$\boldsymbol{P} = \begin{bmatrix} P_{00} & P_{01} & P_{02} & P_{03} \\ P_{10} & P_{11} & P_{12} & P_{13} \\ P_{20} & P_{21} & P_{22} & P_{23} \\ P_{30} & P_{31} & P_{32} & P_{33} \end{bmatrix}$$

The surface patch is transformed by applying transformations to each of the control points.

It is instructive to examine the relationship between control points and derivative vectors at the corner of a patch. For example, consider the corner $u = v = 0$. The relationship between the control points and the vectors associated with the vertex P_{00} is as follows:

$$Q_u(0,0) = 3(P_{10} - P_{00})$$
$$Q_v(0,0) = 3(P_{01} - P_{00})$$
$$Q_{uv}(0,0) = 9(P_{00} - P_{01} - P_{10} + P_{11})$$

Vertex normals and tangents can be calculated at patch corners as, for example:

$$\mathbf{T} = P_{01} - P_{00}$$
$$\mathbf{B} = P_{10} - P_{00}$$
$$\mathbf{N} = \mathbf{B} \times \mathbf{T}$$

A normal can be computed at any point on the patch surface as:

$$\mathbf{N} = \frac{\partial Q}{\partial u} \times \frac{\partial Q}{\partial v}$$

Bézier Patches and Rendering

To render patches using a shader we need to convert them into triangles. This is easily done using a subdivision method (the de Casteljau algorithm) which invokes either uniform or nonuniform subdivision to output a piecewise linear version of the patch made up of rectangles. The subdivision process can proceed to any level of detail. This method would be used to render objects modelled with patches such as the Utah Teapot (Chapter 3).

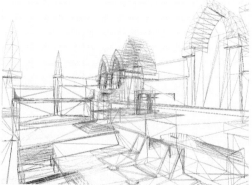

Figure A7.1.7. Quake 3 level modelled with biquadrics and rendered without texture to emphasise the curves.

Alternatively, we can precalculate and store a hierarchy of control points that emerge from the subdivision process—each level representing the patch at a particular level of detail. To render a level, for example, at some LOD means fetching the appropriate control polyhedron from the array of control points representing the patch at its finest level of subdivision. The famous example of levels built from patches is Quake 3, an example from which is shown in Figure A7.1.7—although, in this case, the patches are biquadrics.

With the advent of more and more powerful shaders, it is difficult to predict if there is a future for patch technology in games. After all you can render surfaces that looked curved by using more and more triangles. However, it is surely the case that Bézier technology will persist in game applications like facial animation, as we describe in Chapter 10.

Appendix 7.2: Basic Quaternion Mathematics

Quaternions are 'four-vectors' and can be considered as a generalisation of complex numbers with s as the real or scalar part and x,y,z as the imaginary part:

$$q = s + x\mathbf{i} + y\mathbf{j} + z\mathbf{k}$$
$$= (s, \mathbf{v})$$

Here we can note their similarity to a 2D complex number that can be used to specify a point or vector in 2D space. A quaternion specifies a point in 4D space, and if $s = 0$ a point or vector in 3D space. In this context they are used to represent a vector plus rotation. Variables $i, j,$ and k are unit quaternions and are equivalent to unit vectors in a vector system; however, they obey different combination rules:

$$i^2 = j^2 = k^2 = ij\,k = -1,\ ij = k,\ ji = -k$$

Using these, we can derive addition and multiplication rules each of which yields a quaternion.
For addition:

$$q + q' = (s + s', \mathbf{v} + \mathbf{v}')$$

For multiplication:

$$qq' = (ss' - \mathbf{v} \cdot \mathbf{v}', \mathbf{v} \times \mathbf{v}' + s\mathbf{v}' + s'\mathbf{v})$$

The conjugate of the quaternion

$$q = (s, \mathbf{v})$$

is

$$\bar{q} = (s, -\mathbf{v})$$

and the product of the quaternion with its conjugate defines its magnitude

$$q\bar{q} = s^2 + |v^2| = q^2$$

If

$$|q| = 1$$

then q is called a unit quaternion. The set of all unit quaternions forms a unit sphere in 4D space, and unit quaternions play an important part in specifying general rotations.

It can be shown that if

$$q = (s, \mathbf{v})$$

then there exists a $\mathbf{v}'$ and a $\theta \in [-\pi, \pi]$ such that

$$q = (\cos \theta, \mathbf{v}' \sin \theta)$$

and if q is a unit quaternion, then

$$q = (\cos \theta, \; \sin \theta \, \mathbf{n}) \tag{A7.2.1}$$

where $|\mathbf{n}| = 1$.

We now consider operating on a vector $\mathbf{r}$ in Figure 7.8 by using quaternions; $\mathbf{r}$ is defined as the quaternion $p = (0, \mathbf{r})$ and we define the operation as:

$$R_p(p) = qpq^{-1}$$

That is it is proposed to rotate the vector $\mathbf{r}$ by expressing it as a quaternion multiplying it on the left by q and on the right by q^{-1}. This guarantees that the result will be a quaternion of the form $(0, \mathbf{v})$—in other words a vector; q is defined to be a unit quaternion $(s, \mathbf{v})$. It is easily shown that:

$$R_p(p) = (0, (s^2 - \mathbf{v} \cdot \mathbf{v})\mathbf{r} + 2\mathbf{v}(\mathbf{v} \cdot \mathbf{r}) + 2s(\mathbf{v} \times \mathbf{r}))$$

Using Proposition A7.2.1 and substituting gives

$$R_q(p) = (0, (\cos^2 \theta - \sin^2 \theta)\mathbf{r} + 2\sin^2 \theta \, \mathbf{n}(\mathbf{n} \cdot \mathbf{r}) + 2\cos \theta \sin \theta \, (\mathbf{n} \times \mathbf{r}))$$
$$= (0, \mathbf{r} \cos 2\theta + (1 - \cos 2\theta) \, \mathbf{n}(\mathbf{n} \cdot \mathbf{r}) + \sin 2\theta \, (\mathbf{n} \times \mathbf{r}))$$

Refer again to Figure 7.8 which shows the vector $\mathbf{r}$ being rotated into vector $R\mathbf{r}'$. It can easily be shown as in [WATT92] that:

$$R\mathbf{r} = (\mathbf{r} \cos \theta + (1 - \cos \theta) (\mathbf{n} \cdot \mathbf{r}) + \sin 2\theta \, (\mathbf{n} \times \mathbf{r}))$$

You will notice that aside from a factor of two appearing in the angle the two previous equations are identical in form. Thus, the act of rotating a vector $\mathbf{r}$ by an angular displacement $(\theta, \mathbf{n})$ is the same as taking this angular displacement, 'lifting' it into quaternion space by representing it as the unit quaternion

$$(\cos(\tfrac{\theta}{2}), \sin(\tfrac{\theta}{2})\, \mathbf{n})$$

and performing the operation $q()q^{-1}$ on the quaternion $(0,\mathbf{r})$. We could therefore parameterise orientation in terms of the four parameters

$$\cos(\tfrac{\theta}{2}), \quad \sin(\tfrac{\theta}{2})\, n_x, \quad \sin(\tfrac{\theta}{2})\, n_y, \quad \sin(\tfrac{\theta}{2})\, n_z$$

using quaternion algebra to manipulate the components.

Listing A7.2.1 is a complete library of common quaternion utilities.

Listing A7.2.1

A library of quaternion functions.

```
pQuaternion::pQuaternion(const pMatrix &mat)
{
        float tr,s,q[4];
        int i,j,k;

        int nxt[3] = {1, 2, 0};

        tr = mat.mf[0] + mat.mf[5] + mat.mf[10];

        // check the diagonal
        if (tr > 0.0)
        {
                s = sqrtf(tr + 1.0f);
                w = s/2.0f;
                s = 0.5f/s;
                x = (mat.mf[6] - mat.mf[9]) * s;
                y = (mat.mf[8] - mat.mf[2]) * s;
                z = (mat.mf[1] - mat.mf[4]) * s;
        }
        else
        {
                // diagonal is negative
                i = 0;
                if (mat.mf[5] > mat.mf[0]) i = 1;
                if (mat.mf[10] > mat.m[i][i]) i = 2;
                j = nxt[i];
                k = nxt[j];
```

```
            s=sqrtf((mat.m[i][i]-(mat.m[j][j] +
                    mat.m[k][k])) + 1.0f);

            q[i] = s*0.5f;

            if (s != 0.0f) s = 0.5f/s;

            q[3] = (mat.m[j][k] - mat.m[k][j])*s;
            q[j] = (mat.m[i][j] + mat.m[j][i])*s;
            q[k] = (mat.m[i][k] + mat.m[k][i])*s;

            x = q[0];
            y = q[1];
            z = q[2];
            w = q[3];
        }
    }


void pQuaternion::get_mat(pMatrix &mat) const
{
        float   wx, wy, wz,
                xx, yy, yz,
                xy, xz, zz,
                x2, y2, z2;

        // calculate coefficients
        x2 = x + x;
        y2 = y + y;
        z2 = z + z;
        xx = x * x2;
        xy = x * y2;
        xz = x * z2;
        yy = y * y2;
        yz = y * z2;
        zz = z * z2;
        wx = w * x2;
        wy = w * y2;
        wz = w * z2;
```

```
        mat.mf[0] = 1.0f-(yy+zz);
        mat.mf[4] = xy - wz;
        mat.mf[8] = xz + wy;
        mat.mf[12] = 0.0;

        mat.mf[1] = xy + wz;
        mat.mf[5] = 1.0f-(xx + zz);
        mat.mf[9] = yz - wx;
        mat.mf[13] = 0.0;

        mat.mf[2] = xz - wy;
        mat.mf[6] = yz + wx;
        mat.mf[10] = 1.0f - (xx + yy);
        mat.mf[14] = 0.0;

        mat.mf[3] = 0;
        mat.mf[7] = 0;
        mat.mf[11] = 0;
        mat.mf[15] = 1;
}


void pQuaternion::get_rotate(
                float &angle, pVector &axis) const
{
        angle=acosf(w)*PIUNDER180*2.0f;

        float f=sinf(angle*PIOVER180*0.5f);

        axis.x=x/f;
        axis.y=y/f;
        axis.z=z/f;
}


void pQuaternion::slerp(const pQuaternion& q1,
                const pQuaternion& q2,float t)
{
    float v;         // complement to t
    float o;         // complement to v (t)
```

```
float theta;     // angle between q1 & q2
float sin_t;     // sin(theta)
float cos_t;     // cos(theta)
int flip;        // flag for negating q2

cos_t = q1[0] * q2[0] + q1[1] * q2[1] +
        q1[2] * q2[2] + q1[3] * q2[3];

if (cos_t < 0.0f)
{
    cos_t = -cos_t;
    flip = 1;
}
else
    flip = 0;

if (1.0f - cos_t < 1e-6f)
{
    v = 1.0f - t;
    o = t;
}
else
{
    theta = acosf(cos_t);
    sin_t = sinf(theta);
    v = sinf(theta-t*theta) / sin_t;
    o = sinf(t*theta) / sin_t;
}
if (flip) o = -o;

x = v * q1[0] + o * q2[0];
y = v * q1[1] + o * q2[1];
z = v * q1[2] + o * q2[2];
w = v * q1[3] + o * q2[3];
}
```

Chapter Eight

Real-Time Animation

Introduction

The topic of this chapter is real-time animation. By real-time animation we mean an animation sequence that is created in real time according to the current state of the game together with a set of predefined rules which, given the current state of an object, will calculate its state in the next frame. Applications that fall into this category are many and varied and range from rigid body simulation, which may be used in a racing car game or flight simulator, to particle systems, which may be used to produce an effect,[1] for example, the result of an impact, flame, clouds etc.

Just as the advent of GPU hardware has vastly increased the quality of real-time rendering, so too will it have a significant impact on the quality of real-time animation. Perhaps the best example of this is particle systems whose visual efficacy in many contexts depends on being able to process a large population. As we shall see later in this chapter, we can implement with ease up to one million particles on a GPU.

Because real-time animation in games applications and methods is so diverse, we will deal with the topic by detailing a set of popular examples. We begin by examining one of the most popular genres—simulating the behaviour of water.

Simulating Water

Simulating water falls neatly into two categories: real-time modelling of the waves and rendering issues—mainly reflection and refraction. We begin by considering modelling methods, most of which aim to model a moving height field $H(x,y,t)$

....
[1] Many applications that fall into this category are described as "procedural animation". This is to reflect the fact that many animations can be controlled by a closed functional form or procedure.

in real time. Such methods were first explored in the 1980s, as we detail below, and the renewed interest in them is, of course, due to the fact that they can be implemented in real time.

Modelling Water Waves—Fourier Synthesis

A simple but effective way of simulating water waves is to synthesize a height field by superimposing a set of sinusoidal waves (Fourier synthesis). Animated effects are easily achieved by making such parameters as amplitude, phase and displacement a function of time. This is one of the easiest parametric models to set up, and it produces convincing results. A packet of waves is specified as a spectrum and an inverse Fourier transform generates $H(x,y,t)$ from the spectrum.

The popularity of Fourier synthesis for GPU implementations should be further assured by the availability of FFT (Fast Fourier Transform) implementations on hardware (see, for example, [MORE03]).

Water waves fall into various categories depending on their motivating force. The waves that are usually modelled in computer graphics are surface gravity waves or wind waves which result from the action of the wind. These are the waves that we notice when looking at the sea from a beach. Water waves are usually modelled by using parallel waves—sinusoidally corrugated surfaces in three-dimensional space. These are sometimes called long-crested travelling waves and, for example, a single sine wave would be specified by, a function of a single spatial variable and time:

$$H(x,t) = A \sin(k(x + ct))$$

where A is the wave amplitude, k is the wave number given by $k = 2\pi/L$, L is the wavelength, c is the velocity given by $c = (g/k)^{1/2}$ and g is acceleration due to gravity.

The formula for the velocity is an approximation for small amplitude water waves and makes the assumption that the force due to gravity overrides that of surface tension. It is important to note that we are specifying the motion of waves propagating through water and not the motion of the water.

Extending this to two variables for a surface in three-dimensional space gives:

$$H(x,y,t) = A \sin (\mathbf{k}.(\mathbf{x} + \mathbf{c}t)$$

where $\mathbf{k}$ is the wave vector $(u,v,0)$, $\mathbf{c}$ is a velocity vector and both vectors lie in the direction of the propagating wave and $\mathbf{x}$ is the vector $(x,y,0)$.

Such a wave is shown in Figure 8.1(a). A static wave in three-dimensional space is a sinusoidal corrugation whose contours of constant height are the lines:

$$ux + vy = \text{constant}$$

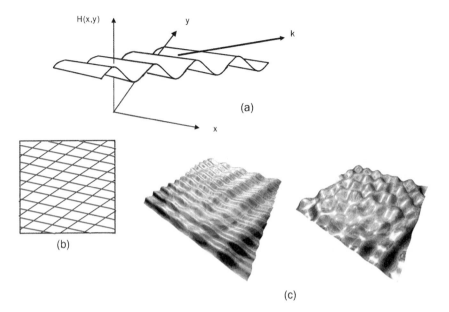

Figure 8.1. (a) A long crested travelling wave. (b) A visualisation of the interaction of two waves. (c) Surfaces rendered with a texture map.

and the equivalent statement in vector notation:

$$\mathbf{k} \cdot \mathbf{x} = \text{constant}$$

The peaks and troughs of the corrugations face a direction that makes an angle

$$\theta = \tan^{-1}(v/u)$$

with respect to the x axis, and the wavelength is

$$\sqrt{\frac{1}{u^2 + v^2}}$$

When implementing this type of travelling wave on hardware, it is common to represent it as a scrolling bump or normal map.

A reasonable surface can be modelled by combining waves moving in different direction. Figure 8.1(b) indicates how two such long crested waves might interact and Figure 8.1(c) shows a surface generated in this way and rendered with a texture map.

We can define radial waves in a similar manner. Each wave is radial with a centre C, amplitude A and wavelength w all specified by the user. We can define a radial travelling wave by

$$H(r,t) = A \sin(\mathbf{k}(|r| + \mathbf{c}t))$$

where $\mathbf{r} = \mathbf{x} - C$

This is useful in simulating the effect of raindrops hitting the surface of the water. Here we define a radial packet as a concentric wave train of length l travelling radially outwards from the centre at start time t_0, say.

We only deform those points r in the annular region $(r_a(t), r_b(t))$. That is:

$$H(r,t) = 0 \qquad \text{for } r < r_a, \text{ and } r > r_b$$

$$H(r,t) = A \sin(\mathbf{k}(|r| + \mathbf{c}t)) \quad \text{for } r \text{ within the annular region } (r_a, r_b)$$

where $r_a(t) = |r| - \mathbf{c}(t - t_0)$ and $r_b(t) = |r| - \mathbf{c}(t - t_0) + 1$.

Due to the obvious discontinuity over the boundary, this method works best when the amplitude of the wave is small.

The extension to this simple single wave model is to generate a wave that consists of the linear summation of a number of sine waves at different frequencies. This gives a better result and seems to approximate what happens in nature:

$$H(x,y,t) = \sum_i A_i \sin(\mathbf{k}_i(\mathbf{x} + \mathbf{c}_i t))$$

It would be a tedious task to individually assign wavelengths, amplitudes etc. to each separate wave, so upper and lower bounds are set for each parameter and a random number generator can be used to choose numbers from within these bounds. Best results are obtained by using a separate low and high frequency group. This is known as Fourier synthesis, and although we notate it as a linear summation, in practice we would generate $H(x,y,t)$ using an inverse FFT.

More sophisticated wave models exist, reflecting more accurately the physical process involved. In a paper entitled "Fourier Synthesis of Ocean Scenes", G. Mastin [MAST87] uses a model based on the work of W. Pierson and L. Moskowitz who use a wind-driven sea spectra, derived from observed data, to describe the motion of deep ocean waves in fully developed wind seas [PIER64]. Wave animation is invoked by manipulating the phase of the Fourier transforms.

Mastin *et al.* point out that ocean waves are not simple spectra but complex waveforms that are influenced by momentum transfer from the wind, and that energy is transferred between spectral components in a nonlinear fashion, making linear superposition models an approximation. In the model of Mastin *et al.*, seas are again constructed in the Fourier domain. They use a formula based on the Pierson and Moskowitz model.

This specifies a particular empirical shape in the Fourier domain for a spectrum which can then be used in a reverse FFT to generate an $H(x,y)$. The spectrum is generated by applying the following filter process to white noise:

$$F_1(f) = \frac{\alpha g^2}{(2\pi)^4 f^5}\left(-\frac{5}{4}\left(\frac{f_p}{f}\right)^4\right) \tag{8.1}$$

where f_p = peak frequency, α = Phillip's Constant (0.0081) and g = gravitational constant.

This equation is used to define a 2D spectrum as follows, and an overall view of this particular form of Fourier synthesis is shown in Figure 8.2. We start with a Fourier transform of white noise, then multiply this to provide a set of frequency components to input to a reverse transform to generate the surface. A packet of waves moving in the same direction is represented in a 2D Fourier transform as a set of frequency terms that will cluster around a diagonal,[2] as shown in Figure 8.2. (Note that since the frequency spectrum of white noise is everywhere uniform, the filter operation is simply defined by the filter itself.) A 2D filter specification to extend Equation 8.1 into a 2D spectrum uses a suggestion due to D. Hasselmann et al. [HASS80]:

$$F_2(f, \theta) = F_1(f)\ D(f, \theta) \tag{8.2}$$

where $D(f, \theta)$ is a directional spreading factor given by

$$D(f, \theta) = N_p^{-1}\ \cos^{2p}\left(\frac{\theta}{2}\right)$$

where

$$p = 9.77\left(\frac{f}{p}\right)^\mu$$

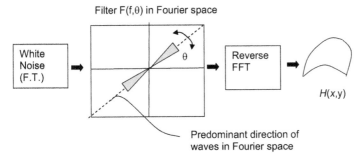

Filter F(f,θ) in Fourier space

White Noise (F.T.)

θ

Reverse FFT

$H(x,y)$

Predominant direction of waves in Fourier space

Figure 8.2. Fourier synthesis from a spectrum defined by Equation 8.2.

....

[2] Fourier theory is beyond the scope of this text, but there are a multiplicity of books on 2D Fourier transforms in the image processing literature.

$$\mu = \begin{cases} 4.06 & f < fp \\ -2.34 & f > fp \end{cases}$$

and N_p is a normalisation constant.

This gives a 2D frequency spectrum whose maximum (along the line $\theta = 0$) is aligned in the wind direction.

However, Fourier synthesis is only adequate for a very basic deep water shape. Our observation tells us that wave profiles are not in general single-valued stationary profiles, but multivalued continuously changing shapes. A sea exhibits a bewildering variety of shapes in a continuum whose extremes we describe as calm and angry. Two important factors that mathematical models cope with are

- propagation speed of the waves, which depends on the current water depth, and

- wave profiles.

The effect of wave speed changing with current depth is predicted by the Airy model [KINS65] and has been implemented in computer graphics by D. Peachey [PEAC86] and A. Fournier [FOUR86]. The consequence of the model is that waves slow down in shallow water. This produces a refractive effect causing the waves to align themselves with the shoreline.

As for wave profiles, a cross-section through a wave in the direction of propagation will not reveal a sine wave. Wind-driven waves have shapes that are a function of wind speed. As wind speed increases, the crests become more sharply peaked and the troughs shallower. This is predicted by the Gerstner/Rankine model [KINS65], which gives a trochoid as the ideal profile. The sine wave shape occurs only for small-amplitude waves under certain conditions. Fournier [FOUR86] also modelled shape change in the wave profile due to wind at the crest of the wave.

Trochoid is the name given to a family of cycloids as shown in Figure 8.3. A cycloid is the locus of a point fixed on a rolling circle and is defined as

$$x = a\theta - b\sin\theta$$

$$y = a\theta - b\cos\theta$$

As a increases, the profile approaches a sine wave, and as it decreases, it tends towards a circle. Note that the limiting point for a wave profile would be $a=b$. Beyond this we get a prolate cycloid.

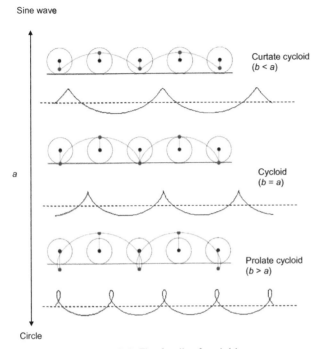

Figure 8.3. The family of cycloids.

The Gerstner wave profile has been implemented on a GPU by M. Finch [FINC04], who notates the height field generation as:

$$P(x,y,t) = \begin{pmatrix} x + \sum_i Q_i A_i \cos(k_i(X + c_i t)), \\ y + \sum_i Q_i A_i \cos(k_i(X + c_i t)), \\ \sum_i A_i \sin(k_i(X + c_i t)) \end{pmatrix}$$

where Q_i is the parameter that controls the sharpness of the peak (if $Q_i = 0$ we have a sine wave as before). Note that the only modification to the previous scheme is the lateral movement of the vertices.

Finch points out a consequential advantage of this profile for computer graphics: the sharper crests are formed by moving vertices towards each crest, automatically giving a better tessellation around the crest.

Waves and Particle Systems

Particle systems (a GPU implementation is introduced later in this chapter) were used by Peachey [PEAC86] and Fournier [FOUR86] to model spray and foam in the animation of wind waves. Peachey uses a sinusoidal profile as a basic model that presupposes that the underlying water motion (as opposed to the wave motion through the water) is a circular or elliptical motion. The average orbital speed of the water in such a model (Figure 8.4(a)) is given by

$$Q = \pi\frac{HC}{L} = \pi SC$$

where C is the wave speed, H is the diameter of the orbit, L is the wavelength and S $(=H/L)$ is the steepness of the wave.

Spray caused by breaking waves occurs when:

$$Q > C$$

$$\text{or } S > 1/\pi$$

(Peachey modifies Q to correct the coarse assumption of uniform circular motion, based on the observation that the maximum value of S does not exceed 0.1.) This model is used as the basis for a particle system for foam. Initial position of a particle is the crest of a wave, and its initial velocity is given by Q. Spray particles can then be assigned a trajectory and their initiation perturbed to prevent visual uniformity.

Peachey also employs a particle system to simulate the spray that results from waves crashing into an obstacle. Particles are generated from an obstacle at a rate

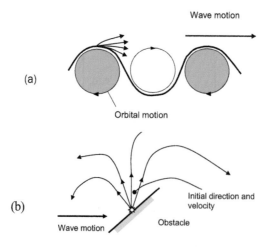

Figure 8.4. (a) Model used to initiate a particle system at the crest of a wave. (b) Initiating a particle system when a crest strikes an object.

that depends on the position of the crest of the wave with respect to the position of the point of impact (that is, maximum when the peak of the crest collides with the object, and zero at some point when the crest has passed the obstacle).

The initial velocities can be chosen from a distribution centred on the orbital speed Q and the initial direction taken by perturbing about the reflected direction for an ideal elastic collision (Figure 8.4(b)).

Rendering Water Waves on the GPU

The usual approach to rendering a perturbed water surface on the GPU is to consider low and high frequency height maps separately. The low frequency content is applied to the vertices, and the high frequency content is rendered into a texture or bump map. Typical of this approach is the implementation described by Finch, who categorises the waves as geometric (low frequency) and texture waves (high frequency). He limits geometric waves to 4 and texture waves to 16. Modulating effects can easily be incorporated in a GPU implementation as offsets to the height fields. An example application is a boat wake.

Reflection and Refraction

The most popular method for GPU implementation (see, for example, [VLAC04]) is to use a surface perturbation model, along with reflection and refraction texture maps. Originally reflection and refraction maps were view-dependent texture maps, meaning that the (u,v) texture access in the fragment program is a function of the view direction vector [WATT92]. The scene was rendered by ray tracing reflected and refracted vectors into the maps.

For example, to render the images in Figure 8.5, we considered the refraction map to be a plane at the bottom of a volume of water. In this case, the map is just a set of colour bars to show the effect of the mapping. The surface is perturbed in one image using longitudinal waves, and in the other with radial waves. View rays are refracted at the surface and index into the refraction map. The surface images show the colour bars breaking up in a convincing manner.

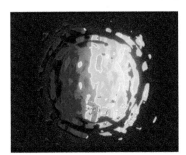  

Figure 8.5. Refraction mapping

In 1987, the progenitor of the current GPU simulations was introduced by P. T'So and B. Barsky [TSO87]. Called the Fresnel Texture Mapping Algorithm, it used an authored reflection map and a refraction map. They cast a view ray per polygon and used Snell's law to calculate the refracted angle. Substituting the incidence and refracted angle into the Fresnel equation

$$R = \frac{\sin^2(\theta_i - \theta_r)}{2\sin^2(\theta_i + \theta_r)} + \frac{\tan^2(\theta_i - \theta_r)}{2\tan^2(\theta_i + \theta_r)}$$

returns the percentage of light reflected from the surface. This value is used to weight the reflection and refraction maps which are then combined.

T'So and Barsky suggest using an approximate form of the Fresnel equation, which is

$$R = \begin{cases} 0.02 & \theta_i < \frac{\pi}{4} \\ \frac{392}{25\pi^2}\left(\theta_i - \frac{\pi}{4}\right)^2 + 0.02 & \theta_i < \frac{\pi}{4} \end{cases}$$

In the GPU implementation of A. Vlachos *et al.*, a refraction map is constructed by rendering all underwater geometry from the camera viewpoint, and the above-water geometry is rendered from the reflected camera viewpoint to construct a reflection map. To render a scene, the reflection and refraction maps are sampled and combined. The refraction texels can be modulated with a water colour, and the reflection texels need weighting with the Fresnel reflectivity term. Vlachos points out that texture interpolation must be linear in screen space since contents of texture maps are already a perspective projection and the projection matrix has to be altered to this effect.

Reflection and Refraction Caustics

The application in this section is an example of using the laws of reflection and refraction to generate an animation. A caustic is the name given to a certain interaction between light and a reflecting or refracting surface. Its most common manifestation is the beautiful animated patterns to be observed on the sides and bottom of a swimming pool. These are produced in bright sunlight when the surface of the water is perturbed—by wind, for example. Light rays from the sun refract at the surface and travel on towards the pool sides and bottom in a manner that causes them to converge or diverge. The result of this is an enhancement

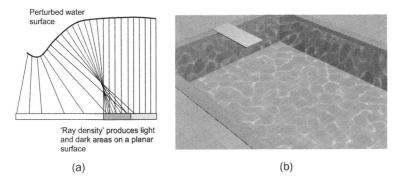

(a)

(b)

Figure 8.6. (a) Light rays striking the surface converge and diverge. (b) Animated caustic patterns appear on the pool sides and bottom.

or diminution of the light reflected from the planar pool surfaces. The resulting patterns twist and move in a sinuous manner due to the continual perturbation of the surface. Such caustics are termed refraction caustics. Their vaguely elliptical shape is a consequence of the wave patterns formed at the surface which have an underlying harmonic basis.

A reflection caustic is produced by light reflecting from the primary surface and travelling towards a secondary surface. Figure 8.7(a) shows the reflected caustic from a spherical mirror. A planar surface intersecting the caustic near the cusp will display an image of the caustic.

The rays, after being reflected or refracted, intersect the closest receiving surface. The vertices are effectively projected onto the receiving surface, as is evident in Figure 8.7(c). This image was rendered using a simple vertex program (Listing 8.1) which casts a ray from the light source through each vertex of the refracting or reflecting surface.

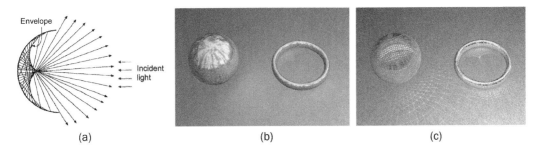

(a) (b) (c)

Figure 8.7. (a) A reflection caustic produced by a spherical mirror. (b) The cusp of the caustic is visible on the flat surface underneath the ring. (c) Showing the projection and concentration of the ring vertices to form a cusp on the flat surface.

Figure 8.7(c) is the same as Figure 8.7(b) except that the vertices are superimposed and connected, using their original connectivity, to make things clearer. The vertices are not moved to the surface solely for visualization of the method, however, but to provide a colour value which is then interpolated for the final rendered image.

First, let us examine the behaviour of a light ray at a surface that is both reflecting and refracting (water, for example). We can easily calculate the reflected vector **R** and the refracted or transmitted vector **T** using the following equations whose parameters are defined in Figure 8.8:

$$\mathbf{R} = (2\mathbf{N} \cdot \mathbf{L})\mathbf{N} - \mathbf{L}$$

$$\mathbf{T} = \left(\frac{\eta_i}{\eta_r}\cos\theta_i - \cos\theta_i \right)\mathbf{N} - \frac{\eta_i}{\eta_r}\mathbf{L}$$

This assumes that the vectors $\mathbf{N}, \mathbf{L}, \mathbf{R}$ and $\mathbf{T}$ are co-planar. For an air-water interface we define:

$$\eta_i = 1 \text{ (air)} \qquad \eta_r = 1.3 \text{ (water)}$$

We now need to assign a colour value to each vertex. Refraction and reflection are treated separately. A 'fake' for refraction caustics is constructed as follows. We observe that, in the case of a local maximum, light rays will tend to converge for overhead light (vertical **L**). For a minimum, light rays will tend to diverge (Figure 8.9).

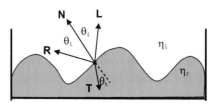

Figure 8.8. Refraction at an air-water interface.

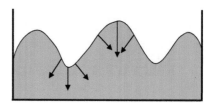

Figure 8.9. Surface normals and thus the refracted rays diverge at minima and converge at maxima.

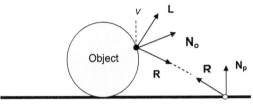

Planar receiving surface

Figure 8.10. Reflection caustics on a planar surface.

This behaviour can be crudely approximated by a simple formula:

$$\frac{(v_z - w_z)^2}{w_h}$$

where v_z is the height of the vertex, w_z is the minimum value of v_z, $w_h = \max (v_z)$ and $\min(v_z)$ is the peak to peak amplitude of the excursion.

For reflection caustics we assume for simplicity that the receiving surface is a plane (Figure 8.10) and the vertex colour is calculated as:

$$(\mathbf{R} \cdot \mathbf{N_p})(\mathbf{L} \cdot \mathbf{N_o})^4$$

Thus, the diffuse reflection at the intersection point on the object is 'transferred' to the receiving surface and weighted by the cosine of the angle between the plane orientation and the reflection vector.

The algorithm for both refraction (five planes in the case of the swimming pool) and reflection (one plane case) is as follows:

for each vertex

      1. calculate **T** (**R**),
      2. ray intersect **T** (**R**) with 1 or 5 planes for closest intersection,
      3. move the vertex to intersect point and
      4. calculate vertex colour.

Code for the reflection caustic shader is given in Listing 8.1

Listing 8.1

Reflection caustic shader (planar surface).

```
// For each vertex, compute the light direction, compute
// the light reflection direction using the vertex normal
// and ray intersect the ground plane for a collision.
// This will project the reflection caustics into the ground.

struct appdata
{
```

```
    float4 pos : POSITION;
    float3 normal : NORMAL;
    float3 color : DIFFUSE;
};

struct vfconn
{
    float4 hpos : POSITION;
    float4 col0 : COLOR0;
};

float plane_ray_intersect(
float4 plane,float3 pos,float3 dir)
{
        float dist = (plane.w - dot(plane.xyz,pos))/
dot(plane.xyz,dir);
        return dist<0?0:dist;
}

vfconn main( appdata IN,
uniform float4x4 modelviewproj,
uniform float3 lightpos,
uniform float3 camerapos,
uniform float4 planes[1],
uniform float4 wave)
{
vfconn OUT;

        float3 lightdir;
        lightdir = normalize(IN.pos.xyz - lightpos);

        float4 pos;
        if (dot(lightdir,IN.normal) > 0)
        {
           pos = IN.pos;
           OUT.hpos = mul(modelviewproj, pos);
           OUT.col0 = float4(0,0,0,1);
        }
        else
        {
           float3 dir = normalize(reflect(lightdir,IN.normal));

           float dist;
           dist = plane_ray_intersect(planes[0],IN.pos.xyz,dir);

           if (dist>1000)
           {
               dist=1000;
               pos.xyz = IN.pos.xyz + dir*dist;
```

```
            pos.z = planes[0].w;
        }
        else
            pos.xyz = IN.pos.xyz + dir*dist;

        pos.w = 1.0;

        if (pos.z > 2)
        {
            pos.z = planes[0].w;
            dist=0;

            OUT.hpos = mul(modelviewproj, pos);
            OUT.col0 = float4(0,0,0,1);
        }
        else
        {
            dist  = dot(planes[0].xyz,dir) *
                     dot(lightdir,IN.normal);
            dist  = dist<0 ? 0 : dist;
            dist *= dist*dist;

            OUT.hpos = mul(modelviewproj, pos);
            OUT.col0.xyz = IN.color.xyz *
                           float3(dist,dist,dist);
            OUT.col0.w = 1;
        }
    }
    return OUT;
}
```

The pool (refraction caustic) shader is Listing 8.2. The water surface is perturbed in the CPU on a per-frame basis (using *Perlin* noise [EBER98]) and this produces the required animation.

Listing 8.2

Refraction caustics on five planes (swimming pool).

```
// For each vertex, compute the light direction,
// compute the light refraction direction using
// the vertex normal and ray intersect the five
// pool planes for the closest collision.
// This will project the water surface into
// the pool walls. The caustic vertex color is
// approximated by the z coord of the water
// vertex within the wave amplitude.

struct appdata
{
```

```
        float4 pos : POSITION;
        float3 normal : NORMAL;
        float3 color : DIFFUSE;
};

struct vfconn
{
        float4 hpos : POSITION;
        float4 col0 : COLOR0;
};

float plane_ray_intersect(
float4 plane, float3 pos, float3 dir)
{
        float dist = (plane.w - dot(plane.xyz,pos))/
                        dot(plane.xyz,dir);
        return dist<0?10000:dist;
}

vfconn main( appdata IN,
                uniform float4x4 modelviewproj,
                uniform float3   lightpos,
                uniform float3   camerapos,
                uniform float4   planes[5],
                uniform float4   wave)
{
   vfconn OUT;

   float3 pos = IN.pos.xyz;
   float3 lightdir = normalize(pos - lightpos);
   float3 dir = refract(lightdir,IN.normal,1.33);

   float dist,d;
   dist = plane_ray_intersect(planes[0], pos, dir);

   d = plane_ray_intersect(planes[1], pos, dir);
   dist = d<dist ? d : dist;

   d = plane_ray_intersect(planes[2], pos, dir);
   dist = d<dist ? d : dist;

   d = plane_ray_intersect(planes[3], pos, dir);
   dist = d<dist ? d : dist;

   d = plane_ray_intersect(planes[4], pos, dir);
```

```
dist = d<dist ? d : dist;

float4 p;
p.xyz = pos + dir*dist;
p.w = 1.0;

OUT.hpos = mul(modelviewproj, p);

dist = (IN.pos.z - wave.x) * wave.y;
dist *= dist*dist;

OUT.col0.xyz = IN.color*dist;
OUT.col0.w = 1.0;

return OUT;
}
```

Particle Systems

A particle system is perhaps the most flexible common games object, and by parameter manipulation it can simulate a wide variety of effects. It is a classic technique that was invented almost two decades ago. The basic idea is that certain phenomena can be simulated by scripting the movement of and rendering a large population of individual particles. In the past, a particle was usually a primitive whose geometrical extent is small or zero—that is many particles can project into a single pixel extent—but which possesses certain fixed attributes such as colour. Now graphics hardware is powerful enough to have particle systems made up of mesh objects where the particle can be the reference point of the object. Each particle is scripted and the idea is that rendering a population of particles, from frame to frame produces a sort of cloud object that can grow, shrink, move, change shape etc. An animation may involve literally tens or hundreds of thousands of particles and supplying an individual script for each one is out of the question. Rather, a general script is provided for each particle with in-built random behaviour which produces the requisite differences for each particle as the position, say, of the particle evolves over time. Different phenomena are modelled by using particle general scripts and varying the attribute of the particle such as colour. For example, in simulating a firework, the basic particle script may be a parabola. Parameters that would be varied for each particle may include the start point of the parabola, its shape parameters, the colour of the particle as a function of its position along its parabolic path and its lifetime (extinction) along the path.

Thus, the dynamic behaviour of the particles and their appearance, as a function of time, can be merged into the same script. Stochastic processes can be used to control both these aspects of particle behaviour. The pioneer in this field is W. Reeves, who published a paper in 1983 [REEV83] that used particle sets to model 'fuzzy' objects such as fire and clouds.

Reeves describes the generation of a frame in an animation sequence as a process of five steps:

1. New particles are generated and injected into the current system.

2. Each new particle is assigned its individual attributes.

3. Any particles that have exceeded their lifetime are extinguished.

4. The current particles are moved according to their scripts.

5. The current particles are rendered.

The instantaneous population of a particle cloud is controlled or scripted by an application dependent stochastic process. For example, the number of particles generated at a particular time t can be derived from

$$N(t) = M(t) + \text{rand}(r)V(t)$$

where $M(t)$ is the mean number of particles perturbed by a random variable of variance V. The time dependency of this equation can be used to control the overall growth (or contraction) in cloud size. Reeves used a linear time dependency with constant variance in the examples given, but he points out that the control can incorporate quadratic, cubic or even stochastic variations. The number of particles can also be related to the screen size of the object—a mechanism that allows the amount of computation undertaken to relate to the final size of the object.

Although this mechanism will clearly contribute something to shape evolution of the particle mass, this is also determined by individual particle scripts. The combination of these two scripting mechanisms was used to animate phenomena such as the expanding wall of fire used in the motion picture *Star Trek II: The Wrath of Khan* and has been used to simulate multicoloured fireworks. Individual particle scripting is based on the following attributes:

- initial position,
- initial velocity and direction,

- initial size,
- initial transparency,
- shape and
- lifetime.

Velocity and lifetime scripts can be based on dynamic constraints. An explosion, for example, may cause a particle to be ejected upwards and then pulled down under the influence of gravity. Associated with both the attribute script and the population script is a generation shape—a geometric region about the origin of the particle cloud into which 'newly born' particles are placed.

Although the applications Reeves described are generally growing phenomena, where the population of the particle cloud tends to increase, the method is general enough to model phenomena where, say, the population remains constant, while the shape of the cloud perturbs or where the population decreases or implodes.

As we have already pointed out, the final object appearance is determined from the net effect of individually rendering all the particles. Rendering is carried out by simply treating each particle as a single light source and using the final value of the appearance parameters.

In a later paper, W. Reeves and R. Blau [REEV85] further develop particle systems. Moving away from using particles to model amorphous and continually changing shapes, they use them as volume filling primitives to generate solid shapes whose forms then remains generally constant, but which have the ability to change shape in such situations as blades of grass moving in the wind. These techniques were used in the film *The Adventures of Andre and Wally B.* to generate the three-dimensional background images of a forest and grass.

The primary significance of particle systems in this context is not their ability to model shape-changing objects, but rather the property of "database amplification"— the ability of a simple database to describe the general characteristics of an object that can then be modelled to the required level of detail. Objects are modelled with a resulting complexity that is far higher than that obtainable by conventional techniques. For example, Reeves states that, in a forest scene, typically well over a million particles will be generated from basic tree descriptions.

A common extension of particle animation alluded to above is to associate geometric entities with a particle using particle animation to control the movement of such primitives. The best example of this is an explosion, where the fragments of the explosion move under a particle script.

Two ways of implementing populations are shown in Figure 8.11(a). The first uses a linear array where each element is a particle class. The process can

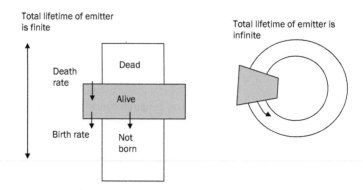

Figure 8.11. Two ways of implementing a particle population: (a) linear array and (b) circular list.

be viewed as a window that moves downwards through the particle array. The length of the array represents the lifetime of the population. The particles inside the window make up the current population. (Note that the birth rate and death rate need not be equal or constant.) A better structure is shown in Figure 8.11(b). This circular structure (see Chapter 11 for implementation details) has an infinite lifetime required in applications where a very long particle display is needed— say, for example, a missile trail.

Depending on the number of particles in a population, we may or may not render them individually. If the particles are a mesh, then by definition they must be rendered individually. The other alternative is to consider a group of particles as a single object and process only the emitter (for visibility and collision detection). This clearly has the disadvantage that if the emitter becomes invisible, then all the particles become invisible. It is easy to imagine applications where we will require partial visibility of a particle set. Examples of a particle system being used in a games object are shown in Chapter 11.

Particle Systems and GPUs

The previous section detailed the implementation of a 'traditional particle system'. In this section we will look at how we can extend the utility of particle systems by using GPU hardware. One of the distinctions between older CPU implementations and newer GPU ones is that the older systems tended to implement stateless particles. A stateless particle is one that does not store its current state, and its behaviour evolves from emission to death under control of a closed form function.

Such particle systems are used, for example, to simulate fire or the result of a weapon impact.

A state-preserving particle, on the other hand, allows new positions, velocities etc. to be calculated from previous ones and opens up the possibility of particles interacting with a (changing) scene through, for example, collision detection and response. (Appendix 8.1 details classical theory for particles and collision detection.)

To implement any type of iterative process on the GPU, we need to re-use or access data output by the fragment program as input, and we require floating point precision. This is done via texture maps using render to texture. Conceptually the texture is seen as an array but the texture coordinates are 2D because 2D texture mapping is the function for which the hardware is designed. The texture pixels can be made of regular 32-bit float values or 16-bit half-float values, resulting in 128 bits/pixel float RGBA texture maps or 64 bits/pixel half-float RGBA texture maps.

In many particle system applications we would want to store the varying particle information—position and velocity—in floating point texture consisting of the (x,y,z) components of these attributes. We also require the static information associated with each particle, such as birth time and particle life. The variable texture maps also need to be double-buffered because we cannot read from, and write to, the same texture map at the same time. Thus, any attributes involved in an iterative process need double buffering whereas static attributes have their current state update using a function of stored attribute values.

The generic pseudocode for a GPU particle system would be:

1. Update velocities.

2. Update positions.

3. Texture to vertex buffer.

4. Render particles.

The fragment program executes for each pixel of the render target, taking input from one of the double-buffered texture maps and outputting to the other. This approach thus enables us to keep the particle system on the GPU and avoid increasing memory bandwidth limitations, which would grow as a function of population size.

Normally, we can only output a single colour buffer from the fragment program, and we will need two different programs: one that outputs the new particle velocity using as input previous particle position and velocity texture maps; and another one for outputting the new particle position using as input the previous position and current (just calculated) new particle velocity. These are given as Listing 8.3.

```
// GPU particle system fragment programs
// computes new particle position and velocity

struct f_vert2frag
{
        float4 hpos : POSITION;
        float4 color : COLOR0;
        float2 texcoord : TEXCOORD0;
};
struct f_frag2screen
{
        float4 color : COLOR;
};

f_frag2screen main_particle_system_pos(
        f_vert2frag IN,
        uniform sampler2D ps_pos:TEXUNIT0,
        uniform sampler2D ps_vel:TEXUNIT1,
        uniform float elapsed_time) // elapsed time in sec
{
        f_frag2screen OUT;

        // get position and velocity
        float4 pos = tex2D(ps_pos,IN.texcoord);
        float4 vel = tex2D(ps_vel,IN.texcoord);

        // compute new position adding vel*elapsed_time
        float4 newpos = pos;
        newpos.xyz += vel.xyz*elapsed_time;

        // decrease particle life
        newpos.w -= elapsed_time;

        // output result (newpos,current_life)
        OUT.color = newpos;

        return OUT;
}

f_frag2screen main_particle_system_vel(
        f_vert2frag IN,
        uniform sampler2D ps_pos:TEXUNIT0,
        uniform sampler2D ps_vel:TEXUNIT1,
        // velocity damping factor (0 for no damping)
        uniform float veldamp,
        // rotation factor (0 for no rot, 1 for rot only)
        uniform float rotfact,
        // elapsed time in sec
        uniform float elapsed_time)
{
```

```
    f_frag2screen OUT;

    // get position and velocity
    float4 pos = tex2D(ps_pos,IN.texcoord);
    float4 vel = tex2D(ps_vel,IN.texcoord);

    // compute vel length and apply damping
    float len = length(vel.xyz);
    len = max(0, len - veldamp*elapsed_time);

    // compute rotation direction
    float3 v = normalize(vel.xyz);
    float3 d = normalize(float3(pos.xy,0));
    float3 s = cross(float3(0,0,1),d);

    // lerp from original vel to rotation vel
    float3 newvel = lerp(v,s,rotfact)*len;

    // output result (newvel,total_life)
    OUT.color = float4(newvel, vel.w);

    return OUT;
}
```

After processing all particles, we use the newly generated pixel buffers as vertex buffers and map the position texture map to the position vertex array and the velocity texture map to the TEXCOORD0 vertex array. Then we draw point sprites at each vertex position using a vertex program that computes colour, pixel size and fade-out intensity for each particle (no fragment program is necessary at this stage). The vertex program for this stage is Listing 8.4. Note that this is a two-pass approach.

Listing 8.4

Vertex program for particle system.

```
// GPU particle system vertex program
// computes particle color, fade and point size

// vertex program input/output structures
struct v_app2vert
{
        float4 pos   : POSITION;
        float4 color : COLOR0;
        float4 vel   : TEXCOORD0;
};
struct v_vert2frag
{
        float4 hpos  : POSITION;
        float4 color : COLOR0;
        float  psize : PSIZE;
};
```

```
v_vert2frag main_particle_system_vert(
       v_app2vert IN,
       uniform float4x4 modelview,
       uniform float4x4 modelviewproj,
       // fade out time in sec
       uniform float fade,
       // point size (const_att,lin_att,quad_att,psize)
       uniform float4 psize,
       // initial and final colours
       // (lerp thought particle life)
       uniform float4 color0,
       uniform float4 color1)
{
       v_vert2frag OUT;

       // vertex position
       float4 pos=float4(IN.pos.xyz,1.0);

       // vertex position in eye coords
       float4 pos_eye = mul(modelview,pos);
       // distance to eye
       float d = length(pos_eye.xyz);
       // time left for this paticle
       float t = IN.pos.w;

       // lerp color from initial and
       //final colors using time left
       OUT.color = lerp(color1,color0,t/IN.vel.w);

       // compute point size using eye
       // distance and attenuation factors
       OUT.psize = psize.w*sqrt(1.0/
                   (psize.x+d*psize.y+d*d*psize.z));

       // compute output vertex position
       OUT.hpos = mul(modelviewproj,pos);

       // if time left less than fade time
       // attenuate output color
       if (t<fade)
              OUT.color.w *= t/fade;

       // if particle's life expired kill vertex
       if (t<0)
              OUT.hpos.w = -1;
       return OUT;
}
```

(a)

(b)

(c)

(d)

Figure 8.12. (a) Two particle system objects built using: 64 x 64 and 256 x 256 RGBA texture maps. (b) The toroidal particle system in context.

Figure 8.12 (a) shows a particle system implemented using 64 x 64 and 256 x 256 RGBA texture maps (4096 and 65536 particles, respectively). In the illustration each particle is moving with a different velocity in the general direction shown (see Chapter 11 for more details on the parameter values used for this demonstration). In Figure 8.12(b) the particle system is shown in a games context.

Using Multiple Render Targets

New GPU systems allow the fragment program to output to multiple colour buffers at the same time (called MRT or multiple render targets). This can optimise our GPU particle system and make the previous two-pass approach for calculating new position and velocity run in single pass, as we can, for example, output to two buffers from the same fragment program. This enhancement is incorporated in Listing 8.5.

```
// GPU particle system fragment program MRT
// computes new particle position and velocity in same pass

// fragment program output structures with two colours
struct f_frag2screenMRT
{
        float4 color0 : COLOR0;
        float4 color1 : COLOR1;
};
```

```
f_frag2screenMRT main_particle_system_vel(
        f_vert2frag IN,
        uniform sampler2D ps_pos:TEXUNIT0,
        uniform sampler2D ps_vel:TEXUNIT1,
        // velocity damping factor (0 for no damping)
        uniform float veldamp,
        // rotation factor (0 for no rot, 1 for rot only)
        uniform float rotfact,
        // elapsed time in sec
        uniform float elapsed_time)
{
        f_frag2screenMRT OUT;

        // get position and velocity
        float4 pos = tex2D(ps_pos,IN.texcoord);
        float4 vel = tex2D(ps_vel,IN.texcoord);

        // compute new position adding vel*elapsed_time
        float4 newpos = pos;
        newpos.xyz += vel.xyz*elapsed_time;

        // decreese particle life
        newpos.w -= elapsed_time;

        // output pos result (newpos,current_life)
        OUT.color0 = newpos;

        // compute vel length and apply damping
        float len = length(vel.xyz);
        len = max(0, len - veldamp*elapsed_time);

        // compute rotation direction
        float3 v = normalize(vel.xyz);
        float3 d = normalize(float3(pos.xy,0));
        float3 s = cross(float3(0,0,1),d);
```

```
// lerp from original vel to rotation vel
float3 newvel = lerp(v,s,rotfact)*len;

// output vel result (newvel,total_life)
OUT.color1 = float4(newvel,vel.w);
return OUT;
}
```

Particle Collisions

As we stated, implementing state preserving particles means that we can calculate interactions between the particle systems and the scene. Both L. Latta [LATT04] and P. Kipfer *et al.* [KIPF04] implement collision detection and response.

Latta considers collisions between particles and a terrain represented by a height field also stored in a texture map, $H(x,y)$ say. If the particle is detected as colliding with $H(x,y)$ then the collision response is calculated using the common game approximation described in Appendix 8.2. The surface normal can be calculated from the height field as we detail in Chapter 3.

Simple constraints can be used to move the particle to a valid position outside the collider when it is detected to be inside of it. The functions given as Listing 8.6 can be used in the fragment program when calculating the new position to collide to a plane, sphere or height-map.

.... Listing 8.6

Post collision constraints.

```
// constrain particle to be outside volume of a sphere
void SphereConstraint(
    inout float3 x, float3 center, float r)
{
    float3 delta = x - center;
    float dist = length(delta);
    if (dist < r)
        x = center + delta*(r / dist);
}

// constrain particle to be above floor
void FloorConstraint(inout float3 x, float level)
{
    if (x.y < level)
        x.y = level;
}

// constrain particle to heightfield stored in texture
void TerrainConstraint(inout float3 pos,
    uniform sampler2D terrain_tex,
    float3 scale, float3 offset)
```

```
{
    float2 uv = (pos.xy - offset.xy) / scale.xy;
    float h = offset.z + scale.z * tex2D(terrain_tex, uv).z;
    if (pos.z < h)
        pos.z = h;
}
```

The familiar problem of a particle penetrating an object due to its proximity to the surface in the previous time step is resolved by calculating the collision detection twice, using both the previous position and the current position. This allows a distinction between particles that are about to collide and particles that have already penetrated.

Particle Initiation and One Million Particles

The above shaders will handle up to one million particles at 80 fps, an astonishing number given that each particle is an independent entity, albeit subject to the same processing. It is a good demonstration of the power of the GPU.

However, as we increase the number of particles, the initialisation phase (the initial position and velocity of each particle) takes longer and longer. This is important when a particle system has to be initiated as part of another animation, say, for example, when an explosion is required from a collision, or the situation shown in Figure 8.4(b) where a wave strikes an obstacle and spray is required.

Each particle consumes a calculation involving several random values, and for one million particles, this extends to a CPU time of about five seconds. The initialisation phase could, however, be implemented in a fragment program by using a predefined texture map with each texel storing a random value. This will take the same time as one particle system step.

Distance Sorting

An optional addition to a GPU particle system is to distance-sort the particles. Latta uses this for alpha blending, and Kipfer *et al.* [KIPF04] use sorting in an ingenious algorithm that implements interparticle collision detection.

Most sorting algorithms have a structure that renders them unsuitable for implementation on the GPU; however, an algorithm developed by K. Batcher [BATC68] is suitable for GPU implementation because of its inherent parallelism. This algorithm has recently been implemented on hardware by I. Buck [BUCK04} and Latta [LATT04]. The algorithm also exhibits a constant number of iterations, as a function of the data size.

Following the terminology in [BUCK04], we describe the algorithm as a bitonic merge sort which repeatedly merges sorted sequences resulting in a bitonic

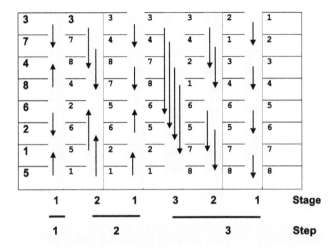

Figure 8.13. A simple example of a bitonic merge sort—the column on the left is sorted in six steps. *Based on an illustration in [BUCK04].*

sequence. A bitonic sequence is one that increases then decreases or *vice versa*.

Figure 8.13 shows a simple example. The column on the left is sorted in six steps of up to three stages. The head and tail of each arrow indicates the cells to be compared, and the direction of the arrow corresponds to the direction of the swap.

The sorting is performed in a fragment shader with the intermediate results from one step stored in a texture which is read in the next step. Each step comprises a pass in the fragment program. The sort requires $(\log n(\log n + 1)/2$ steps or passes where n is the number of elements in the sort. This implies, for 10^6 particles, a texture map of dimension 1024 x 1024 and 210 passes per frame. This is too expensive and Latta suggests spreading the sort over say 50 frames which reduces the sort workload to four per frame. The efficacy of this elaboration depends on the frame-to-frame coherence, which in turn is a function of the velocity of the particles and viewer.

Appendix 8.1: Basic Classical Theory for Particles

The basic familiar law of motion—Newton's Second Law—is:

$$\mathbf{F} = m\,\mathbf{a}$$

and this is easiest to consider in the context of a particle or a point mass. $\mathbf{F}$ is a 3D vector as is $\mathbf{a}$ the acceleration that the point undergoes. A point mass is an abstraction that can be used to model simple behaviour—we can assume that a rigid body that has extent behaves like a particle, because we consider its mass concentrated at a single point—the centre of mass. A point mass can only undergo translation under the application of a force.

Newton's Second Law can also be written as:

$$\mathbf{F} = m\frac{d\mathbf{v}}{dt} = m\frac{d^2\mathbf{x}}{dt^2}$$

where $\mathbf{v}$ is the velocity and x the position of the particle. This leads to a method that finds, by integration, the position of the particle at time $t + dt$ given its position at time t as:

$$\mathbf{v}(t + dt) = \mathbf{v}(t) + \frac{\mathbf{F}}{m}dt$$

$$\mathbf{x}(t + dt) = \mathbf{x}(t) + \mathbf{v}(t)dt + \frac{1}{2}\frac{\mathbf{F}}{m}dt^2$$

$$= \mathbf{x}(t) + \frac{1}{2}\mathbf{v}(t) + \mathbf{v}(t + dt)dt^2$$

In practice we would have three equations—one for each dimension:

$$x(t+dt) = x(t) + \frac{1}{2}v_x(t) + v_x(t + dt)dt^2$$

$$y(t+dt) = y(t) + \frac{1}{2}v_y(t) + v_y(t + dt)dt^2$$

$$z(t+dt) = z(t) + \frac{1}{2}v_z(t) + v_z(t + dt)dt^2$$

This method is called Euler's method, and it is generally too inaccurate for serious applications, but it is widely used in games. Its inaccuracy is a function of the step length dt.

For a given $\mathbf{v}(0)$ and a constant $\mathbf{F}$ the above will always produce the same particle motion and in most applications of interest, $\mathbf{F}$ is a function of time. Also, we may have more than one force acting on the body, and in that case we simply calculate the net force using vector addition. If the mass of the body changes as it travels—the case of a vehicle burning fuel, for example, then the second law is expressed as:

$$\mathbf{F} = \frac{d(m \cdot \mathbf{v})}{dt}$$

As a simple example, consider a cannonball being fired from the mouth of a cannon (or any ball/projectile problem). This could be modelled using the above equations. The cannonball is acted on by two forces—the constant acceleration due to gravity and an air resistance force that acts opposite to the velocity and is a function (quadratic) of the velocity and the square of the cross-sectional area. A simulation would be provided with the initial (muzzle) velocity and the inclination of the barrel and Newton's Second Law used to compute the arc of the missile. What we have achieved here is a simulation where at each time step the program computes continuous behaviour as a function of time.

Appendix 8.2. Particle Collision Detection

Collision detection and response (although a fairly complex operation for an arbitrary polygonal object, particularly the response) are straightforward for a particle. Consider the collision of a particle with a static object such as a wall (Figure A8.2.1). The particle is initially positioned at p_0 with velocity v_0 and is moving to position p_1:

$$p_1 = p_0 + v_0 \, dt$$

If we assume that p_1 is coincident with the surface then an easy solution is to compute the new velocity at point as follows:

$$v_r = f(v_0, N, \text{bump\_factor}, \text{friction\_factor}) \qquad (A8.2.1)$$

where N is the surface normal at the point of intersection.

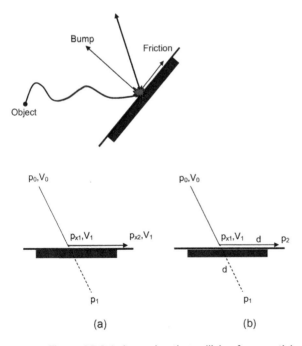

Figure A8.2.1. Approximating collision for a particle.

The response behaviour as a function of *bump_factor* and *friction_factor* is a much loved hack detailed in Table 8.1

Bump	Friction	Effect
0	1	Object moves along the collision plane. The objects component normal to the collision plane has been destroyed. There is no resistance to the component parallel to the plane.
1	0	Object moves along the collision normal. The object's velocity component parallel to the collision plane is destroyed by infinite friction.
Non-zero	Non-zero	Objects move along a direction between the collision normal and the colliding surface plane. The angle depends on the relative values of the two factors.
0	0	Object 'sticks' to the surface.

The problem with this simple solution is demonstrated in Figure A8.22(a). Consider point p_x a small distance from the intersection point. The time at which we position the particle at p_x is the time it would have taken to travel to position p_1 had the collision not occurred. If we use this, we have effectively 'lost' time. At this time the particle must have already collided, responded and moved some distance out of the collision point p_x.

To solve this inadequacy, we need to enter a loop at every collision point. Consider the sequence shown in Figure A8.2.2(b). After we find the first collision at point p_x we compute a new velocity at point p_x based on Equation A8.2.1. Say for simplicity the bump factor is 0 and friction factor is 1. The new velocity will be parallel to the plane. We calculate distance d and use this to move the particle to position p_2. We now do exactly the same collision detection and response from p_x to p_2. Thus, we must loop until no further collisions are found from one point to the other before returning the final point and velocity. This approach means that no time is lost and the particle will exhibit correct sliding motion (to within the limitations of the simple physics of the simulation model). Pseudocode for this process is:

```
compute_collision(p0,v0,p1,v1)
{
    p=p0
    repeat
    {
        dir = p1-p
```

```
            if (dir length is 0) break
            normalize dir
            if (no collision from p to p1) break

            p0 = intersectpoint

            compute_reflection(dir,normal,bump_factor,friction_
factor,refdir);

            v1 = refdir*v1
            normalize refdir
            p1 = refdir*length(p1-p0)
        }
    }
```

Chapter Nine

Character Animation— Using MoCap and Skinning

Introduction

Character animation is perhaps the last frontier in computer graphics. To imitate human behaviour has long been a goal in many applications, particularly in computer games. Currently, we tend to regard body animation as a solved problem, and this is certainly true as far as motion and rendering is concerned, but many problems remain. In particular if AI in games is going to develop and increase the 'play complexity', we need event driven animation where game logic, events, etc. can call for animation to be created in real time as required. This is particularly so in visual speech, which by definition is event driven and which we examine in Chapter 10.

Skeleton Animation

We begin by looking at how to animate human-like bodies. This is almost always based on a simplified human skeleton—a stick figure. The bones in the stick figure receive animation control, and a skin or mesh, representing the outer garments of a clothed character, are attached to the bones and rendered. The issue of separation of the mesh and the animation, which skeleton animation facilitates, is of crucial importance in almost all contexts in which figure animation is used.

Consider first the skeleton structure. There are several options possible. The simplest way to store the structure is; for each node, set up a matrix representing the rotation and translation from the origin. Note that this method does not explicitly link the nodes together, nor does it reflect the fact that the skeleton is a hierarchy. If each bone is specified by a position and orientation, then there need to be constraints that keep the bones joined together. All of these constraints need to be applied when any motion is applied.

Now consider the conventional tree structure which does set up an explicit hierarchy. Each child node possesses a single matrix which represents its rotation and translation (or offset) from its parent node. Global positioning and orientation is applied to the root node (usually the hip), and all other motion is specified relative to the root node.

An example skeleton is shown in Figure 9.1 in its base position and for the first key in an animation sequence. The labelling and structure of this skeleton are designed for the BVH MoCap file format. Such data structures are unique to a particular MoCap format, but all are based on a hierarchical model. A small sample of a BVH file is given as Listing 9.1.

Listing 9.1

A small sample of a BVH file that would be applied to the skeletal structure shown in Figure 9.1.

```
ROOT Hips
{
OFFSET  0.00     0.00     0.00
CHANNELS   6   Xposition  Yposition  Zposition  Zrotation  Xrotation
Yrotation
JOINT LeftHip
    {
        OFFSET    3.430000     0.000000    0.000000
        CHANNELS 3 Zrotation Xrotation Yrotation
        JOINT LeftKnee
        {
            OFFSET   0.000000   -18.469999      0.000000
            CHANNELS 3 Zrotation Xrotation Yrotation
            JOINT LeftAnkle
            {
                OFFSET   0.000000   -17.950001   0.000000
                CHANNELS 3 Zrotation Xrotation Yrotation
                End Site
                {
                    OFFSET    0.000000    -3.119996       0.000000
                }
            }
        }
    }
JOINT RightHip
    {
        OFFSET -3.430000     0.000000    0.000000
        CHANNELS 3 Zrotation Xrotation Yrotation
```

```
JOINT RightKnee
{
    OFFSET   0.000000   -18.809999      0.000000
    CHANNELS 3 Zrotation Xrotation Yrotation
    JOINT RightAnkle
    {
        OFFSET   0.000000   -17.570000   0.000000
        CHANNELS 3 Zrotation Xrotation Yrotation
        End Site
        {
            OFFSET   0.000000   -3.250000       0.000000
        }
    }
}
}
```

In a hierarchical structure the local transformation of a bone describes its orientation within its own local coordinate system, which is itself subject to the parent's local transformation. Consider that if we move a leg, the attached foot must also move—any part of the structure has to inherit the motion of all its parents. To obtain a global matrix for a given bone, the local transform needs

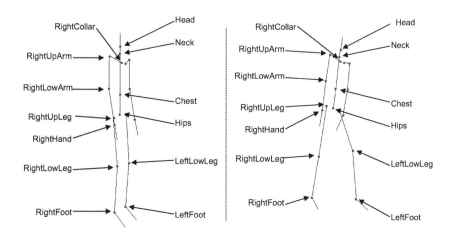

Figure 9.1. Skeletal structure of the sample BVH file: (a) base position and (b) first frame of the animation.

to be premultiplied by its parent's global transform, which is itself derived by multiplying its local transform by its parent's global transform and so on. Thus for any bone n we have

$$M^n_{global} = \prod_{i=0}^{n} M^i_{local} \tag{9.1}$$

Using MoCap

MoCap has become an increasingly popular way of creating motion for characters. The reasons are obvious—by definition it produces very high quality animation for little effort, but at high cost. Compared to the long and intricate process of designing static poses, it is immediate and speeds up the production of a game.

Although the first uses of MoCap were to be found in the television and film industry, the games industry was the first to embrace the technology as a routine method for animating human-like characters. Now the games industry accounts for around 90 percent of the total usage and almost all games that employ such characters use MoCap to drive the animation.

The quality and convenience of MoCap are convincing. Consider Figure 9.2. Although the figure is a simple stick skeleton, the resulting animation from MoCap data exhibits complex and expressive motion.

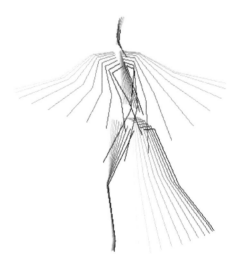

Figure 9.2. Superimposed frames of MoCap data applied to a stick figure.

This 'ghost' sequence shows sets of superimposed frames at equal sampling intervals. Providing the motion is sampled at a sufficiently high rate, the technology captures all the subtlety of the human performance. Examine the illustration: here is easily seen in the left leg, the deceleration in the motion towards the extreme position. Using keyframe animation from two key positions at the start and end of the ghost frames would not result in the correct motion. To imitate such a sequence using a keyframe system, the animator must position the keys appropriately so that the required accelerations and decelerations are present in the final sequence. It is precisely the difficulty and cost of accomplishing this that motivates the use of MoCap data.

One of the disadvantages of MoCap is that it requires semi-manual postprocessing. This is extremely important and demands much effort. The operations are mainly clean-ups and involve noise removal, filling in gaps caused by a marker going out of view for a period and eliminating confusion when two markers become coincident in a view. Another important low level processing operation is converting the data—which specify the position of markers as a function of time—into joint rotation form suitable for driving a skeleton hierarchy.

Time consuming and complex operations, such as retargetting are at the moment, performed offline. This situation is likely to change as the technology develops, with more complexity moving into the real-time domain. For example, in a report published in 2001, H. Shin *et al.* [SHIN01] handle both the low-level preprocessing operations and the retargetting operation in realtime. Their application is computer puppetry, by definition a real time application. Here, the movements of a performer are mapped to an animated character, and a prototype system has been used successfully to create a virtual character for a children's TV program as well as a virtual news reporter. Computer puppetry may find applications in the future in multiplayer applications, but for now, the lesson that all conventional MoCap processing can be done in realtime has significance for the games industry.

The main drawbacks of MoCap technology are the following:

- We can only activate prerecorded scripts in a game—an obvious statement but one that needs emphasis. Although a large number of sequences are stored and selected in realtime according to game logic, this is still an inherently limiting process. We would like to have facilities so that MoCap sequences continually adapt themselves to the developing game, altering themselves and producing new sequences from existing material.

- MoCap data is only valid for a virtual character who possesses the same scale as the real human from which the data was recorded. When we try to use the data on a character of different scale, we encounter problems. This is known as the retargeting problem.

- MoCap for facial expressions and visual speech is difficult.

There are many other subtle problems in the technology. A quality consideration, which has meant less take-up from the film industry (cf. the games industry), derives from the fact that sampling the motion of points on the surface of the skin of a character does not lead to a completely accurate script with which to animate a skeleton composed of rigid links. Currently, the aesthetic demands in character animation are lower for games than for film, and this has meant the wholesale take-up of MoCap technology in games.

The motivation for dealing with MoCap in a text which purports to deal with real-time aspects of game technology is that many of the manipulation techniques developed for MoCap data can be applied at interactive rates, and many are by definition techniques that are applied as the game is executing. Ideally, we would like a human-like game character to have his motion characteristics altered according to events as the game develops. The simplest manipulation may be just to speed up or slow down the action. Alternatively, we may want the character to react by becoming angry or tired, and that characteristic is reflected in the way he walks or runs. We would like to generate such motions in realtime by altering in some way the existing MoCap data beyond that available from blending existing sequences.

Another common requirement is to alter the motion so that a constraint is satisfied. Motion data may have been acquired for a character picking up an object. What if the object a character has to pick up in the game is larger or in a different relative position? Consider, for example, a football game. The goalkeeper character may be animated by a MoCap vocabulary of saves: "dive downwards to the ground", "dive upwards to the corner". So that the goalkeeper reaches the ball, the game may simply 'teleport' or translate the motion. A more correct approach would be to use inverse kinematics, altering the pose of the goalkeeper in the motion sequence so that he strives to reach the ball. And, of course, such situations depend on the demands of the game logic. It may be that we *require* the goalkeeper to catch the ball, but there is no MoCap sequence—even with inverse kinematic adaptation—that will position his hands at the ball position. We may then have to use a teleport. Alternatively, we have to cover all possible ball positions and trajectories with an (adaptable) MoCap sequence.

Applying MoCap to a Skeleton

MoCap data consist of separate channels which are joint angles as a function of time. The data are sampled at between 30 and 60 frames per second, although violent movement like karate actions may have to be sampled at a higher rate. Currently in games, we aim for a frame rate of around 100. Because the MoCap rate is generally lower, the data is then regarded as a set of keys, and quaternion interpolation is applied, as explained in the previous chapter.

Figure 9.3 is a visualisation of the process. Three channels are controlling the three degrees of freedom (DOFs) of a shoulder joint which moves the upper arm. The sequence is part of a goalkeeper's catch and throw. Although this is a

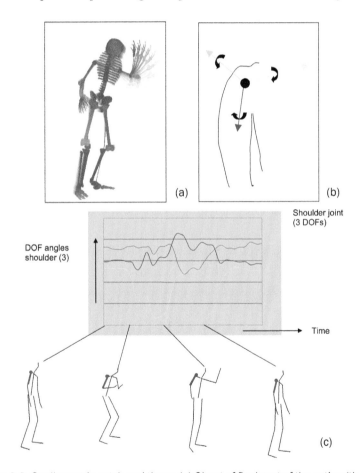

Figure 9.3. Goalkeeper's catch and throw. (a) Ghost of final part of the action (the throw). (b) Shoulder joint has three DOFs. (c) MoCap functions applied to a stick figure (upper right arm highlighted).

very short sequence, you can see by examining the joint angle functions that they contain very fine detail—precisely the detail which would be time consuming to author. Applying the MoCap to the shoulder DOFs produces the motion shown in the ghost sequence (Figure 9.3(a) which shows the final part of the action and in Figure 9.3(c) which shows the motion of the right upper arm).

Skinning

Skinning, as the name implies is the process of adding a skin to a skeleton character.

We now look at the detail of applying motion to a skeleton. First, we need to evaluate the local transform of each bone by composing a matrix $M = TRS$ containing translation, rotation and scale. BVH format MoCap information does not contain any scaling, and in that case we need only consider rotation and translation. Other formats, for example, HTR, do provide scaling information for each bone. Our examples above are based on BVH format where the rotation is given as three separate channels. We calculate the rotational component of M as

$$R = R_x \, R_y \, R_z$$

Now consider translation T. The root node accepts per frame translation to move a character forward. In addition each bone has an offset representing its distance from the parent node, thus T is the sum of the root translation and its offset. M is of the form:

$$M = \begin{bmatrix} R_{00} & R_{01} & R_{02} & T_x \\ R_{10} & R_{11} & R_{12} & T_y \\ R_{20} & R_{21} & R_{22} & T_z \\ 0 & 0 & 0 & 1 \end{bmatrix}$$

Using

$$M^n_{global} = \prod_{i=0}^{n} M^i_{local}$$

we can calculate for each bone its matrix M_{global} and for every frame in the animation we transform the bones into the global or world coordinate system for rendering. The organisation of the animation then would proceed as follows. We define a skeleton as a structure of

$$n \text{ bones} * (1 \text{ quaternion} + 1 \text{ translation}).$$

Note that the quaternion is derived from R as discussed in Chapter 7. The animation sequence for such a structure consists of

$$m \text{ keys} * (1 \text{ time} + n \text{ bones}).$$

To calculate the skeleton pose at time t, we find keyframes around this time to compute unit time u:

$$u = \frac{(t - t_1)}{(t_2 - t_1)}.$$

The keys are defined as:

$(q_1$ (quaternion) and p_1 (translation)) and $(q_2$ (quaternion) and p_2 (translation))

Then for every bone we apply

$$q = \text{slerp}(q_1, q_2, u) \text{ and}$$
$$p = p_1(1 - u) + p_2 u$$

Blending Animation—General Considerations

The established usage of MoCap in the games industry consists of storing a vocabulary of sequences in the game and blending and adapting these in realtime as the game progresses (Figure 9.4). Game events, which emerge from the game logic and player interaction, cause a particular sequence to be selected and blended with the previous sequence.

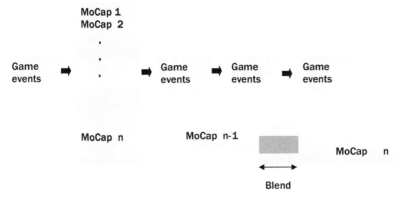

Figure 9.4. Blending MoCap sequences.

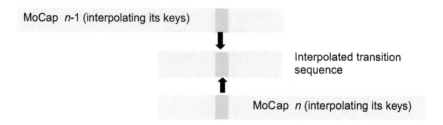

MoCap *n*-1 (interpolating its keys)

Interpolated transition sequence

MoCap *n* (interpolating its keys)

Figure 9.5. Three sequences are active during interpolation.

Note that blending implies that there are three interpolations active during the transition time of the blend (Figure 9.5). MoCap *n*-1 is interpolating its keys as is MoCap *n*. The interpolated transition sequence, the one we display, lasts for the transition time, which may be around 250 milliseconds, say.

Alternatives to MoCap

MoCap is an established technology that enables realistic animation with little effort beyond the data collection process. It is a matter of debate, therefore, if there are viable alternatives to this approach. We have emphasised MoCap in some detail because it is currently the mainstream method for character animation in games. There are, however, motivations for using alternatives, and the two most important of these are necessity and expense. Necessity covers cases that are impossible to MoCap (creature motion, for example), and expense comes into play in situations where, for example, we may want to animate a crowd in the background, where the visual quality of the motion is less important.

For simple cyclic motion such as running and walking, we can animate a skeleton by using a procedural or analytic method in realtime or more cheaply by using the same methods to create skeleton scripts offline. These scripts can also be individualised (old person, young person, tired, energetic etc.) to make them more convincing.

Although the production of animation for games is dominated by MoCap and pre-authored methods, automatic script generation for skeletal characters is worthy of exploration and perhaps exploitation in the future by the games community. Scripts generated by a program are much more amenable to real-time modification—the significant omission in MoCap. Real-time adaptation of motion to a changing environment is surely going to be an important requirement in future games. We will concentrate in this section on one of the most powerful techniques—inverse kinematics—demonstrating how to use it to construct cyclic motions such as walking.

Explicit Scripting by Forward Kinematics

We already alluded to this technique in Chapter 7. It involves an animator effectively replacing a MoCap studio and posing a skeleton per keyframe. This is done either in authoring software or by using a digital input device. It goes without saying that creating poses manually is very labour intensive, and the motivation for it is simply that the motion of dinosaurs, or for that matter of living animals, cannot be captured in a MoCap studio.

Simulating Dynamics

Although many commercial systems are currently available,[1] systems that simulate the dynamics of human body motion have not (yet) been taken up by the games community. This is in contrast to rigid body dynamic simulator, such as Havok,[2] which has been used in recent productions. Again, this may be due to the quality and dominance of MoCap or the perceived lack of efficacy of such systems.

Procedural Generation of Cyclical Motion using Inverse Kinematics

This is the approach that in our opinion is of greatest potential for automatic script generation and is the MoCap alternative to which we shall devote most space. The foundation technique in the procedural generation of human figures is Inverse Kinematics (IK). This is a powerful technique which can be used to generate, and also stylise, cyclical motions such as running and walking, and is one of the easiest approaches to retargetting and stylising MoCap.

Procedurally generated scripts are potentially useful for background characters. They can be generated offline for common cyclic motions, like walking and running, and applied in real time. Sameness can be ameliorated by stylising the motions but there is a memory cost as we store more and more scripts. For background characters sameness may not be a problem. Another not insignificant advantage of procedurally generated motion is that we avoid having to retarget the MoCap data. Inaccurately applied MoCap data for a walk results in the well-known foot sliding effect.

. . . .

[1] See www.washedashore.com/Humans/Commercial.

[2] See www.havok.com.

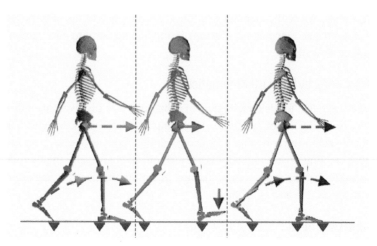

Figure 9.6. From left to right: start of walk cycle, start of the post flight phase and start of the cycle on the other foot. *Courtesy Michael Meredith, University of Sheffield.*

As an example, we describe how to generate leg motion for a walk cycle. The method is based on work carried out by M. Meredith at the University of Sheffield [MERE04] which uses an IK solution based on Jacobian inversion. (See Appendix 9.1 for a basic treatment and [WATT92] for a more detailed explanation of differential methods for IK.)

Consider Figure 9.6 which shows three (extreme) frames of a walk cycle. These are, from left to right: start of walk cycle, start of the postflight phase and start of the cycle on the other foot. The red triangles represent the foot plants at the extremes of the cycle. Defining a foot flight path between these extremes gives us the information we need to input into an IK solver which produces the required joint angles. The hip joint can move forward in a horizontal plane, or its height can be controlled by a low-amplitude sine wave.

A foot flight path can be defined parametrically, and Figure 9.7(a) shows such a curve defined by :

$$y = 1 - \cos(x) \qquad x \leq \pi$$

$$y = 1 - \cos\left(\frac{\pi + x}{2}\right) \qquad x > \pi$$

For comparison, Figure 9.7(b) shows an actual foot flight curve extracted from MoCap data. The difference between the two curves is obvious: there is noise apparent in the recorded motion and also a plateau on the negative side of the

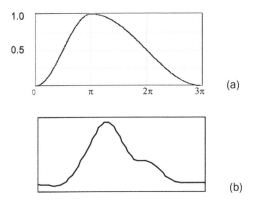

Figure 9.7. Foot flight path. (a) A path defined by a parametric function. (b) A path extracted from MoCap data. *Courtesy Michael Meredith.*

curve indicating that the walker has levelled his foot before planting. The foot flight gives us control over length, height and speed of the stride, and the IK enables control over the style of the walk.

The walk cycle is divided into two IK phases. The first is the flight of the foot as the character performs a stride and the second is a postflight phase that rolls the foot from a heel supporting phase to a foot supporting phase. This is summarised in Table 9.1.

In each phase, the IK solver returns the knee angle and the angle the upper leg makes with the hip. Figure 9.8 shows the output from the IK solver. The curve adopts the expected cyclical behaviour after starting from a straight-legged

Table 9.1.

IK phase of the walk cycle.

		Phase 1	Phase 2
starting Configuration	Left foot	Heels and toes on floor	Toes on floor
	Right foot	Toes on floor	Heel on floor
Movement		Hips move forward	Hips move forward
		Right heel follows foot flight path	Right toes move to floor
		Left toes remain planted	Left toes remain planted

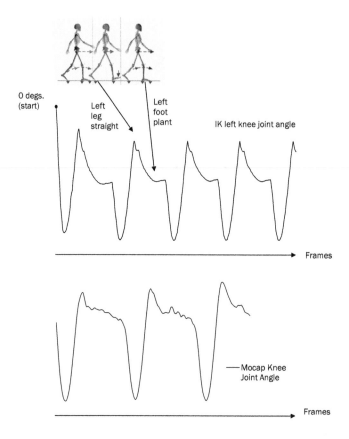

Figure 9.8. Comparing procedurally generated motion with MoCap for knee joint angle. *Courtesy Michael Meredith.*

position (knee angle = 0). This can be compared with a segment of MoCap data from the same joint captured from a walking subject. Again the motion is cyclical as expected, but now with noise variations. Also, the profile of the cycle is somewhat different with the tendency to level the foot before planting occupying a larger proportion of the cycle.

Animation control is achieved by controlling any or all of the parameters described in Table 9.2. This gives a rich set of parameters for artistic control. Hip rotation and arm swing can easily be defined with a user defined cyclic script curve. In the case of the arm swing we do not need an IK solution—there are no floor constraints as is the case with the feet. However, for actions like a hand moving to grasp an object IK is relevant.

Walking action	Assigned parameter
Height and stride length	Foot flight path parameters
Walk style	Joint angle constraints (see Appendix 9.1)
Walk individualisation	IK weight coefficients
Hip rotation (about vertical axis)	Rotation parameter
Arm swing	Swing parameter

Table 9.2

Controlling a walk cycle.

Weighting the IK solution means applying a weighting coefficient to the iteration (see Appendix 9.1):

$$\theta = \theta + J^{-1}\Delta x$$

is replaced with

$$\theta = \theta + wJ^{-1}\Delta x \qquad \text{where } w \in 0,1$$

This trivial addition is surprisingly effective. For example, we can apply low weighting values to simulate sluggish motion suggesting a limb with low muscle tone and higher weights to suggest more powerful muscle motivation. Decreasing weights (and adjusting control parameters) can also be used to simulate injury where a character reduces joint motion to minimise pain that would otherwise occur in normal motion. In a walk motion, this is limping.

Figure 9.9 attempts to show the method applied to a figure to simulate a limp.[3] In the illustration, the stick figure is a (normal) MoCap walk. For the coloured skeletons, altered control parameters are applied to the left leg to make it limp. Control parameter alterations include reducing the maximum height of the foot flight and the stride length by 50 percent, while increasing the stride speed by 30 percent. The red figure has even weights applied, and the green and blue figures have altered weights. The trails are the foot and knee paths.

....

[3] It is difficult to demonstrate this with a static image; see www.dcs.shef.ac.uk/~mikem to view the animations.

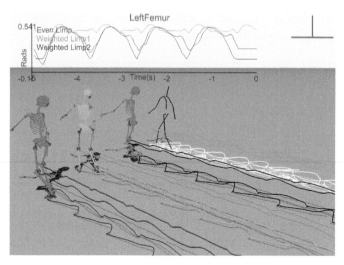

Figure 9.9. Stick figure: MoCap. Red figure: even weight + altered control parameters. Blue and green figures: altered weights + altered control parameters. *Courtesy Michael Meredith, University of Sheffield, UK.*

Retargetting a MoCap Walk

Retargetting a MoCap walk is trivial using this method; all we have to do is extract the foot flight curve from the MoCap data then apply the same algorithm. The foot flight curve in Figure 9.7 was extracted from MoCap data using simple gradient analysis, full details of which are given in [MERE04].

Higher Level Control of Background Groups

A crowd or a herd can be made up of characters regarded as single entities with their own autonomous behaviour but whose root motions are globally controlled at a higher level so that the crowd or herd moves with its own behaviour.

An example of a simple, but highly effective, form of high level control is the flocking model first proposed by C. Reynolds [REYN87][4]. This behaviour has been used in many different applications: stampeding herd in the film *The Lion King*, and to a bicycle race in [HODG95]. It is implemented using simple social rules/strategies, which in order of precedence are:

- collision avoidance (avoid collision with nearby flock mates),
- velocity matching (attempt to match velocity with nearby flock mates),
- flock centring (attempt to stay close to nearby flock mates) and
- random wandering.

....

[4] See also Craig Reynold's excellent website: http://www.red3d.com/cwr/boids/

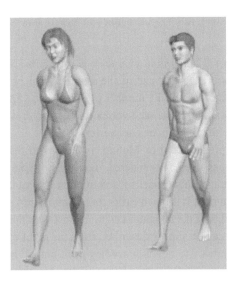

Figure 9.10. Skinned games characters (circa 2004). *Characters courtesy Tony Lupidi, Rio de Janeiro.*

Skinning Skeletal Characters

Skinning is the name given to the process that converts a simple articulated model, which accepts the animation control, into a complex (usually humanlike) character. The skin object is a mesh of triangles of high complexity (10^5 is not uncommon), and we can look upon the process as an example of that well-established paradigm in deformation animation where a high resolution mesh is deformed by a much simpler control structure which accepts the animation control. Figure 9.10 shows skinned characters whose similarity to reality is perhaps typical of games characters at the time of writing. We know that they are obviously computer graphics constructions, but nevertheless, they look sufficiently real to serve contemporary games culture.

Whereas the notion of a skeleton with bones is intuitively appealing, the actual model consists of a mesh and a large set of matrices (equivalent to the bones) which are associated with the mesh vertices. Each vertex is connected to a number of matrices. This connection is via a weighting factor which determines the how much that matrix influences the vertex. The mesh is originally constructed in a default state, usually with legs apart and arms outstretched. This is called a rest pose or bind pose.

271

The visual quality of a humanlike character is, of course, a function of the number of vertices, as is also the size of the skinning task. In the case of the characters shown in Figure 9.10, the number of vertices is 15,936 (female) and 16,588 (male). As we explain later, each vertex in a character will be associated, or attached, to no more than four bones per vertex.

Animation control, pre-authored or MoCap, is applied to the matrices in real time, and the character, skinned and rendered, moves accordingly. Apart from its visual complexity leverage, this model of deformation animation has significant advantages for pre-authoring. It is much easier for an animator to set up poses using a skeleton than it would be if the animator had to interact with the complete mesh.

The overall process can be simply described from the point of view of a single vertex. We require a vertex v to be influenced by positions of the bones to which it is attached. That is, v moves to a new position v' say. We also require that v' be in global or world space for rendering.

There are two popular ways of authoring the process called the "vertex offset method" and the "bone offset method". The sequence of transformations that we have to perform is easier to explain using variable names, and we will now go through the operations required in that manner. We start with the character mesh and bones in a rest position (usually legs apart and arms outstretched). In that position, we define the bones affecting each vertex. We need to represent the vertices in relation to the rest position of the bones, so we compute the offset from the vertex to the bone (by transforming the vertex into bone space). To do this, we multiply the vertex position by the rest-pose bone inverse matrix (if no scale is used in the bones we can use a simple affine inverse).:

$$offset = vertex * inverse\_restpose\_bone\_matrix$$

Then, after applying the animation which consists of the matrices for the skeleton bones, we compute the new vertex position by applying the offset to the current bone matrices:

$$new\_vertex = offset * new\_bone\_matrix$$

We must also transform the normals for the original rest pose mesh so we can illuminate the object while it animates. To do this, we compute the normal in rest-pose bone space, just as we did for the vertices. But for normals, we only use the rotation part of the matrices (3 x 3 submatrix). To compute the normal in bone space, we multiply the rest-pose normal by the inverse of the rest-pose bone matrix (using the rotation part only):

$$normal\_in\_bone\_space = normal\_in\_object\_space *$$

$$inverse\_restpose\_bone\_matrix^{(3x3)}$$

For rotation matrices, the inverse rotation is simply the transpose matrix, and we can optimise this by using a special multiply transpose method that does the multiplication directly with the transpose without the need to swap the values around.

When we animate the skeleton, we can compute the normal in relation to the new animated bone position by multiplying the normal in bone space with the new bone matrix rotation part only (3 x 3 submatrix):

$$\text{new\_normal} = \text{normal\_in\_bone\_space} * \text{new\_bone\_matrix}^{(3\times3)}$$

The above formulation will produce what is called a rigid vertex (a vertex that is associated to a single bone). The vertex will behave as if it was connected to the bone with a rigid link and will always maintain the same distance and relative position to the associated bone matrix whereever it moves.

Rigid vertices might be good for robots and other rigid characters, but for humans and soft deformable characters, we need blended vertices. The so-called blended vertices are vertices which are connected to more then one bone. For that, we specify weights w_i for each vertex/bone connection so that the sum of all weights for a given vertex adds up to 1.

So now one vertex may be associated with multiple bones (usually four as we justify in the next section), each with a different weight factor. Thus, we need one offset and normal (in bone space) for each vertex/bone connection. When computing the new vertex and normal we add together all contributions, each multiplied by its weight:

$$\text{new\_vertex} = \sum_{i=0}^{3} (\text{offset}(i) * \text{new\_bone\_matrix}(i) * \text{weight}(i))$$

or:

$$v = \sum_{i=0}^{3} w_i M_i o_i \qquad \text{where} \quad \sum_{i=0}^{3} w_i = 1$$

$$\text{new\_normal} = \sum_{i=0}^{3} (\text{normal\_in\_bone\_space}(i) * \text{new\_bone\_matrix}(i)^{(3\times3)} * \text{weight}(i))$$

or:

$$\mathbf{N} = \sum_{i=0}^{3} w_i \mathbf{R}_i \mathbf{N}_i \qquad \text{where} \quad \sum_{i=0}^{3} w_i = 1$$

The advantage of this method is that we can do all the skinning in the GPU using the animated bone matrices for a given frame as constants for the shader. However, the disadvantage is that we need many per-vertex variable parameters to pass in, as we need the vertex and normal in bone space for each vertex/bone connection.

Another common way of organising skinning is called the bone offset method. Here v is specified in the model space of the rest pose of the mesh. This reduces the size of the variable data needed at each vertex. In this method, we premultiply the inverse rest-pose matrices by the current frame matrices before passing them into the shader as constants. The inverse rest-pose matrices can be pre-calculated at load time. After interpolating the new bones from our keyframe animation we postmultiply them with the stored inverse rest-pose matrices. This allows us to use the original rest-pose vertex positions and normals at the skinning phase. Thus, we do not need to calculate the vertex and normals in bone space; we can use the object space version from the rest pose mesh directly. Also, from a modelling point of view, attachments such as hair and eyes are defined and exported in rest-pose space.

The bone offset method also allows us to apply deformations to the rest pose mesh prior to the skinning phase (say morph targets for facial animation). It would be difficult to do that in the vertex offset method, since in that method we have vertices in bone space duplicated for every vertex/bone connection. However, the bone offset method adds an extra matrix multiplication per bone per frame in order to add the rest pose inverse matrices. To animate the skeleton we interpolate new bone matrices for the current frame as follows:

for every bone i

$$new\_bone\_matrix(i) = inverse\_restpose\_matrix(i) *$$
$$new\_bone\_matrix(i)$$

$$new\_vertex = \sum_{i=0}^{3} (vertex\_in\_restpose * new\_bone\_matrix(i) *$$
$$weight(i))$$

or:

$$v = \sum_{i=0}^{3} w_i M_i M_{i\,ref\,i}^{-1} v_i \qquad where \quad \sum_{i=0}^{3} w_i = 1$$

$$new\_normal = \sum_{i=0}^{3} (normal\_in\_restpose * new\_bone\_matrix(i)^{(3 \times 3)} *$$
$$weight(i))$$

or:

$$\mathbf{N} = \sum_{i=0}^{3} w_i R_i R_{i\,ref\,i}^{-1} \mathbf{N} \qquad where \quad \sum_{i=0}^{3} w_i = 1$$

Notice that the vertex and normal (from the rest pose) used in above sums are constants for all bones associated to a given vertex.

Current Hardware Limitations on Character Complexity

Current hardware limitations effectively limit the complexity of skinned characters in terms of the number of bones per character and the complexity of the skinning (number of bones associated with a single vertex). Figure 9.11 shows a typical data structure that we require in a vertex program for skinning using the vertex offset method.

The variable parameter structure limits the number of bones associated with one vertex, and the uniform parameter structure limits the number of bones. Good quality skinning ought to be achievable with no more that 4 bones associated with each vertex. The bone data are a uniform array of 4 x 4 matrices, and a typical hardware limit would be 128 matrices. However, a good-quality character can be achieved by a smallish number of bones, say 20 to 50. This figure excludes fully articulated fingers and toes, which if included would imply say 100 bones. (Note that number of bones is not the same as number of DOFs.) C. Beeson and K. Bjorke in [BEES04] report a character of 180,000 triangles being controlled with 98 bones and no more than 4 bones per vertex. They also point out that you can sort bone weights and use a vertex shader to truncate the number of bones acting on a vertex according to the hardware/performance state, but a disadvantage of this is that the active bone weights must be rescaled so that they always sum to 1.

As we do not require the last column of the bone matrices—which are always (0,0,0,1), it is possible to use only three vectors to store the bone matrix if we use

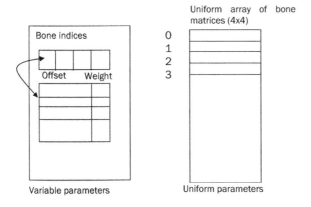

Figure 9.11. A typical data structure for skinning using the vertex offset method.

a 3 x 4 transposed matrix. Multiplication in shader must then be adapted to use the transposed matrix instead.

Listing 9.2 gives a CPU program for skinning. This will consume large amounts of CPU time for large meshes, and it is, of course, better to offload the work onto the GPU (Listing 9.3).

Listing 9.2

CPU skinning.

```
void pMeshSkeleton::build_mesh()
{
    int i,j,c,p;
    pVector v,n,vv,nn;
    float f;

    p=0;
    for( i=0;i<nvert;i++ )
    {
        // vertex position
        vv=pVector(vert[i].pos[0],vert[i].pos[1],vert[i].pos[2]);
        // vertex normal
        nn=pVector(vert[i].norm[0],vert[i].norm[1],vert[i].norm[2]);

        // apply morph target animations
        // (accumulated from all active morph targets)
        vv+=m_phy.voffset[i];

        v.vec(0);
        n.vec(0);
        // number of bones associated to vertex
        c=m_phy.vweightcount[i];
        for( j=0;j<c;j++ )
        {
            // weight for this bone
            f=m_phy.wfactor[p+j];
            // accumulate vertex
            v += m_phy.bmat[m_phy.wboneindx[p+j]]*vv*f;
            // accumulate normal
            n += f*m_phy.bmat[m_phy.wboneindx[p+j]].
```

```
    multiply_rotation(nn);
    }
    p+=c;

    // store accumulated vertex position
    m_mesh.vert[i].pos[0]=v.x;
    m_mesh.vert[i].pos[1]=v.y;
    m_mesh.vert[i].pos[2]=v.z;

    // normalize accumulated normal
    f=n.x*n.x+n.y*n.y+n.z*n.z;
    f=1.0f/sqrtf(f);
    m_mesh.vert[i].norm[0]=n.x*f;
    m_mesh.vert[i].norm[1]=n.y*f;
    m_mesh.vert[i].norm[2]=n.z*f;
    }
}
```

Listing 9.3

GPU skinning.

```
struct app2vert
{
    float4 pos : POSITION;
    float4 color : DIFFUSE;
    float2 texcoord : TEXCOORD0;
    float3 normal : NORMAL;
    float4 bone_indices : TEXCOORD1;
    float4 bone_weights : TEXCOORD2;
};

struct vert2frag
{
    float4 hpos : POSITION;
    float4 color : COLOR0;
    float2 texcoord : TEXCOORD0;
};

vert2frag main_vert_skinning(
    app2vert IN,
    uniform float3 camerapos,
```

```
    uniform float4 specular,
    uniform float3 skincolor,
    uniform float3 lightcolor,
    uniform float4 lightpos,
    uniform float4x4 bones[MAX_BONES],
    uniform float4x4 viewinverse)
{
vert2frag OUT;

    float4 v = float4(0,0,0,1);
    float3 n = float3(0,0,0);

    int i,j;
    for( i=0;i<4;i++ )
    {
      j = (int)IN.bone_indices[i];

      v.xyz += mul(bones[j],IN.pos).xyz*
             IN.bone_weights[i];

      n += mul(float3x3(bones[j]),
           IN.normal)*IN.bone_weights[i];
    }

    n=normalize(n);

    float3 viewdir = normalize(v.xyz-camerapos);

    float4 color;
    color.xyz = lightcolor * illuminate(v.xyz,
              lightpos, viewdir, n, IN.color,
              specular, skincolor);
    color.w = IN.color.w;

    OUT.hpos = mul(glstate.matrix.mvp,v);
    OUT.texcoord = IN.texcoord;
    OUT.color = color;

    return OUT;
}
```

Figure 9.12. The effect of the $1 - (\mathbf{N} \cdot \mathbf{V})^2$ term. *Character courtesy Tony Lupidi, Rio de Janeiro.*

When using a vertex program for skinning, we must also implement lighting in the vertex program (or in a separate fragment program) as the standard pipeline lighting will not be available. For human characters a skin term can be added to the illumination function to give it a softer look. Rendering skin, so that it looks like skin rather than plastic, is a fairly well researched topic. Many, if not all, of the approaches attend to a physical model which implements, in some way, subsurface scattering—the predominant phenomenon that makes skin look like it does. A good example of this approach is given in [HANR93]. However, such models are computationally expensive and, with the current level of reality in

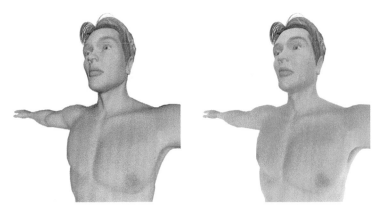

Figure 9.13. A character rendered without (left) and with (right) the skin term added to the diffuse term. *Character courtesy Tony Lupidi, Rio de Janeiro.*

games characters, perhaps not justified. Therefore, we can use a crude but effective imitative model consisting of the term

$$1 - (\mathbf{N} \cdot \mathbf{V})^2$$

This gives a kind of 'glowing' effect near the silhouette edge of the character as shown in Figure 9.13.

This term is multiplied by the skin colour and added to the diffuse term. The illumination code is given in Listing 9.4 can be used in a vertex or fragment program and includes the skin term.

Listing 9.4

Skin illumination code (can be used in vertex or fragment program).

```
float3 illuminate(
        in float3 objpos, in float4 lightpos,
        in float3 viewdir, in float3 normal,
        in float4 diffuse, in float4 specular,
        in float3 skincolor)
{
    float3 lightdir;
    float dist;

    lightdir = lightpos.xyz-objpos.xyz;
    dist = length(lightdir);
    lightdir /= dist;
    dist /= lightpos.w;
    dist = max(0.0,1.0-dist*dist);
    if (lightpos.w==0.0)
        dist=1;

    float3 halfdir = normalize(lightdir-viewdir);

    float HdotL = saturate(dot(halfdir,normal.xyz));
    float NdotL = saturate(dot(lightdir,normal.xyz));

    float skin = saturate(1.0+dot(normal.xyz,viewdir));
    skin *= skin;

    return dist*(diffuse.xyz*(NdotL+skin*skincolor)+
            specular.xyz*pow(HdotL,specular.w));
}
```

Figure 9.14. Using morph targets for facial animation. *Character courtesy Tony Lupidi, Rio de Janeiro.*

Using Morph Targets

Morph targets are minor deformations that are superimposed on the main mesh deformation which is implemented by the skinning operation. They are commonly used for facial expressions and/or local deformations that correct the unwanted effects that skinning produces in certain joint locations in the body mesh—such as the elbow (see Figure 9.15). Although we can implement the fine deformations that are required using bones or deformers in the head—that is in principle the same paradigm that we use for skeleton controlled body mesh deformation—it is easier to use morph targets [BEES04]. (Facial animation using deformers is dealt with in detail in Chapter 10.) As we have already mentioned,we can apply morph targets *prior* to skinning by using the bone offset method. The morph targets are applied to the rest pose and are thus automatically incorporated into the skinning. A typical morph target for facial animation is shown in Figure 9.14.

To manage the animation, we consider that a morph target consists of a list of offsets to be applied to a subset of the mesh vertices. Each morph target can modify a different set of vertices in the mesh. In our implementation (Listing 9.5), we identify each morph target by a name and can store multiple morph targets in the same data file. Adding the offsets to the associated vertices before skinning will make the morph target visible. For a smooth transition, we can fade in or out the offsets through time to make the morph target modification appear and disappear without discontinuities.

Listing 9.5.

Implementing morph
targets.

```cpp
// morph target
class P3D_API pMSMtg
{
    friend pMeshSkeleton;

protected:
    // morph target name
    pString name;
    // number of total vertices in mesh
    int nvert;
    // number of vertices with offset
    int noffset;
    // vertex id for each offset
    int *offsetvert;
    // vertex offsets
    pVector *offset;

public:
    pMSMtg();
    ~pMSMtg();

    pMSMtg(const pMSMtg &in);
    void operator=(const pMSMtg &in);

    // free all data
    void reset();
    // sets number of offsets
    void set_noffset(int n,bool keep_old=false);
};
```

A morph target animation is made of a list of morph targets, each with a 1D animation for its weight. Thus, at any given time, we can evaluate the weighted animation for each morph target and add together all offsets.

Listing 9.7

Morph target
animation.

```cpp
// morph target animation
class P3D_API pMSMtgAni
{
        friend pMeshSkeleton;
```

```
protected:
        // num animations
        int nanim;
        // morph target id for each animation
        int *animmtg;
        // animation keys for each animation
        pAnimation *anim;

public:
        pMSMtgAni();
        ~pMSMtgAni();

        pMSMtgAni(const pMSMtgAni &in);
        void operator=(const pMSMtgAni &in);
        // free all data
        void reset();
        // sets number of animations
        void set_nanim(int n,bool keep_old=false);
};
```

Usually for a character, we will have multiple morph target animations active at the same time, each affecting a different region of the character mesh. Each of the animations will be doing a weighted blending of all its component morph target poses. Listing 9.7 evaluates the animations and accumulates into a single array of vertices offsets for all morph target animations. When skinning each vertex, we simply add this accumulated offset, which will contain all active morph target animations.

Listing 9.7

Handling multiple morph target animations.

```
void pMeshSkeleton::update_mtgani(
                pMSMtgAni *ma,float time,float weight)
{
        int i;
        float f;
        // for each active morph target animation
        for( i=0;i<ma->nanim;i++ )
                if (ma->animmtg[i]!=-1 &&
                    ma->anim[i].numkey>1)
```

```
{
        // evaluate weight from animation keys
        // at current time
        ma->anim[i].update(time,&f);

        // if weight >0 then blend morph target
        if (f>0.0001f)
                blend_mtg( m_mtg[ma->animmtg[i]],
                        f*weight);
        }
}


void pMeshSkeleton::blend_mtg(pMSMtg *mtg,float weight)
{
        int i;
        // for each offset vertex in morph target
        for( i=0;i<mtg->noffset;i++ )
                // Accumulate offset for this vertex
                // with current weight
                m_phy.voffset[mtg->offsetvert[i]] + =
                        mtg->offset[i]*weight;
}
```

Skinning Defects

In this section, we examine in more detail the nature of the deformation due to skinning and explain why we need to 'tie' a vertex to more than one bone. Consider implementing skin deformation around a joint when it rotates. For example, we can consider an approximation of the elbow as a hinge joint (1 DOF). When an elbow bends, the skin folds on the acute side and stretches on the other side. If skin vertices at the joint region are associated with only one bone, as in Figure 9.15(a) then it is obvious that an unsatisfactory deformation occurs . In Figure 9.15(b) the centre vertices (coloured blue) are attached to each bone. If the blue vertices are transformed by each bone matrix this is effectively the same as inserting two new vertices (coloured red). The resulting position of the blue vertices will lie on a straight line joining the split components. In general then, skin behaviour will be satisfactory on the obtuse side of such a joint and will shrink on the acute side.

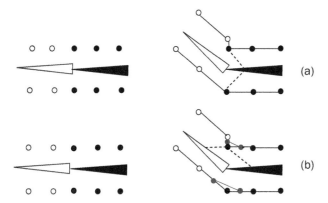

Figure 9.15. (a) One vertex to one bone attachment causes bad deformation. (b) One vertex to two bones attachment.

Another serious effect comes as a consequence of rotating one bone about the common axis joining two extended bones. For example, rotating the forearm with respect to the upper arm will result in a total collapse for a rotation of 180 degrees. Such visual inconsistencies are characteristic of a simple skinning scheme. An important observation is that the extent of the problem is a function of joint angle. The undesirable practical consequence is that animators cannot directly manipulate the deformation and indeed may be unsure if continuing to manipulate the weights w_i will result in any improvement.

Finally consider why there are problems with this scheme. All of the problems emerge from the fact that we are trying to choreograph the deformation of a polygon mesh model by moving the vertices individually and without regard to the context in which they are embedded. We can apply fixes and relate vertices by tying them to more than one bone. This helps but all of such fixes are context dependent and somewhat unsatisfactory. Obviously morph targets can also be used to correct unwanted deformations.

Appendix 9.1: Inverse Kinematics—the Theory

We begin by considering the difference between forward and inverse kinematics by distinguishing between the spaces that they operate in:

1. Joint space is the multidimensional space of joint angles. With a dimensionality equal to the number of DOFs of the computer graphics skeleton, the pose of a figure is a single point in this space. As a figure moves a path, is traced out in this space.

2. End effector space is the m dimensional space of the end effector (where m = number of end effectors times their DOFs.

3. World space is the space in which the character is visualised.

Considering the first two spaces, this concept leads to a useful model of the relationship between forward and inverse kinematics.

Thus we write for forward kinematics:

$$\mathbf{X} = f(\theta)$$

meaning that the position of any point $\mathbf{X}$ on the skeleton (usually an end effector) is some function of the joint angles θ. This expression controls the pose of the skeleton, and we animate the character by injecting joint angles as a function of time into the forward kinematics equation. This is the model used by MoCap control.

For IK we write:

$$\theta = f^{-1}(\mathbf{X})$$

and here $\mathbf{X}$ is normally used to specify a required position for an end effector, in the case of character animation—the hands or feet. The expression models the notion that if the hands are to be moved to grasp an object, say, then we specify $\mathbf{X}$ as the goal and the IK calculates the θ required to meet the goal. (Although for simplicity, we will continually refer to θ as determining the pose of the character, we also have to consider the position of the root node. In a grasping scenario, if the object is in range then only θ need be altered; if it is out of range, then the IK solution will involve also a change in position of the root node.)

An Example—the Two-Link Arm

The simplest possible example is a two-link arm moving in 2D space as shown in Figure A9.1.1. Simple link mechanisms are studied by setting up a coordinate frame at each joint and expressing the overall movement of a structure as a concatenation of a series of transformations that express the movement of the origin of frame n with respect to frame n-1. This enables us to express the motion of an end effector—the origin of frame n with respect to the base frame 0 as:

$$_n^0T = {}_1^0T\,{}_2^1T\,{}_3^2T\ldots{}_n^{n-1}T$$

(This expression is just a different way of notating the expression given as Equation 9.1.) The position and the orientation of the end effector is given by the concatenation of the individual link transformations.

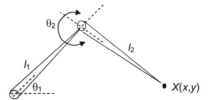

Figure A9.1.1. A simple two-link arm.

For the two-link planar mechanism we set up four frames: frame 0 which is the base frame and cannot move; frame 1, which shares an origin with the base frame and can rotate in the plane of the paper; frame 2, which can also rotate in the plane of the paper; and finally the end effector which we designate as frame 3. This is fixed to the end of the final link and cannot move. Thus, the arm exhibits two DOFs, the same as the dimensionality of the space in which it moves.

We develop the transformation as follows. First, we consider how frame 1 moves with respect to frame 0. It can only rotate, and we have:

$$
{}^0_1T = \begin{bmatrix} c_1 & -s_1 & 0 & 0 \\ s_1 & c_1 & 0 & 0 \\ 0 & 0 & 1 & 0 \\ 0 & 0 & 0 & 1 \end{bmatrix}
$$

similarly

$$
{}^1_2T = \begin{bmatrix} c_2 & -s_2 & 0 & l_1 \\ s_2 & c_2 & 0 & 0 \\ 0 & 0 & 1 & 0 \\ 0 & 0 & 0 & 1 \end{bmatrix}
$$

where c_1, c_2, s_1 and s_2 are abbreviations for $\cos\theta_1$, $\cos\theta_2$, $\sin\theta_1$ and $\sin\theta_2$. And

$$
{}^2_3T = \begin{bmatrix} 1 & 0 & 0 & l_2 \\ 0 & 1 & 0 & 0 \\ 0 & 0 & 1 & 0 \\ 0 & 0 & 0 & 1 \end{bmatrix}
$$

reflects the fact that the end effector is rigidly attached to this link—the end effector has two DOFs only.

In the case of the two link trigonometric manipulation give the closed form solution as:

$$\theta_2 = \cos^{-1}\left(\frac{x^2 + y^2 - l_1^2 - l_2^2}{2l_1 l_2} \right)$$

$$\dot{\theta}_1 = \tan^{-1}\left(\frac{-l_2 \sin\theta_2 x + (l_1 + l_2 \cos\theta_2)y}{l_2 \sin\theta_2 y + (l_1 + l_2 \cos\theta_2)x} \right)$$

Finding a closed-form solution becomes progressively more difficult as the chain becomes more and more complex—that is, as the number of DOFs increases. Another problem with closed-form solutions is that they are difficult to generalise to multiple constraints, particularly if these are interacting. Their significant advantage is that they are fast. The application of a single formula results in a solution. This contrasts with all other approaches, which are iterative.

The Jacobian

Now, in the case of applications that do not have a closed-form solution, we can implement inverse kinematics solutions by exploiting the fact that for small movements of the end effector we can assume a linear relationship between joint velocity and the velocity of the end effector. This is written as

$$\dot{\mathbf{X}} = J \dot{\theta}$$

J is known as the Jacobian and is a multidimensional derivative relating the end effector velocity to the velocity of the joints. It is an $m \times n$ matrix, where n is the number of joint variables (the total number of DOFs) and m is the number of DOFs of the end effector. The ith column of J represents the incremental change in position and orientation of the end effector caused by an incremental change in θ_i. If the inverse of J exists then we can write:

$$\dot{\theta} = J^{-1}\dot{\mathbf{X}}$$

We will now consider again the two-link arm and develop its Jacobian. We do this by developing an expression for the linear and rotational velocity of each frame then expressing the velocity of the end effector with respect to the base frame. The base frame has zero linear and rotational velocity and we start with frame 1. This has zero linear velocity—it can only rotate—and we have

$$^1\omega_1 = \begin{bmatrix} 0 \\ 0 \\ \dot{\theta}_1 \end{bmatrix}$$

$$^1v_1 = \begin{bmatrix} 0 \\ 0 \\ 0 \end{bmatrix}$$

To calculate the angular velocity of frame 2, we only augment its angular velocity with that of frame 1:

$$^2\omega_2 = \begin{bmatrix} 0 \\ 0 \\ \dot{\theta}_1 + \dot{\theta}_2 \end{bmatrix}$$

$$^2v_2 - \begin{bmatrix} 0 \\ 0 \\ 0 \end{bmatrix} + \begin{bmatrix} c^2 & s^2 & 0 \\ -s^2 & c^2 & 0 \\ 0 & 0 & 1 \end{bmatrix} \begin{bmatrix} 0 \\ l_1\dot{\theta} \\ 0 \end{bmatrix} = \begin{bmatrix} l_1s_2\dot{\theta}_1 \\ l_1c_2\dot{\theta}_1 \\ 0 \end{bmatrix}$$

The linear velocity of the origin of frame 2 is that of the origin of frame 1 plus the component caused by the angular velocity of frame 1/link 1:

$$^3\omega_3 = {}^2\omega_2 = \begin{bmatrix} 0 \\ 0 \\ \dot{\theta}_1 + \dot{\theta}_2 \end{bmatrix}$$

Finally we have:

$$^3v_3 = \begin{bmatrix} l_1s_2\dot{\theta}_1 \\ l_1c_2\dot{\theta}_1 \\ 0 \end{bmatrix} + \begin{bmatrix} 0 \\ 0 \\ \dot{\theta}_1 + \dot{\theta}_2 \end{bmatrix} = \begin{bmatrix} 0 \\ l_1c_2\dot{\theta}_1 + l_2(\dot{\theta}1 + \dot{\theta}_2) \\ 0 \end{bmatrix}$$

Now we need to express the linear velocity of the end effector in the base coordinate system, and for this we need the rotation matrix:

$$^0_3R = {}^0_1R \, {}^1_2R \, {}^2_3R = \begin{bmatrix} c_{12} & -s_{12} & 0 \\ s_{12} & c_{12} & 0 \\ 0 & 0 & 1 \end{bmatrix}$$

giving

$$^0v_3 = \begin{bmatrix} -l_1s_1q.1 - l_2s_{12}(\dot{\theta}_1 + \dot{\theta}_2) \\ l_1c_2\dot{\theta}_1 + l_2c_{12}(\dot{\theta}_1 + \dot{\theta}_2) \\ 0 \end{bmatrix}$$

This leads directly to the Jacobian using the chain rule for differentiation:

$$J = \begin{bmatrix} -l_1s_1 - l_2s_{12} & -l_2s_{12} \\ l_1c_1 + l_2c_{12} & l_2c_{12} \end{bmatrix}$$

Finding the Jacobian by differentiation becomes more and more difficult as the complexity of the structure increases, and in practice it must be constructed geometrically. We will first state the general principles then use the approach to evaluate the Jacobian for the two-link planar arm. The principle of this approach extends in a straightforward manner into 3 space, and a more detailed treatment of the general case is given in [WATT92].

We consider the motion of the end effector in terms of velocities propagated from the base of the chain to the end. Each link in an n link chain will in general be subject to a linear velocity (as its joint translates) and an angular velocity (as the link rotates about the joint). We state without proof that

- the angular velocity at the end of the chain is equal to the sum of all local angular velocities (evaluated in the base frame), and

- the linear velocity at the end of the chain is the sum over all intermediate frames of the cross product of the local angular velocity with the vector from the end of the articulation to the origin of that frame.

Now before we move on we should point out the Jacobian in this case is valid for all θ. In most cases of interest the Jacobian is a function of θ and in an iterative approach it has to be continually re-evaluated.

Approaches to IK

Accepting the notion that most systems of interest are too complex to possess a closed-form solution, we look in general terms at the various ways in which the problem can be approached.

- A geometric/analytical method generates a goal state in a single step and is hence fast. Although, as we have discussed, it cannot form a solution for a structure of any complexity, it can used as part of a solution in a hybrid method.

- Differential algorithms are used to linearise the problem for small changes using the Jacobian and generate a solution by iteration. In other words, the Jacobian can be embedded in an iterative approach that, exploiting the linearity of small changes, moves the end effector towards a solution. The performance of any iterative approach is a function of its convergence properties.

- Unconstrained optimisation methods instead of finding a solution which *must* satisfy the constraints, operate by associating a cost or penalty with the nonsatisfaction of a constraint.

- Cyclic coordinate descent is an algorithm which again moves towards a solution in small steps. This time, however, the steps are formed heuristically.

- Hybrid methods use a combination of approaches. Their motivation is usually real-time performance.

Differential Methods using the Jacobian

We begin by restating the enabling equation:

$$\dot{\theta} = J^{-1}\dot{X}$$

which in an iterative framework becomes

$$\Delta\theta = J(\theta)^{-1}\Delta X$$

At each iteration we move the end effector ΔX nearer to its goal and calculate the corresponding change $\Delta\theta$ in the state vector. The iteration is complete when the end effector reaches its goal. We can proceed as:

$\Delta X =$ small movement in the direction of the goal

repeat

$\Delta\theta = J^{-1}(\theta)\,(\Delta X)$

$X = f(\theta + \Delta\theta)$

calculate new value of J and invert

$X = X + \Delta X$

until goal is reached

An iteration for a three link arm is shown in Figure 11.4. Problems in the iteration can arise from tracking errors which is when the desired change in X is different from the actual change. Tracking errors will occur when ΔX is too large and are given by:

$$\|J(\theta) - \Delta X\|$$

A more intelligent iteration must then be employed which involves starting with a ΔX, evaluating the tracking error and subdividing ΔX until the error falls below a threshold.

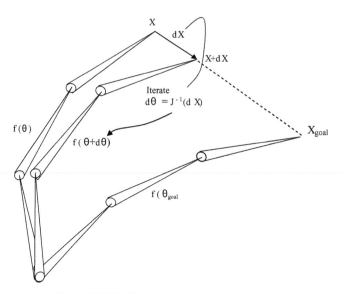

X

dX

$X+dX$

Iterate
$$d\theta = J^{-1}(d\ X)$$

$f(\theta)$

$f(\theta+d\theta)$

$f(\theta_{goal})$

X_{goal}

Figure A9.1.2. One iteration in a 3 link arm

A major difficulty with this approach is that for any system of interest, the Jacobian is not square—for practical structures the dimension of X is less than that of θ—and hence it cannot be inverted. The practical reason for this is that skeletons are highly redundant—they possess more degrees of freedom than they require to reach their goal. A good example is the human arm. If we consider, without concerning ourselves with the complexity of the hand, that the end effector has six DOFs (for position and orientation), then this is one less than a simple seven DOF skeleton for the arm. This consists of two spherical joints (shoulder and wrist) plus one hinge joint (the elbow). This is reflected in the physical situation that if we fix the hand and the shoulder in a desired position the elbow is free to swivel in an arc which is constrained by a plane normal to the line from the shoulder joint to the wrist joint (Figure A9.1.3). This motion is caused by the redundant DOF in the shoulder joint. This is called the elbow circle.

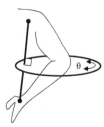

θ

Figure A9.1.3. The elbow swivel angle. The elbow is free to move in a plane normal to the line from the shoulder to the wrist without affecting the position of the hand.

The extra degree of freedom means that there is an infinity of solutions, and we say that the structure can undergo self-motion. That is, the structure can move and take up a new pose without moving its end effector. Alternatively, we can say that the Jacobian transformation has a null space containing an infinite number of joint space rates that result in no end effector motion. For a redundant structure, whatever method we use will result in a single solution out of an infinity of solutions. We exploit this by choosing a solution that satisfies some desirable constraints. In other words, we incorporate the constraints into the solution method.

Kinematically redundant manipulators offer certain critical advantages over nonredundant ones. In particular, we can include obstacle avoidance, self-collision avoidance and singularity avoidance into the solution. In general terms, we say that a redundant structure is more dexterous.

This situation can be modelled mathematically as

$$\Delta\theta = J^+ \Delta X + (IJ^+ J) \Delta Z$$

where J^+ is a square matrix known as the pseudo-inverse, ΔX is referred to as the main task, I is the identity matrix of joint space dimension and ΔZ is known as the secondary task.

The pseudo inverse J^+ of the Jacobian J (an mxn matrix of rank r) is given by:

$$J^+ = \begin{cases} (J^T J)^{-1} J^T & \text{if } m > n = r \\ J^T (J J^T)^{-1} & \text{if } r = m < n \end{cases}$$

The first part of the solution is called the pseudo-inverse, and the second part the homogeneous solution. The homogeneous component results in no end-effector velocity. This is diagrammed in Figure A9.1.4. In the upper diagram, the Jacobian J relates n-dimensional joint space to m-dimensional end effector velocity space $(n > m)$. In the second diagram the pseudo inverse J^+ relates m dimensional end-effector space to an m dimensional subspace of the joint velocity space. (IJ^+J) is an operator that selects those components of ΔZ that lie in the set of homogeneous solutions. That is, we can set ΔZ as a secondary task because it projects into the null space the end effector .

Secondary tasks can thus be used to satisfy constraints other than the goal. This is known as exploiting the redundancy. For example, we can change the pose of a figure without altering the end-effector position. To do this we proceed as follows:

evaluate $\quad\quad \Delta\theta = J^+ \Delta X$

evaluate $\quad\quad \theta_t = \theta_{t-1} + \Delta\theta$

evaluate $\quad\quad \Delta Z \quad$ (see next section for an example)

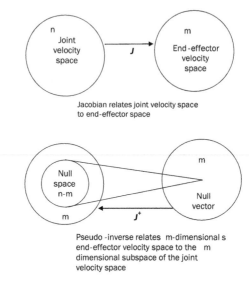

Jacobian relates joint velocity space
to end-effector space

Pseudo -inverse relates m-dimensional s
end-effector velocity space to the m
dimensional subspace of the joint
velocity space

Figure A9.1.4. The Jacobian and the pseudo-inverse.

project into null space by evaluating

$$(I - J^+J)\, \Delta Z$$

add result to θ_t

Secondary Tasks—Joint Limits

Possibly the most common secondary task is to ensure a good joint angle pose. For example, generate a pose that minimises the joint angle motion away from some desired configuration—say the mid-range angles. To do this, we set ΔZ to be the gradient:

$$\Delta Z = -2(\theta - \theta_M)$$

where θ is the current pose and θ_M is the mid-range pose.

More generally we can write:

$$\Delta Z = \nabla H \qquad \text{where } H = \sum_{i=1}^{no\_of\_DOFs} \alpha_i(\theta_i - \theta_i^M)$$

where α_i $(0 \le \alpha_i \le 1)$ is a gain value defining the stiffness of the joint.

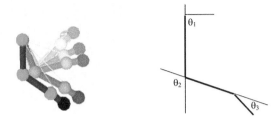

Figure A9.1.5. A differential IK solution for a three-link structure using joint angle constraints. *Courtesy Michael Meredith, University of Sheffield, UK.*

Figure A9.1.5 shows the influence of joint angle constraints injected into a differential solution. The end effector (coloured blue) of the three-link planar structure is moved to simulate an animated goal, and the constraints are

$$-90° \leq \theta_1 \leq 90°$$

$$0 \leq \theta_2 \leq 140°$$

$$-10° \leq \theta_3 \leq 10°$$

Figure A9.1.6 shows the same structure with its end effector placed in (approximately) the same positions, but this time with the joint constraints removed.

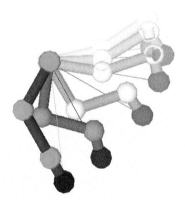

Figure A9.1.6. The three-link structure with all joint constraints removed. Compare with previous solution. *Courtesy Michael Meredith, University of Sheffield, UK.*

Chapter Ten

Facial Animation

Introduction

Believable character animation is perhaps the last frontier in computer graphics, and within that field, facial animation has proven to be the most challenging. The difficulties are obvious and do not need to be stated in much detail. Facial expressions are quite subtle, and this implies that we must use a very high resolution mesh. And controlling the motion of, say, 10^4, using a number of control points two to three orders of magnitude less is a difficult problem and one that is still a vigorous research area.

We can say that facial animation and associated body gestures fall into five categories:

- simple global movement of the head;
- simple movement of the eyes;
- complex simultaneous deformation of different parts of the face to form expressions;
- speech—complex deformation/movement of the lips, jaws and tongue; and
- appropriate gestures particularly of, but not restricted to, arms and hands that accompany speech.

In this chapter we will be examining the third and fourth categories. A brief description of the main difficulties now follows.

- **Integration.** Expressive visual speech involves all of the above movements, and a believable model has to integrate them into a whole, driven by appropriate parameters.

- **Identity/uniqueness.** A second difficulty arises from the uniqueness of faces. Ideally, we would like an underlying deformation model which admitted different 'masks'. Currently the most common manifestation of this approach is (photographic) texture mapping onto a generic polygon mesh. The mesh vertices are then animated. The identity problem is absent from, or does not concern us to the same extent in other aspects of human animation (body and fabric for instance).

- **Rendering quality.** The detail of expressions (wrinkles etc.) is difficult to render convincingly using standard geometric and shading models. At a finer level of detail, rendering of skin texture is also not currently accomplished to high quality. And in the absence of convincing photorealistic quality, we sometimes resort to cartoon-like characters.

Facial animation has a long history, and most models fall into the two-level paradigm with a low-resolution controller level accepting the animation and controlling the deformation of a high resolution mesh. This idea was first implemented by K. Waters in 1987 [WATE87]. Waters used a controller that attempted to imitate, to some extent, the action of facial muscles in deforming the skin of a face. He used two types of virtual muscle models: a linear muscle that pulled and a sphincter muscle that squeezed. The field of influence associated with a particular muscle controlled the movement of vertices in the mesh as a function of their position relative to the reference point or attachment point of the muscle in the mesh. Although the resolution of the facial mesh was low (see Figure 10.6) this model was successful in animating expressions such as anger and joy, albeit in a somewhat cartoonlike manner. This was the classical approach of a deformer whose range of influence controls many mesh points. Its importance at the time was that it showed the potential of this animation method rather than providing a high-quality solution.

Perhaps the most important aspect of facial animation is visual speech, and it is the case that this area, of high importance across all computer applications, has lagged behind progress in audio speech synthesis. Figure 10.1 emphasises this point and shows a visual speech module as part of an 'anthropomorphic' interface. Such interfaces must eventually predominate in man-machine communication; the implications of this technology for computer games are obvious.

Using MoCap to record facial motion is difficult because, unlike the motion of limbs, the motion of the face surface is subtle and involves important small-scale movement, such as creases and wrinkling, which is impossible to capture from the limited spatial density of markers. This, of course, contrasts with the quality of captured body motion, whose success has spawned an entire industry.

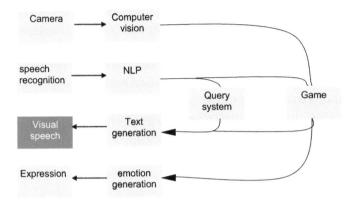

Figure 10.1. An 'anthropomorphic' interface with visual speech as one of the modules.

On the other hand we can use MoCap to record large-scale motion of the lips and jaw. Because of these difficulties, the current methodology in games is for artists to model static poses as keys or morph targets—see, for example, Chapter 9 and[BEES04]. These then form keys and in between expression motion is interpolated in real time. This system enables good artistic control, but using this method for visual speech is problematic.

Despite the drawbacks of MoCap, we shall examine the use of the technology to capture speech motion and using the data to generate visual speech on arbitrary facial meshes.

This chapter is not meant to be a comprehensive treatment of facial animation [1], but is a description of techniques that may be of use in the games industry, in particular the use of MoCap. We now look at a range of surface deformers which have or can be used to control large-scale (lips and jaw) facial motion.

Surface Deformers

Free-Form Deformers (FFDs)

As we stated above, subtle facial expressions require high resolution meshes and deformation control system of low resolution (small number of control points) capable of deforming a very large number of vertices (say $>10^4$). The generic technique that best satisfies that requirement is SOFFDs, or Surface Oriented Free Form Deformers.

. . . .

[1] A comprehensive introduction into the literature of facial animation and its applications is given at mambo.ucsc.edu/psl/fan.html.

SOFFDs developed out of a method called Free Form Deformation (FFD), introduced into the graphics community in 1986 by T. Sedeburg *et al.* [SEDE86]. Sedeburg's breakthrough was to realize that an object model of any representation—say for example—a triangular mesh could be 'embedded' in the space of a tricubic parametric patch or volume and be deformed in an 'expected' manner as the patch was deformed by its control-point motion.

We can define a tricubic Bézier (see also Appendix 7.1) patch as:

$$Q(u,v,w) = \sum_{i=0}^{3} \sum_{j=0}^{3} \sum_{k=0}^{3} P_{ijk} B_i(u) B_j(v) B_k(w) \qquad (10.1)$$

where

P_{ijk} are a lattice of 4x4x4 control points

$B_i(u) = B_j(v) = B_k(w)$ are the Bézier basis functions:

$$B_0(u) = (1-u)^3$$
$$B_1(u) = 3u(1-u)^2$$
$$B_2(u) = 3u^2(1-u)$$
$$B_3(u) = u^3$$

This control grid is the volumetric equivalent of a planar patch—where the 16 control points lie in the plane of the patch. Now, if we move points in the lattice, we deform the volume. The FFD model of surface deformation is a three-step method:

1. We embed a polygon mesh object in the tricubic volume. To do this we express the vertex coordinates in lattice space. If (x,y,z) is the position of vertex p we have:

$$p = X_0 + uU + vV + wW$$

and

$$u = u(x - X_0)$$
$$v = v(y - Y_0)$$
$$w = w(z - Z_0)$$

where (X_0, Y_0, Z_0) defines the origin of UVW space.

2. The lattice is deformed by moving the control points pulling each vertex p to a new position p'.

3. The value of p' is obtained by evaluating Equation 10.1 with the (u, v, w) coordinates of p and the new control point positions.

The particular advantage of FFDs is that the number of lattice points can be, and generally is, much lower than the number of object vertices. Effectively, a FFD acts as a device that accepts linear transformations on its controls points and transmits these to the vertices of the object to be deformed. Although FFDs provide an elegant shape deformation model, they do have disadvantages. There is a relationship between the complexity of the deformation required and the difficulty of achieving this by deforming a FFD lattice, and for highly complex deformations we need a dense control lattice. Figure 10.2 shows an FFD being used to deform facial features. The upper illustration shows an FFD emplaced in the face mesh, and the lower illustration shows how moving the control points deforms the face. In this simple example, the number of control points is very low and we can only alter facial features at a large scale.

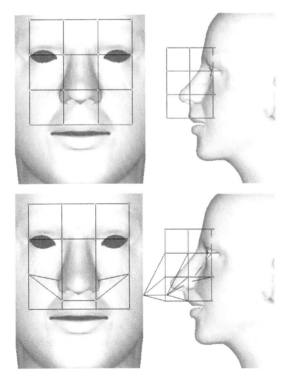

Figure 10.2. An FFD applied to the nose region of a face mesh. *Courtesy James Edge, University of Sheffield.*

Surface-Oriented Free Form-Deformers (SOFFD)

In 2000 K. Singh *et al.* developed a related technique called a SOFFD (surface oriented free form deformer)[SING00]. This deformer is also implemented in the modelling and animation system *Maya* (wherein they are termed wrap deformers) and can be used as a general deformation technique, although the authors emphasise its utility in automating the skinning of characters. The technique relates to FFDs in that the deformation motion is controlled by the relationship between a reference (control) surface, originally bound to the object to be deformed, and a movable surface.

Comparing it with an FFD, we say that it emphasises deformation based on surfaces whereas the FFD is based on a volume.[2] The motivation for this is that we end up with a deforming control—in this case a surface—which visually correlates with an underlying object to be deformed. This contrasts with a conventional FFD where the deforming entity is a 3D lattice of control points. This means that it is clearer how to move the deforming structure to effect the desired change in the deformed structure. Another advantage over the FFD is that the equivalent of the control points can be arbitrarily distributed, making it easy to introduce local control where required.

In SOFFDs the deformer is a triple $\{D,R,\text{local}\}$ where:

D is the *driver* surface,

R is the reference surface originally bound to and registered with the object surface and

local is a scalar.

A reference surface R will usually be a low resolution scaled version of the object mesh, and originally R and D are coincident. D is then moved, and the deviation between R and D controls the deformation of the object. The parameter local controls the locality of the deformation. The registration phase of the process calculates influence weights based on a distance metric which controls, along with the R-D deviation, the deformation of object points by a control element. A control element on R is a triangular facet and the function

$$f(d, \text{local}) = \frac{1}{1 + d^{\text{local}}}$$

is calculated for each point on the object surface, where d is the closest distance from the object point to a face of R. For each point x and each control element k a weight:

$$w_k^x = f(d_k^x, \text{local})$$

....

[2] A consequence of the volume nature of the FFD is that we may have to control all the points in the lattice as if the object we are deforming was a volume rather than a surface.

is determined so that each x has associated with it a weight vector. In practice the number of control elements associated with each object point will be small.

The faces of R—the control elements—also define, for each face, a face coordinate system derived from two edges and their cross product and in addition to calculating the influence weights the registration phase computes the coordinates of the undeformed objects points x in this local face coordinate system.

The deformation phase proceeds with faces in D changing shape, position and orientation and maps each object point x to x^{def}. A point moves such that its local position in the face coordinate space of D remains the same as D moves. This is achieved as follows. The world space position of x^{def} deformed by face element k is given by:

$$x_k^{\text{def}} = x_k^R M_k^D \qquad \text{where } x_k^R \text{ is the local coordinate of } x \text{ in } R$$

M_k^D is the transformation matrix for face k of the driver

x^{def}, the deformed position of x taking into account the n faces it is associated with, is then:

$$x^{\text{def}} = \sum_{k=1}^{n} w_k^x x_k^{\text{def}}$$

A simple example using spheres is shown in Figure 10.3. The object mesh is contained within the deformer mesh, which is also a sphere.

This method is also suitable for skinning. The driving surface D is bound to the skeleton—rather than the skin of the object. D then controls the animation of the skin as the skeleton is animated. In this context, D is a low resolution version of the skin, and an artist is faced with the task of associating D, which will bear a close resemblance to the skin surface but is low resolution, with the skeleton instead of the skin.

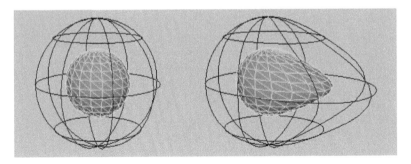

Figure 10.3. As simple example of SOFFDs using a sphere object.

Bézier-Triangle Induced Deformation (BIDs)

We now move on to a type of SOFFD called BIDs (Bézier-Triangle Induced Deformations) [EDGE04], which has been found to be suitable for controlling facial expressions. It is particularly suitable for facial MoCap, where the number of face markers with the corresponding animation control is likely to be very low compared to the facial mesh. The BIDs patch topology is similar to that of the facial mesh enabling motion of the BIDs vertices to control the facial mesh in a manner that is visually convincing. In our application MoCap markers on a face correspond to the control points—the vertices—of the BIDs surface.

The BIDs deformation technique constructs a deformer surface as a triangulation of the control points and proceeds by defining a one-to-one mapping from vertices in the target surface onto the deformer surface. Due to the fact that the deformer is composed of Bézier triangles, a certain degree of surface and deformation continuity can be maintained. Two stages are required by the BIDs deformation technique, projection, and reconstruction.

BIDs Projection

In order to define a parameterisation of the target geometry, each vertex is projected onto the deformer surface along the surface normal N of the closest point (Figure 10.4). This is possible because the deformer surface is constrained such that its unitary normal map is at least C^0 continuous, and provides a full coverage of the target mesh.

For a vertex, p, the closest point in the parametric domain of the ith Bézier triangle can be found by minimizing the squared distance. This problem is equivalent to finding the root of Equation 10.1, where B_i is the biparametric

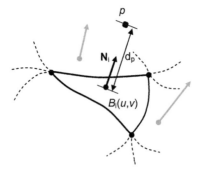

Figure 10.4. Projection of vertex p onto the closest triangular patch B_i.

expression of the ith triangular patch.

$$\left(\frac{\partial\|p - B_i(u,y)\|^2}{\partial u}\right)^2 + \left(\frac{\partial\|p - B_i(u,y)\|^2}{\partial v}\right)^2 \qquad (10.1)$$

Solutions may be found for (u_p, v_p) that fall out of the parametric domain of the patch, however, taking into account a coverage property, it can be stated that at least one of the tuples found will lie inside its respective domain triangle. It must be noted that in the case of cubic and quartic Bézier surfaces, the degree of this expansion prevents us from using an analytical solution. In these cases, a numerical approach must be taken. Due to the regularity of low-degree Bézier triangles, a Newton-Raphson gradient descent approach should be capable of finding the correct minima of Equation 10.1. To ensure convergence, the starting point for the optimisation procedure is derived from a coarse sampling of the surface. To complete the parameterisation for a vertex, p, the projected distance along the surface normal, d_p, is stored. Given a parameterisation, (u_p, v_p, d_p), each of the target vertices can be directly reconstructed from the deformer surface as described in the next section. The fact that a parameterisation now exists can be used in several contexts, as we shall see.

There are continuity issues—we need to move the control points in the BIDs surface such that the mesh deforms with at least C^0. This means that the BIDs surface must exhibit G^1 continuity.

BIDs Reconstruction

The second step of the algorithm makes use of the defined parameterisation to reconstruct the deformed target geometry over the control surface spanned by the displaced control points (displaced in subsequent frames of animation). This is the inverse process to the projection described in the previous section. The deformation of a vertex, p, projected onto the ith Bézier triangle is defined as:

$$p_{def} = B_i'(u_p, v_p) + d_p n_i'(u_p, v_p)$$

where d_p is defined in Figure 10.4, and B_i' and n_i' are the deformed Bézier triangle and normal respectively, i.e., deformed according to the displaced control points and additional continuity considerations.

Thus, given a parameterisation of a target surface, the deformed surface can simply be reconstructed by re-evaluating the necessary Bézier triangle patches.

Figure 10.5 shows BIDs in action. Figure 10.5(a) shows markers on the face of a MoCap subject. These form the vertices of the BIDs surface (Figure 10.5(b)) whose motion produced the two images in Figure 10.5(c). This solves the obvious

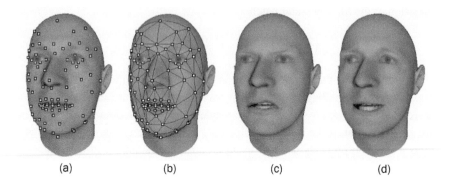

(a)   (b)   (c)   (d)

Figure 10.5. BIDs and MoCap. (a) MoCap markers. (b) The BIDs surface. (c) Motion of the vertices of the BIDs surface. *Courtesy M. Sanchez and J. Edge, University of Sheffield.*

problem that distinguishes facial MoCap from body MoCap, which is, the system only records the motion of sparse markers, not the motion of the entire face. This contrasts with body MoCap, where we record the motion of all the bones in the skeleton.

Visual Speech from Static Poses—Dominance Functions

As we discussed in the introduction, visual speech is a long-awaited milestone in Human Computer Interfaces (HCI) which also has implication in game player interfaces. Currently, the topic is very much a research area, and there are significant difficulties in producing convincing visual speech.

We begin by examining the use of static poses called visemes (visual-phonemes). A viseme is a static pose of the face when uttering a single phoneme, and the idea is to create animation by using visemes as keys and interpolating. The data flow in such a system is shown in Figure 10.6 (the head is the low resolution face mesh created by Waters as discussed in the introduction.) At run time, visemes are already stored as muscle parameters, although they have been shown as two separate stages in the diagram.

Visemes can be considered as the basic unit of visual speech and can be described as the extreme lip shapes that correspond to basic auditory speech units. They form a minimally distinct set representing the sounds in a language. To drive visual speech from text, a sentence is broken into a sequence of phonemes for each of which we have an equivalent viseme. We then need some method for interpolating the visemes.

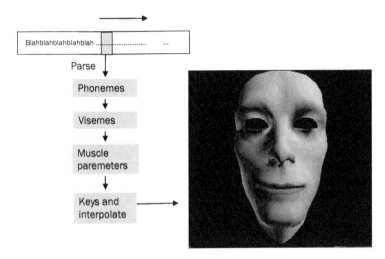

Figure 10.6. An ideal talking head system with (arbitrary) text as input.

Thus, in theory all we have to do is to parse the text for phonemes and the head will talk. The question is: how convincingly?

The biggest problem in visual speech is handling the coarticulation effect. Coarticulation refers to changes in the audio signal, and consequently in the facial shape, for a particular sound which are a function of what sounds have come before and what sounds are going to follow. The apparent importance of this phenomenon means that using phonemes, in the form of independent discrete units, as a basis for driving visual speech cannot be correct.

The extent of the time window over which coarticulation effects can occur can be up to five phonemes before (backward coarticulation) and after (forward coarticulation) the current one. Forward coarticulation often occurs when a series of consonants is followed by a vowel. Coarticulation effects have, of course, a visual as well as an auditory context. Different sounds for the same phoneme imply different lip shapes. A good example (in English) is the rounding of the lips at the beginning of the word "stew" in anticipation of the "ew" sound.

A scheme for morphing target values of the parameters of visemes was introduced by M. Cohen *et al.* [COHE93]. This assigned a dominance function for every parameter of every viseme. The idea is that coarticulation effects can be modelled combining the target values by a factor which is the sum of the dominant functions that are currently active. Figure 10.7 shows an example of three dominant functions for targets T_0, T_1 and T_2. The functions have a range that encompasses adjacent targets and, in this example, cause target T_0 to be interpolated exactly, whereas T_1 and T_2 'suffer' from the dominance of T_0 and are not interpolated exactly.

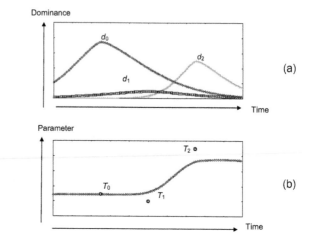

Figure 10.7. (a) Dominance functions for three targets. (b) Interpolated parameter using the dominance functions.

Visual Speech from MoCap

In the previous section, we stated that the main problem in creating visual speech from static poses was implementing coarticulation. The dominance function solution, although simple in concept, requires much detailed tuning to produce visually correct speech. A way to sidestep the coarticulation problem is to use MoCap fragments for visual speech. Figure 10.8 shows an illustration of facial MoCap for speech showing the number and position of the markers and a head frame for capturing global head motion.

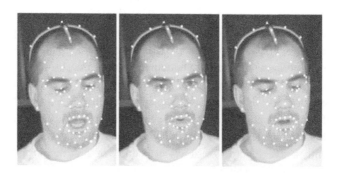

Figure 10.8. Facial MoCap for speech.

As we have discussed, although MoCap cannot capture subtle motion of the face, it can be used to capture the motion of speech, which involves large-scale motion of the lips and jaw. The advantage that accrues is that if we can use 'atomic' units of sufficient length (whole words and phrases) we do not have to cater for coarticulation—since this will already be contained, to a greater or lesser extent, within the MoCap fragments.

Audio speech synthesis is now a highly developed technology and one of the reasons for the high quality of current synthesizers is that they concatenate speech fragments of varying length to make a sentence. Using the same concatenation approach in visual speech can achieve high quality results in the animation. This is a compromise approach that limits the size of the databases (for both motion and audio) to manageable extents. For example, storing diphones (phone to phone transitions) requires about 1500 units for British English. Storing syllables, words, phrases and sentences for a particular context increases the volume substantially, and a balance must be struck between the quality of the concatenation of speech fragments and the size of the database.

The same consideration applies to speech facial motion; obviously, we can only capture the motion of speech fragments for a limited domain—an example of which is a talking head clock which tells the time on demand. Such applications build novel utterances from prerecorded fragments. So in this case, we would construct a sentence such as:

"the time is now/exactly one/in the afternoon"

from three fragments.[3] Although this application in practice would be accessed by a single request for the time, it is easy to see how this approach could be extended to function as Figure 10.1 suggests, where the input would come from game logic and user interaction.

In this application, MoCap fragments of varying length drive a BIDs control surface, which then controls lip and jaw motion of the target head. Examples from this approach are shown in Figure 10.9 at intervals of five frames. The MoCap data has already been retargetted as we discuss later.

Recording the motion fragments for the application domain is only part of the story. We cannot simply bind the audio to the motion fragments and then replay the fragments as the original speaking clock did. This would give poor quality fragmented speech. Instead, we must build a speech synthesiser system which

. . . .

[3] This technology has a longer history than you might have expected. In 1935, the GPO (General Post Office) in the UK developed an electromechanical talking clock for telephone subscribers. The kernel of the system was a set of four continually rotating glass discs on which was recorded a female voice—a circular version of the linear optical recording on film. The discs were accessed by electromechanical relays, and when a subscriber dialled the talking clock number, the relays would connect to the discs in sequence, constructing the reply: *"The time is now/hours/minutes/seconds"* See http://web.ukonline.co.uk/freshwater/clocks/spkgclock.htm for an illustration of this massive machine.

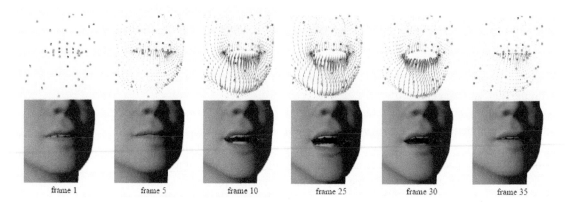

frame 1   frame 5   frame 10   frame 25   frame 30   frame 35

Figure 10.9. Extracts from a speech animation driven by retargetted MoCap fragments. Also shown are corresponding vertex trajectories. *Courtesy M. Sanchez and J. Edge, University of Sheffield.*

assembles and blends fragments to produce reasonably natural sounding speech. This can be done using Festival,[4] a powerful tool for constructing user-specific synthesisers.

A number of considerations are involved in both processing the MoCap and building the speech synthesis. For motion, we have the following:

- **Preprocessing.** Rigid motion of the head is removed from the data (this is captured from the motion of an attached head frame).

- **Unit generation.** The motion data is chopped up into fragments representing sentences words and diphones (phone to phone transitions).

- **Motion synthesis.** Combinations of motion fragments are concatenated and synchronised with the audio to generate novel speech utterances.

- **Retargetting.** The motion is retargetted onto the desired facial mesh.

- **Animation.** The retargetted motion animates the BIDs control surface and produces facial motion of the high resolution mesh.

For speech synthesis, we have these considerations:

- **Unit selection.** Units must be selected from the database to generate the utterance. Given a target utterance, we need to find a selection   of units

....

[4] Festival offers a general framework for building speech synthesis systems as well as including examples of various modules. As a whole, it offers full text to speech through a number of APIs: from shell level, through a scheme command interpreter, as a C++ library, from Java, and an Emacs interface. Festival is multilingual (currently English (British and American), and Spanish) though English is the most advanced.

to synthesise it. The key factor here is to choose fragments of as long a duration as possible to match with the capture motion data.

- **Alignment and resampling**. Each of the selected units must be phonetically aligned such that the motion is synchronised with the speech. As a consequence of this alignment, speech and motion fragments must be resampled to give a consistent frame-rate for animation. Resampling is carried out using radial basis functions.

- **Blending**. Having aligned and resampled the motions, overlapping sections must be blended to achieve a consistent trajectory over the synthesized utterance. This is done using a nonlinear blending function.

Retargetting Facial MoCap Data

The difference between a head used to MoCap and a target head in a game is likely to be substantial and for artists to be able to use facial MoCap, accurate retargetting is necessary. This is particularly critical when using MoCap fragments for visual speech—inaccuracies in lip and jaw movement are highly noticeable and persist in many current games.

Retargetting MoCap for body animation is a well researched problem and real-time solutions now exist (see, for example [SHIN01]). This involves dealing with the change in the relative scale of bones in the skeleton. However, we cannot use these techniques in facial MoCap. The dimensions of the different faces vary, and so also does the scale of the motion. We have to deal with the different motion within the marker set between different faces, where the correspondence between different faces is highly nonlinear. These factors are clearly visible in Figure 10.10.

A significant advantage of the BIDs controller, which is used as a deformer, is that it is also used for the retargetting of facial MoCap data. It controls the deformation of the mesh due to marker motion and it also facilitates the necessary change in scale between the captured head and the target head.

In this context, retargetting means:

- adapting the (BIDs) control surface to the target geometry and

- scaling the motion of the markers according to the change of the physiognomy between the MoCap subject and the target mesh.

The first stage involves finding the correspondence between two static meshes—a reference mesh and the target mesh. The reference mesh is a base mesh with vertices corresponding to the marker positions in the MoCap set-up and is deformed to fit the target model. This warp is initiated by an initial manual

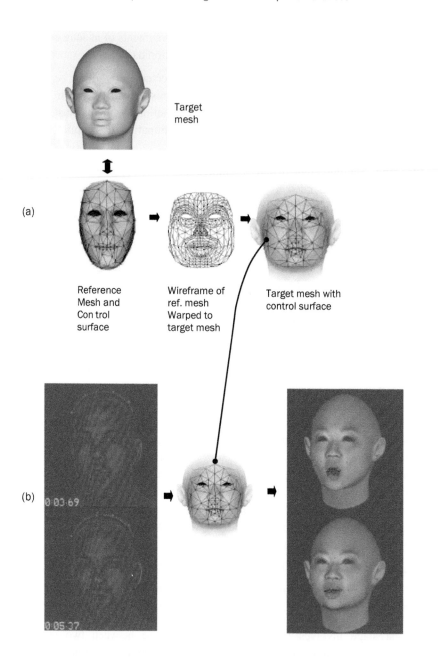

Figure 10.10. Retargetting facial animation. *Images courtesy M. Sanchez and James Edge, University of Sheffield.*

correspondence and subsequently uses radial basis functions (for scattered data interpolation) and an energy minimisation to maintain the structural integrity of the reference mesh while minimising the distance between the two surfaces. The vertices of the target mesh then acquire a labelling which defines the correspondence between the MoCap markers and the target mesh.

The process is analogous to the well-known method where B-splines adapt to image contours in 2D space. The internal energy maintaining the structure of the 3D surface snake is formed by the combination of the strain and bending terms, and the external energy is the distance term pulling the surface as close as possible to the target mesh. The process is described in full detail in [JUNY01] where it is described as 'expression cloning'.

A visualisation of this correspondence is shown in Figure 10.10(a) where the images from left to right are:

1. a rendered reference mesh with the control surface superimposed,

2. wireframe of the reference mesh adapted to the target mesh and

3. the adapted reference mesh which enables the control surface to be bound to the target mesh.

Figure 10.10(b) is a visualisation of the adaptation which is in effect a volume warp. The markers on the subject bind to the vertices on the target mesh. As the markers move on the MoCap subject's face, these are applied to the vertices of the target control surface, and hence the same volume warp is undergone and the goal of transforming the animation from the MoCap subject to the target subject is achieved. An example frame from a speech animation using this method is shown in Figure 10.10(b).

Small Scale Motion—Wrinkling

It does not have to be emphasised that the modelling of facial expressions is an important part of the believability of facial animation. We have seen that the BIDs method gives good control over the deformation of the facial mesh, and in this respect, it can be used to model the large-scale deformation as has been demonstrated. Small-scale motion—wrinkling—needs to be included in any accurate modelling of the face and needs to be a process operating in parallel with large-scale deformation.

The need to model small-scale deformation is clearly shown in Figure 10.11, which shows the BIDs controller deforming static expressions retargetted from photographs of a head with markers. Here, it can be seen that the lack of wrinkling on the synthetic head detract from its realism compared with the photographs (see [SANC04] for a detailed explanation). Compare this image with Figure 10.14, which has normal mapped wrinkles implemented.

Figure 10.11. Comparing wrinkled reality with a synthetic head driven by BIDs (cf. Figure 10.14). *Courtesy M. Sanchez and J. Edge, University of Sheffield.*

Wrinkling has been implemented on high resolution polygon meshes by perturbing the geometry, using bump maps or photographic textures. Photo-texture has perhaps been the most popular of these options, but it suffers from the obvious disadvantage that the lighting is fixed at the time of creation.

Another possibility is to use normal maps. These are effectively static representations of wrinkles and can be captured using shape from shading techniques. See, for example, [RUSH98], which reconstructs normal maps from an object. This method only requires a moderately priced camera and lighting set-up.

The theory of this approach is straightforward. We begin by defining the reflected radiance, L_r, from the point on a perfect Lambertian[5] surface which is illuminated by a distance small source (Figure 10.12):

$$L_r = \rho\left(\frac{L_i \Delta\omega}{\pi}\right)\mathbf{N}\cdot\mathbf{l}$$

where ρ is the reflectance, $\mathbf{l}$ is the light direction vector, $\mathbf{N}$ is the surface normal and $\Delta\omega$ is the solid angle, which can be considered over the surface for a distant light source.

Consider that we have three light sources and three images of the object, illuminated by each light source in turn. Then we define $L_{r,i}$ to be the reflected radiance when light source i is active. An approximation of the surface normal

....

[5] The assumption of a Lambertian surface implies zero specular component, which in the case of the face can be achieved with matte make-up.

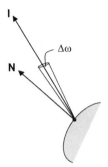

Figure 10.12. Reflected radiance from a point.

N is then given by

$$
\begin{bmatrix} N_x \\ N_y \\ N_z \end{bmatrix} = \frac{1}{\rho L'_0} \begin{bmatrix} I_1^x & I_1^y & I_1^z \\ I_2^x & I_2^y & I_2^z \\ I_3^x & I_3^y & I_3^z \end{bmatrix} \begin{bmatrix} L_{r,1} \\ L_{r,2} \\ L_{r,3} \end{bmatrix}
$$

where $L'_0 = L_0 \Delta\omega/\pi$ is the constant radiance emitted by each light source.

This procedure captures the normal map at a point, and in order to evaluate a map over an entire face a 3D model has to be provided. This can be done by reverse stereoscopy from a rig of three cameras and stick-on face markers. The markers are used to specify a BIDs surface, which then provides the required 3D surface. An illustration of a normal map extracted using this method is shown in Figure 10.13.

Sanchez *et al.* state [SANC04] that although this procedure is not accurate enough to extract good quality static maps, it enables the differences between

Figure 10.13. A normal map of an expression extracted using shape from shading. *Courtesy M. Sanchez, J. Edge, University of Sheffield.*

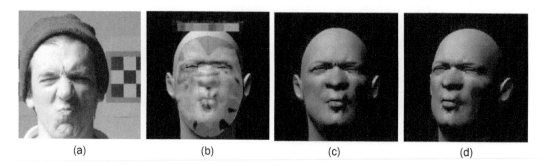

(a) (b) (c) (d)

Figure 10.14. Wrinkle model. (a) Reality. (b) Strain analysis of BIDs deformed model. (c) and (d) Results rendered with normal map. *Courtesy M. Sanchez and J. Edge, University of Sheffield.*

normal maps from different facial poses to be measured and facilitates a dynamic functional model.

The ideal is to model the dynamic behaviour of skin tissue as it moves from one expression to another and Sanchez *et al.* suggest modelling the driving mechanism of the wrinkling process. They conclude that wrinkling, is a local phenomenon that forms into patterns determined by the position of permanent crease lines and by the magnitude of the compressive force in specific directions. To model the dynamic behaviour of skin wrinkling they define a functional model of the variations in the normal map across different expressions, parameterised on the magnitude and direction of compression.

The markers on the captured head enable not only a representation of a 3D model as described but can also be used to analyse the deformations in the captured poses. Sanchez *et al.* use the Cauchy infinitesimal strain tensor [SANC04], which represents both the magnitude and direction of the strain. This is done in tangent space. Now that compression data is available a polynomial approximation to the normal maps based on the components of the strain tensor can be built. And in this way we obtain a sampling space for 16 poses. Some results are shown in Figure 10.14.

For the sake of brevity, missing from this explanation are details on the division of the face into patches and parameterisation issues; again, see the original report for a full explanation.

Chapter Eleven

Managing Game
Development

Introduction

In this chapter, we describe a system for managing game development. In particular, we describe how to bring various elements together to build a game system beginning with the management and integration of shaders. In the course of the chapter, we will demonstrate the construction of an actual system that will facilitate the development of games that require high-quality animation and rendering. Important code fragments for this system will be given in the text; the full source code can be found on the CD-ROM. We will also look at the design of common game objects and their behaviour.

Integrating Shaders into a System

Shaders are not isolated entities but are elements that will eventually be used in a game. There are a number of problems involved in the integration of shaders into a game or a similar application as a CAAD (Computer-Aided Architectural Design) system. As we have seen, shaders require unique parameter sets from the application in the form of uniform and variable parameters. These requirements vary amongst different shaders. For example, a shadow volume shader requires the application to render the geometry in a specific way, which is totally different to the lighting shader requirements.

Render Profiles

Ideally we would like a game Software Development Kit (SDK) to be as general as possible and to allow the end user—developer or programmer—to add new shaders, modify existing shaders according to the demand of each particular game object and effect. And such a system is what we attempt to do in this chapter.

The simplest approach would be to have the engine itself know about all shaders and manipulate them (load and set their parameters) as needed. But adopting this approach would mean that the system would not be amenable to modifications.

A better approach, that goes some way to realizing the ideal goal, is to use a render profile manager. This means we define a base class for a render profile with virtual functions such as test/load/reset/draw. We can then derive different render profile objects, each having a different set of hardware requirements. At load time, the engine can query each render profile for its availability in current running hardware. Each render profile is responsible for interfacing the shaders required for that profile, and the engine does not have to know specific details about shader parameters and attributes. In this way, we can add and modify shaders by working with a single class.

Figure 11.1 shows render profile architecture. Using this we can have multiple render profiles, each derived from the same base render profile class and each interfacing with different shader sets. Different render profiles will require a different set of shaders, and some shaders will be common to more than one set. For example, two lighting shaders working in eye space could share a common vertex program for transforming data into eye space. The general idea is to have

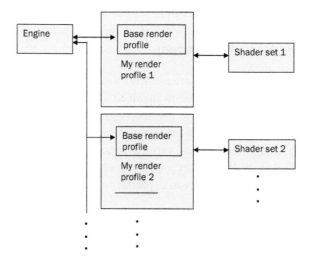

Figure 11.1. Render profile architecture.

shaders, of minimum complexity, which perform an elemental task rather than unique, complex shaders that have been developed for a particular game.

Another important facility that this architecture enables is the creation of multiple instances of the same render profile, each using a different Cg profile. For example, we may have multiple instances of myRenderProfile1 using the same shaders but running on a multivendor ARB_FP1 Cg profile or a custom vendor NV_FP30 Cg profile.

It is important to carefully design the base render profile, as this is the main interface with the engine. Although the custom render profile to shader interface is open and customisable by the user when creating the new render profile, the engine to base render profile interface is fixed. Changes in the base render profile class will propagate to every profile created and should be avoided. Also, the generality of this interface determines the flexibility of the render profiles users will be able to implement.

An implementation for this base render profile class is shown as Listing 11.1. The full implementation and different derived render profiles can be seen in files pRenderProfile.h, pRenderProfile.cpp, pRenderProfileVert.h, pRenderProfileVert.cpp, enderProfileFrag.h and pRender ProfileFrag.cpp.

.... Listing 11.1

```
class P3D_API pRenderProfile
{
    public:
            pString name;    // profile name

    pRenderProfile()
    { }
    virtual ~pRenderProfile()
    { }
    // test is this profile can run in current hardware
    virtual         int         test()         const=0;
    // return profile capabilities
    virtual int get_caps() const=0;
    // prints profile debug info
    virtual void print(pString& str) const=0;
    // reset all loaded profile data (free shaders, etc...)
    virtual void reset()=0;
```

Base render profile class.

```
                    // load all profile data (load shaders, query parametersm, etc…)
                    virtual void load()=0;
                    // multi pass draw (draw all objects for given light)
                    virtual void draw_mp(pLight *l)=0;
        // single pass draw (draws a set of object each with its set of lights)
                    virtual void draw_sp(pArray<pRenderObject *>& o)=0;
        // draw shadows for given light
                    virtual void draw_shadows(pLight *l)=0;
                    // setup shader for given material
                    virtual void load_mat(const pMaterial *mat,int rendermode)=0;
                    // reset material setting for given material
                    virtual void unload_mat(const pMaterial *mat)=0;
    };
```

For example, the `load_mat()` and `unload_mat()` virtual methods would enable us to create a `myRenderProfile` which would pass the standard material values such as diffuse color, texture map etc. to the specific shader parameters for that render profile without having to have any knowledge of how geometry is rendered. The idea is to have all functionality common to all render profiles (such as geometry drawing loops) moved outside, and only specific code like material set-up included at each custom render profile.

Note that the two rendering structures discussed in Chapter 2 are implemented by the render profile draw methods as follows.

The first structure:

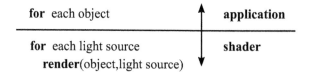

is implemented by

```
    void pRenderProfile::draw_sp(pArray<pRenderObject *>& o)
```

This method renders all objects in the list, each with a set of associated lights. In a single pass for each object, we can render multiple lights.

The second structure:

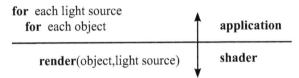

is implemented by

```
void pRenderProfile::draw_mp(pLight *l)
```

This method renders all objects illuminated by a single light source (a list of objects associated with each light is included in light object). Here, we draw the object once per light to illuminate it (multipass lighting).

When the application is initialised, we query each of the implemented render profiles for its availability in current running hardware. The profiles that are available are added to a list, and we can only have one profile loaded at a time. All geometry in a frame will be rendered with the same profile. The motivation for a profile change will come from the user of the application. It may be that a simpler profile will perform better even though a more advanced profile is available.

One alternative to this approach, which would allow per-object profile change, would be to load all available profiles at initialisation time so that we could switch profiles in-between object draws. This enables us to have objects that are not visually important using a simpler and therefore faster profile. Not all objects in a scene may need complex lighting with specular and/or advanced effects such as parallax and relief mapping. However, that would require a separate list of visible objects categorized by render profile so that we could draw them in separate batches using separate render profile objects. Per-material render profile changes would require an even more complex organization of visible objects. We would have to fragment the mesh by different materials, implying an even larger overhead.

Render Objects

The motivation for using a render object architecture (Figure 11.2) is to enable us to create and modify game objects without needing to make any modification to the rest of the engine and user interface.

Render objects are a class that defines the base object interface through which the render object manager will handle interaction between the user/engine and the game objects. To create new render objects, we derive a new class from the base render object class and implement the required virtual methods.

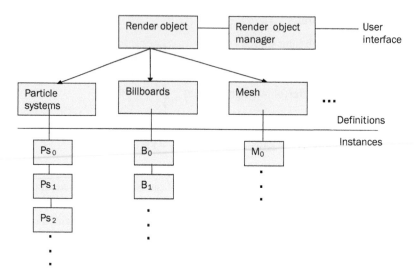

Figure 11.2. Render object architecture.

Common parameters shared by all game objects should be included in the base render object class. For example, an object name and bounding box must be present in all objects.

```
class P3D_API pRenderObject
{
    public:
        unsigned int m_type;    // object class type
        unsigned int m_id;          // object unique id
        unsigned int m_flags;   // bit flags

        // transformation matrix (translate/rotate)
        pMatrix m_transform;
        // global transformation matrix (translate/rotate)
        pMatrix m_transform_global;

        // bound box in local space
        pBoundBox m_bbox;
        // bound box in global space
```

```
pBoundBox m_bbox_global;
// bound box in global space including all children
pBoundBox m_bbox_global_childs;

// object name
pString m_name;
// lights illuminating object
pArray<pLight*> m_light;
// array of child objects
pArray<pRenderObject *> m_child;
// pointer to parent object
pRenderObject *m_parent;

// Default constructor.
pRenderObject();

// Destructor.

virtual ~pRenderObject();
...
}
```

Listing 11.2 shows a typical set of common base object parameters. Each object deriving from the base object has a unique type identifier (m_type), a unique object identifier for each instance (m_id), and general bit flags (m_flags) indicating whether an object is enabled, visible etc. Each object has a transformation matrix relative to its parent (m_transform) and also a global transformation matrix accumulating all parent transforms (m_transform_global). It has a bounding box (m_bbox) in its local space and a bounding box in global space (m_bbox_global), which takes into account the accumulated parent transforms, and a bounding box enclosing all its children (m_bbox_global_childs). This enables efficient hierarchical culling and collision detection. The efficient implementation of both of these utilities is a mandatory requirement demanded by the complex geometry in modern games. The base object also has a string name (m_name), a list of lights currently illuminating it (m_lights), a list of child objects (m_child) and a pointer to a parent object (m_parent).

Virtual methods included in the base class must be implemented by the game objects so that they can function and appear in the game. Common virtual methods are the init, step, and draw among many others. The method init is called when a new object is activated, and the object initializes all its variables in this method. The method step is called to update the object state. The object may change its parameters in this method and react to other objects and the elapsed time. The draw method is where the object renders itself.

Step is an important method wherein the object updates its local transformation matrix (move and rotate) and its local bounding box, among other things. At some point after this, the object must call the base object step method that will calculate the object's global transformation matrix and global bounding boxes and recurse down its children. Only after calling the base object step method can the global object parameters be used. Listing 11.3 shows a simple example of a step method for the skeleton animation object.

Listing 11.3

A simple step method.

```
void pROMeshSkeleton::step(
const float elapsed_time,const pMatrix& global)
{
    if (m_mesh)
    {
        m_mesh->update(g_romanager->m_time,m_timefactor);
        m_bbox=m_mesh->bbox;
    }
    pRenderObject::step(elapsed_time, m_transform*global);
}
```

Other useful virtual methods are the parameter description and parameter change notification methods. The parameter description method lists all external object parameters that can be modified by the user. It uses a parameter description class that must be filled in for every available parameter as shown in Listing 11.4.

Listing 11.4

Parameter description class.

```
//  Parameter Descriptor class
/*
This class holds information on object parameters.
Each class derived from pRenderObject can have any
number of parameters. Each parameter must have an
associated pParamDesc class describing its data.
The pParamDesc class encloses the parameter's name,
type and value, and is very useful in parameter-editing
```

```
front-ends, like editors.
*/
class P3D_API pParamDesc
{
    public:
        pString name;          // parameter name
        int type;              // parameter type
        void *data;            // parameter value
        pString comment;       // parameter comments

        // Retrieves the value of associated
        // parameter in a string-form.
        const char *get_string() const;

        // Stores the value of associated parameter
        // in a binary buffer.
        void get_binary(void *bin) const;

        // Updates the value of associated parameter
        // from the str string.
        void set_string(const char *str);

        // Updates the value of associated parameter
        // from the bin binary buffer.
        void set_binary(const void *bin);
};
```

Listing 11.5 shows a typical parameter description implementation for the light render object. For every parameter, we define its type (bool, float, vector, color and string, among many others). Its name is used for access and modification of the parameter and the parameter data address.

....

Listing 11.5

```
// light object parameter description implementation
int pROLight::get_custom_param_desc(int i,pParamDesc *pd)
{
        if (pd)
        switch(i)
        {
        case 0:
```

Parameter description
implementation for a
light object.

```
            pd->type='b'; // bool
            pd->name="enabled";
            pd->data=&m_enabled;
            pd->comment="Turn on/off source light";
            break;
    case 1:
            pd->type='f'; // float
            pd->name="radius";
            pd->data=&m_radius;
            pd->comment="Light's radius";
            break;
    case 2:
            pd->type='f'; // float
            pd->name="multiplier";
            pd->data=&m_multiplier;
            pd->comment="Multiplier of light's intensity";
            break;
    case 3:
            pd->type='c'; // colour
            pd->name="color";
            pd->data=&m_color;
            pd->comment="Light's color";
            break;
    case 4:
            pd->type='e'; // periofic function
            pd->data=&m_func;
            pd->name="function";
            pd->comment="Function to animate color of light";
            break;
    case 5:
            pd->type='f'; // float
            pd->data=&m_angle;
            pd->name="angle";
            pd->comment="Angle in degrees";
            break;
    case 6:
            pd->type='b'; // bool
            pd->data=&m_shadow;
            pd->name="shadow";
            pd->comment="Shadow casting flag";
```

```
        break;
    }
    return 7;
}
```

When a parameter is modified by the game logic (other objects) or the user, the object being modified will receive a notification before and after the parameter is modified through two virtual methods.

```
virtual void pRenderObject::on_pre_parameter_change(int i);
virtual void pRenderObject::on_pos_parameter_change(int i);
```

The `on_pre_parameter_change` is called just before the parameter is modified and the `on_pos_parameter_change` is called after it. The object then has the opportunity to update itself in response to the parameter modification.

Render Object Manager

The object manager is the main user interface to the render objects. Through it, the user can load new objects, modify their parameters and destroy them. The manager will handle updating and drawing of the active render objects automatically.

Managing object creation is a somewhat complex task and must be implemented in a manner that enables the user to exploit the potential object behaviour to the full. The source of every render object is a text description. An example of part of the text file for the object shown in Figure 11.3 is given in Listing 11.6. This object is a combination of meshes, a particle system (the trails) and a billboard (the flares).

Figure 11.3. Sample object described in Listing 11.6.

```
[Space_Scene]
classtype=group
child=Space Dust Catfish

[Space]
classtype=panorama
transform=4.594 -99.993 7.849 0.000 0.000 0.000
tile=2.000
up=data\bg_space.jpg
down=data\bg_space.jpg
left=data\bg_space.jpg
right=data\bg_space.jpg
front=data\bg_space.jpg
back=data\bg_space.jpg

[Dust]
classtype=spacedust
count=100
pixelsize=1.500

[Catfish]
classtype=mesh
child=conn_eng-conn_eng_right conn_eng-conn_eng_left
mesh=data\catfish\catfish.p3d

[conn_eng-conn_eng_left]
classtype=group
child=Catfish_Engine
transform=30.304 51.851 20.398 0.000 -90.000 0.000

[conn_eng-conn_eng_right]
classtype=group
child=Catfish_Engine
transform=-30.304 51.851 20.398 0.000 90.000 0.000

[Catfish_Engine]
classtype=mesh
child=Catfish_EnginePS Catfish_Trail
mesh=data\catfish\engine.p3d
```

```
[Catfish_EngineBB]
classtype=billboard
flags=7
blendadd=1
sizex=30.000
sizey=30.000
texture=data\whitelen.tga
color=0.969 0.792 0.576
transp=0.750


[Catfish_EnginePS]
classtype=particle_system
child=Catfish_EngineBB
flags=7
transform=0.000 12.500 1.500 90.000 0.000 0.000
texture=data\smoke.tga
total=50
life=1.000
color=1.000 0.000 0.000
colorf=0.000 0.502 0.753
colorvar=0.302 0.302 0.302
function=5 0.500 0.500 0.000 1.000
transp=0.200
radius=5.000
radiusvar=2.000
speed=25.000
ax=0.250
ay=0.250
```

We can now see that the flow of information through the render object manager will be as shown in Figure 11.4.

The manager allows the loading of multiple text files containing object descriptions. The `create` method parses the text files and generates 'stock' objects. The stock objects can be removed using the manager `destroy` method and are organized in a hash list for fast access by name or identifier. Each stock object has a unique identifier (returned by the `create` method) that allows read/write access to its parameters. When created from its text representation, all

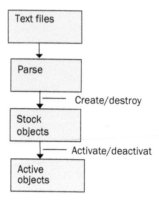

Figure 11.4. Information flow in the object manager.

child objects referenced by it will also be created so that all the object hierarchy is available in the stock. For example, in the case of the spaceship, the stock manifestation will be the main body and one engine (which is referenced three times by the body at different locations). The engine is made of a mesh, a billboard and a particle system that will also have a single instance created in the stock.

The stock objects are not present in the game simulation and are just an inventory of available objects—hence the name. The manager method `activate` receives a stock object identifier and will clone all the object hierarchy into the active hash table. Here, objects referenced multiple times (like the engine in the ship example) will be invoked as different instances. In the case of the ship, for example, three separate engines will be created, each with their own independent simulation. This enables the particle system in each engine to be running its simulation independently of the others. Figure 11.5 shows the exhaust simulation for the same particle system objects activated three times by its parent and using independent particles differentiated by the use of randomized control parameters.

Active objects can be removed from the simulation using the manager `deactivate` method. Deactivating an active object will also deactivate all the children in its hierarchy. In addition destroying a stock object will also deactivate all active instances of it.

Accessing Object Parameters

Methods must be available to set and get the common and custom object parameters. Common parameters are parameters available to all objects, and custom parameters are unique to each different type of object.

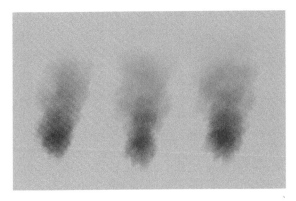

Figure 11.5. Particle system objects activated three times.

Access to common parameters is necessary, for example, if we want to move or rotate the object or query its current transformation. These methods accept stock or active objects as input, but when setting a parameter from a stock object, all active copies of it will also have the same change applied to them (changing an active object parameter only affects that unique active copy). The methods to get and set the object bitfield flags and to get and set the object transformation matrix (translation/rotation) are as follows:

```
bool pRenderObjectManager::set_object_flags(
unsigned int obj,const unsigned int flags);
bool pRenderObjectManager::get_object_flags(
unsigned int obj,unsigned int& flags);

bool pRenderObjectManager::set_object_transform(
unsigned int obj,const pMatrix& m);
bool pRenderObjectManager::get_object_transform(
unsigned int obj,pMatrix& m);
```

The custom object parameters can be set/get given a parameter name (string) or parameter index (integer). Also, parameter values can be set/get by string or binary format. Every parameter type must be able to convert to/from a string in order to be saved in a text format. The integer parameter index is faster than the string parameter version, but knowledge of the parameter index might not be possible at all times. The methods to set/get an object parameter by string or binary data are the following:

```
bool pRenderObjectManager::set_object_param(
unsigned int obj, const char *param, const char *value);
bool pRenderObjectManager::set_object_param(
unsigned int obj, int param, const char *value);
bool pRenderObjectManager::set_object_param(
unsigned int obj, const char *param, const void *value);
bool pRenderObjectManager::set_object_param(
unsigned int obj, int param, const void *value);


bool pRenderObjectManager::get_object_param(
unsigned int obj, const char *param, pString& value);
bool pRenderObjectManager::get_object_param(
unsigned int obj, int param, pString& value);
bool pRenderObjectManager::get_object_param(
unsigned int obj, const char *param, void *value);
bool pRenderObjectManager::get_object_param(
unsigned int obj, int param, void *value);
```

Objects can be from stock or active hash lists. The parameter to be set/get can be specified by name (string) or parameter index (integer).

The following can be used to recursively set/get object parameters in a hierarchy:

```
bool pRenderObjectManager::set_param(
unsigned int obj, const pString &string, const char *value);
bool pRenderObjectManager::set_param(
unsigned int obj, const pString &string, const void *value);
bool pRenderObjectManager::get_param(
unsigned int obj, const pString &string, pString &value);
bool pRenderObjectManager::get_param(
unsigned int obj, const pString &string, void *value);
```

We pass the root object identifier, a string with a chain of object names, a parameter name at the end and the desired value. For example, we could modify the ship's left engine particle system color using the following string:

```
Catfish.conn_eng-conn_eng_right.Catfish_Engine.Catfish_EnginePS.color
```

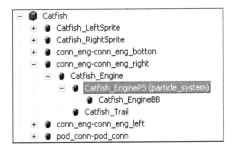

Hierarchy Manipulation

Object hierarchy is an important feature in modern games which enables us to cull and detect collisions efficiently. Hierarchy manipulation means that we need to be able to insert a new object into an existing hierarchy. This can be done with a method that receives a parent and a child object and links them using a transformation matrix to position the child in relation to the parent.

Figure 11.6 shows two objects with a set of attach points. An attach point is defined by a transformation matrix local to the object. If we want object 2 (the child) to have attach point M_4, connected to object 1 (the parent) at attach point M_2 we need to calculate the transformation matrix for the connection, which is $M_2M_4^{-1}$. The following are the appropriate methods:

```
bool pRenderObjectManager::attach_objects(
unsigned int parent, unsigned int child,
const pMatrix& child_transform);

bool pRenderObjectManager::attach_objects(
unsigned int parent, const char *par_dummy_name,
unsigned int child, const char *ch_dummy_name);
```

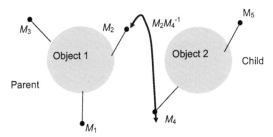

Figure 11.6. Attaching a new object to an existing hierarchy.

It is also useful to have a tool analogous to cut/copy/paste which enables us to move around or duplicate subtrees of the hierarchy with a very simple interface. We can implementt this idea as

```
void pRenderObjectManager::cut(unsigned int active_obj);
unsigned int pRenderObjectManager::copy(unsigned int active_obj)
void pRenderObjectManager::paste(unsigned int active_obj_parent,
unsigned int active_obj_child)
```

Cutting uses an object identifier for a non-root active object, releases the given object from its parent and adds it to the root active objects list, along with the objects beneath it in the hierarchy.

Copying creates a copy of the object along with its complete downward hierarchy and adds the copy to the root active objects list, returning the identifier for the newly created object.

Pasting uses two object identifiers for two active objects and adds the second one (along with its complete downward hierarchy) to the child list of the first. The second object must be a root active object.

Main Application Loop and Parameter Modification

The main per-frame loop for most game applications will consist of the kernel

update
draw

At the update stage, all active objects will update their states according to their parameters and individual behaviours—for example: object motion, object deformation, camera motion, particle system simulation etc. At the draw stage, all visible objects will be displayed, and no object parameters can be modified at this point.

Therefore, user interaction and changes in object parameters must always happen between a draw and update pair, and never between an update and a draw. This is because making changes after an update and before a draw will desynchronize the objects. For example, if a camera tracking an object updates its position and orientation in the update step to look at the object, and the object's position is modified after the update step, the camera will end up in the wrong position at the draw stage. This applies to all interdependent objects.

Animating

Every frame, the render and object manager must be updated:

```
g_render->update();
g_romanager->step(g_render->curdtf);
```

The call:

```
void pRender::update();
```

computes the elapsed time from last frame.

The call:

```
void pRenderObjectManager::step(float elapsed_time);
```

updates all objects currently active in object manager. The elapsed time in seconds from last frame must be passed in as a float. Not calling this method for some frames will stop all simulation over those frames.

Drawing

Drawing is independent from animation; you can draw and animate, or draw and not animate or animate and not draw. First, 3D objects are drawn followed by 2D objects drawn in an overlay.

```
g_render->begin_draw();
g_render->draw3d();
g_render->set_draw2d();
g_render->draw2d();
g_render->end_draw();
```

Then we set up the camera and initial render states for starting a frame using:

```
void pRender::begin_draw();
```

All render objects visible to the current camera are then drawn in 3D mode:

```
void pRender::draw_3d();
```

followed by all render objects visible to the current camera being drawn in 2D mode:

```
void pRender::set_draw2d();
void pRender::draw_2d();
```

Frame drawing is completed with:

```
void pRender::end_draw();
```

and we swap buffers.

Behaviour of Common Game Objects

Many current games share a set of common game objects, and in this section we give a selection of the most common ones as well as some developed for a space game. They are all implemented as render objects and can be combined together in the aforementioned hierarchical system.

Billboard

Billboard is the name given to a technique where a 2D image is considered as a 3D entity and placed in the scene. It is a simple technique that implements the emplacement in the scene by rotating the plane of the image so that it is normal to its viewing direction (the line from the viewpoint to its position). Probably the most common example of this technique is the image of a tree which is approximately cylindrically symmetric. Such complex objects are slow to render in real time, and the visual effect of this trick is quite convincing providing the view vector is close to the horizontal plane in scene space. The original 2D nature of the object is hardly noticeable in the two-dimensional projection, presumably because we do not have an accurate internal notion of what the projection of a tree should look like anyway. The billboard is in effect a 2D object which is rotated about its y axis through an angle which makes it normal to the view direction and translated to the appropriate position in the scene. The background texels in billboard images are usually set to transparent.

One modelling rotation for a simple z-axis aligned billboard is given as:

$$\theta = \pi - \cos^{-1}(\mathbf{V} \cdot \mathbf{B_n})$$

where $\mathbf{B_n}$ is the normal vector of the billboard, say $(0,0,1)$, and $\mathbf{V}$ is the viewing direction vector from the viewpoint to the required position of the billboard in world coordinate space.

Given θ and the required translation we can then construct a modelling transformation for the geometry of the billboard and transform it. Figure 11.7 is an example of a static billboard object and an animated one.

Clearly, the parameters that control the behaviour of game objects should be sufficiently flexible to allow a variety of different behaviours, which may be required within a game and between games. A billboard can easily be animated either by varying the parameters as indicated below or by playing a precalculated animation from texture map(s) as shown in Figure 11.7. The parameter list for the bilboard shown in the figure is now explained.

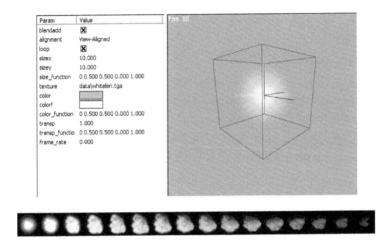

Param	Value
blendadd	☒
alignment	View-Aligned
loop	☒
sizex	10.000
sizey	10.000
size_function	0 0.500 0.500 0.000 1.000
texture	data\whitelen.tga
color	
colorf	
color_function	0 0.500 0.500 0.000 1.000
transp	1.000
transp_functio	0 0.500 0.500 0.000 1.000
frame_rate	0.000

Figure 11.7. An example of a billboard object and a billboard animation.

- **blendadd**—This parameter is used to select the blending mode. When checked, additive blending (1, 1) will be used and transparency is multiplied into the billboard's color. When not checked, standard transparency is used (src_alpha, 1-src_alpha).

- **alignment**—Three options are available: *none,* where the billboard is drawn in the local *xy* plane and the object orientation will be defined by its rotation from its user defined transformation matrix; *view-aligned* which will make the billboard align normal to the camera view direction (this is the most used option); *axis-aligned* which makes billboard align to the local *z* axis and rotates around it to align to the camera view direction (this option can be used to implement a billboard tree for example).

- **sizex and sizey**—Billboard width and height.

- **size_function**—Periodic function which modulates the billboard's size.

- **texture**—Billboard's texture map.

- **color and colorf**—Billboard's main color and secondary color.

- **color_function**—Periodic function f to modulate primary and secondary colors:

$$(1-f)*color+f*colorf$$

- **trasp**—Billboard's opacity value (1.0 full opaque, 0.0 fully transparent).

- **transp_function**—Periodic function modulating opacity.

- **frame_rate**—For animated billboards, it is the rate in which images are updated. Setting it to 0.0 will disable animation. Setting it to 30.0 will change the image 30 times per second.

- **loop**—For animated billboards, will loop animation when checked. If not checked billboard will die after last animation frame.

Composite Dynamic Billboards

This object shown in Figure 11.8 is made up of two billboards. The final effect can be used as a missile trail or as an entity in its own right. The object was built of two cross-sectional planes that are maintained orthogonal to each other as shown in the illustration. To a certain extent, this solves the 2D problem that is common to all billboards. This object is blended into the frame buffer, with the fire added to the current frame buffer and with the black background having no effect.

The key to making the object appear 3D is to rotate it about its current position so that the longitudinal cross-section is normal to the plane containing the camera point, the current position of the fire object and the vector joining them. The spatial relationship of the camera point and direction and the current position of the fire and its direction is constantly changing as we assume in general that the

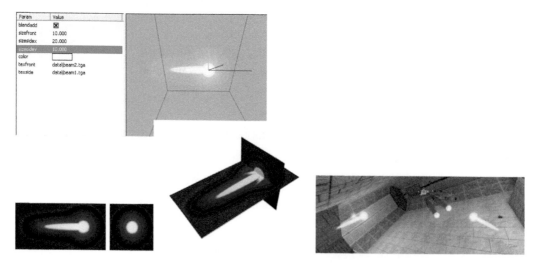

Figure 11.8. A composite dynamic billboard.

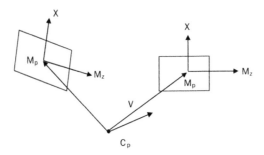

Figure 11.9. Dynamic billboard vectors.

vessel that fired the weapon can immediately change direction before the fire has struck home.

This orientation of the billboard is calculated as follows. First we evaluate **V** (Figure 11.9) the vector containing the current positions of both the camera and the fire object.

$$\mathbf{V} = \mathbf{C_p} - \mathbf{M_p}$$

Then **X** is a vector normal to **V** and $\mathbf{M_z}$ given as:

$$\mathbf{X} = \mathbf{V} \times \mathbf{M_z}$$

where $\mathbf{M_z}$ is the direction of fire (the missile z axis).

We embed the longitudinal cross-section in the plane containing **X** and $\mathbf{M_z}$. This then ensures that, irrespective of the constantly changing spatial relationship between the fire and the viewer, the viewer always sees the billboard cross-sections oriented exactly as if they were the cross-section of a 3D object representing the fire.

An optimisation used by this object and other similar objects (which have hundreds of instances in the game) is to use a single object definition and an array of transformation matrices. Instead of having hundreds of instances activated, we can pass a single instance and the array of transformation matrices so that we draw on copy of the object with each transformation matrix. In the render object manager, a special method is available for that called `render_projectiles`.

Lens Flare Billboards

Lens flare is an effect that is not perceived in reality. It only shows up in recorded images; however, despite originally being perceived as an unwanted effect, that is due to inadequacies in the lens, it has come to be embraced as an artistic effect in films and photography. A professional camera lens contains many elements

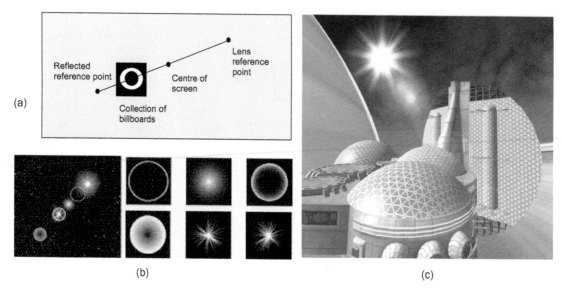

Figure 11.10. (a) Billboard placement geometry. (b) A selection of typical billboards. (c) Lens flare in games level.

which, depending on the nature of the lens, produce a particular type of image of reality—zoom lens, fisheye lens etc. To prevent internal reflections amongst these elements, lenses are coated with an anti-reflective material, but when the camera is viewing bright lights, this lens coating is not fully effective and secondary reflections occur, manifesting as lens flares in the image.

Lens flare can easily be faked in computer graphics by simply superimposing a selection of billboards along a line through the centre of the screen, from the lens reference point to its reflected position, as shown in Figure 11.10.

Camera Object

This object implements a 3rd person camera that tracks its parent object. The user can rotate the camera position around the object and also zoom in and out. We can implement it using two floats to define the camera direction (rotation angles around target object) and one float for the distance to the target object.

In this way, after we can update the camera position, the target object is moved and/or rotated using the predefined camera angles and distance. We can use the target object transformation matrix as the base for the camera orientation.

Listing 11.7 computes the camera position given two angles around target (m_angle_x and m_angle_y) and the distance to target (m_dist):

Listing 11.7

Computes camera
position.

```
// X local axis
pVector tx=m_target->m_transform_global.get_column3(0);
// Y local axis
pVector ty=m_target->m_transform_global.get_column3(1);
// Z local axis
pVector tz=m_target->m_transform_global.get_column3(2);
// translation
pVector tt=m_target->m_transform_global.get_translate();

float cosa=cosf(m_angle_x*PIOVER180);
float cosb=cosf(m_angle_y*PIOVER180);
float sina=sinf(m_angle_x*PIOVER180);
float sinb=sinf(m_angle_y*PIOVER180);

pVector to(cosa*cosb, sina*cosb, sinb);
to *= m_dist;

pVector newpos = tt + tx*to.y + ty*to.x + tz*to.z;

camera.pos = newpos;
```

Although the above camera can smoothly rotate/zoom around the target object, it is effectively a totally rigid link. When the target object moves, the camera follows it with infinite velocity, repositioning itself to the same relative position around the new target. It is sometimes better to have a more flexible link between the camera and its target so that the camera has a delay when responding to target position/orientation changes.

A simple way to implement a more flexible camera attachment is to include a response factor that would modulate the camera movements. Say we set such parameter to 0.9 (equivalent to a 90 percent rigid link). Then when we compute the new camera position, instead of moving directly to the new calculated position, we move only 90 percent of the distance from new and old camera positions. As we set this parameter smaller, we get looser camera behaviour, while setting it close to 1.0 gets it more rigid (totally rigid at 1.0).

The following code replaces the last line from the previous camera position calculation adding a flexible movement controlled by the parameter m_factor (0 < m_factor <= 1.0).

```
camera.pos += (newpos - camera.pos)*m_factor*elapsed_time;
```

After updating the camera position, we must then rotate it to look at the target object. We can use a simple look-at matrix to define the camera rotation, which aligns the camera *z* axis to face the desired position in the target object. Listing 11.8 generates a look-at matrix for a given look direction and up vector.

Listing 11.8

Generating a look-at matrix.

```
void align_z(const pVector& Z, const pVector& up, pMatrix& M)
{
    pVector X,Y;

    Y=up-z*VECDOT(z,up);

    Y.normalize();
    X.cross(Y,z);

    M.set_column3(0,X);
    M.set_column3(1,Y);
    M.set_column3(2,Z);
}
```

Explosion Object

The explosion object, when activated, will release all its children at the explosion point. It acts as a container of other objects that are activated at the explosion point. An example of this object is shown in Figure 11.11; the parameters should be self-explanatory.

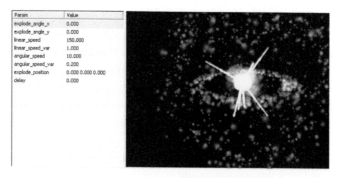

Param	Value
explode_angle_x	0.000
explode_angle_y	0.000
linear_speed	150.000
linear_speed_var	1.000
angular_speed	10.000
angular_speed_var	0.200
explode_position	0.000 0.000 0.000
delay	0.000

Figure 11.11. An explosion object.

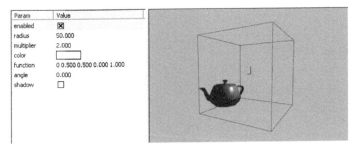

Param	Value
enabled	☒
radius	50.000
multiplier	2.000
color	[ ]
function	0 0.500 0.500 0.000 1.000
angle	0.000
shadow	☐

Figure 11.12. A simple light object.

Explode Object

The explode object is a container for other objects and includes parameters such as velocity, rotation velocity and life. When an explosion is activated and one of its children is an explode object, the object's velocity and rotation velocity will be set according to its position in relation to the explosion point. In this way we can have any type of object being ejected from the explosion. The explode object has a life parameter and will deactivate itself when its life has expired, fading out at the end.

Light Objects

Light objects (Figure 11.12) are covered extensively in Chapter 2, and the interpretation of most parameter lists should be obvious. In the illustration, the spotlight is positioned at the origin shown, and the bounding box is constructed with dimension 2*radius.

The parameter angle specifies whether the light is a spotlight or a point source. If angle is zero then the light is a point source, otherwise it is a spotlight whose frustum is specified by angle. The parameter multiplier sets the fade out towards the bounding box faces.

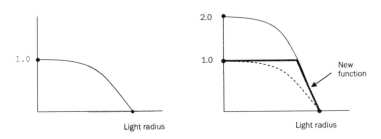

Figure 11.13. Fall-off function for the light object.

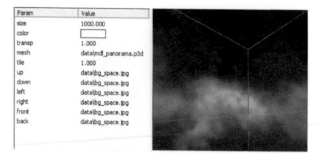

Figure 11.14. Panorama object.

All objects in the bounding box are illuminated to an extent depending on their distance from the light source. Within the bounding box, the field of influence of the light is defined by a function of the radius of light—a fall-off function. This acts in conjunction with the multiplier parameter. If the multiplier is 1 then the base function shown in Figure 11.13(a) is applied, if it is 2, however, a new function is constructed as shown in bold in Figure 11.14(b). Compared to the base function, the new function 'pushes' the fade out closer to the bounding box faces.

Panorama Object

The panorama object (Figure 11.14) represents very distant objects. It is always centred at the camera position so that you can never move closer to it. It uses the same transformation matrix as the camera excluding rotations. It usually takes the form of a cube with six images. It can have a color and opacity value so that we can compose multiple panoramas if needed. Another option is to use a generic 3D mesh (usually a sphere with a single texture map) as the panorama object.

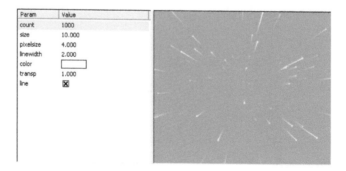

Figure 11.15. Space-dust object.

Space-Dust Object

A space-dust object is a box of random points in space that tiles infinitely. As the illustration shows (Figure 11.15), there is an option for drawing lines from the current point to the previous last frame's point position to give an impression of moving through space.

Obfuscating Point

This is a point in space which when looked at, will add a full screen color blend. Its parameters are color, opacity and angle, which defines a frustum centred on the camera in the direction of the camera look direction. If the point is inside this region, color is blended to full screen fading out at the extremities of the frustum. Looking directly to the point gives the highest obfuscation.

Trail Object

A trail object (Figure 11.16) is constructed from a particle system and is mainly controlled by the threshold parameter. If the last trail point distance to emitter is bigger than this threshold, a new point is emitted. If object is stationary and no velocity is set, the trail will not be visible.

Particle System

An example of a particle system is shown in Figure 11.17. This is a GPU implementation and is fully described in Chapter 8.

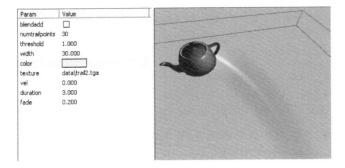

Figure 11.16. Trail object.

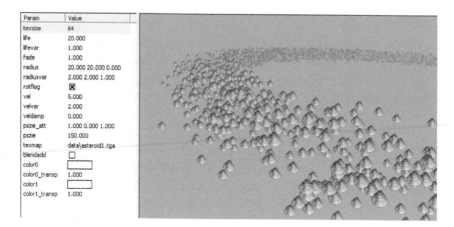

Param	Value
texsize	64
life	20.000
lifevar	1.000
fade	1.000
radius	20.000 20.000 0.000
radiusvar	2.000 2.000 1.000
rotflag	☒
vel	5.000
velvar	2.000
veldamp	0.000
pszie_att	1.000 0.000 1.000
pszie	150.000
texmap	data\asteroid1.tga
blendadd	☐
color0	
color0_transp	1.000
color1	
color1_transp	1.000

Figure 11.17. Particle system.

The parameters are as follows:

- **texsize**—float texture maps resolution (for example, 64 means 64x64 texture or 4096 particles; 128 means 128x128 or 16,384 particles and 256 implies 65,536 particles).

- **life**—total life in seconds for all particles.

- **lifevar**—variance to randomly add to life of each individual particle (so they die at different times).

- **fade**—time to fade out at end of particle life (0.5 will fade out for half a second at end of particle life).

- **radius**—initial position radius - which defines an ellipsoid (x,y,z) that contains the initial position. To simulate an explosion a small value would be used. The ring shown in Figure 11.18 was generated by using large *x,y* and small z (see also Figure 8.12).

- **radius_var**—a random number (-1 to 1) which is multiplied by radius and added to each particle position (radius 10,10,0 with radius var of 1,1,1 will make something like a torus).

- **rotflag**—a boolean indicating if particles should rotate around a centre point or just follow their initial velocity.

- **vel**—initial particle velocity

- **velvar**—a random number (-1 to 1) which is multiplied by `vel` and added to variance to randomly add to each particle velocity.

- **veldamp**—damping factor to subtract particle velocity.

- **pzise_att**—point size attenuation factor (constant, linear and quadratic).

- **psize**—max point size.

- **texmap**—point sprite texture map.

- **blendadd**—a boolean to select additive blending (no depth write) or standard alpha blending (with depth write and alpha test).

- **color0, color1**—initial and final colors linearly interpolated though particle life (particle is born with `color0` and dies with `color1`).

Finally, Figure 11.18 shows three of the above objects used in a game.

Figure 11.18. Trail, panorama and space-dust objects used in a game. *Courtesy Hoplon Infotainment and Taikodom www.hoplon.com.br and www.taikodom.com.br*

Utility Classes

The common utility classes used in the system number four, and these are now explained.

pString

This is a dynamic string class that simplifies the manipulation of text. You can add strings together, use pString like formatting and you do not have to worry about allocation size.

```
pString a,b="test string ";
b.format("%i",100);
b+=a; // b holds "test string 100"
```

pArray<T>

This is a template based dynamic array class supporting any object type. You can add objects to the array, and it will reallocate automatically when needed.

```
pArray<int> a;
a.add(10);
a.add(25);
printf("%i",a[1]-a[0]); // prints 15
```

pCircularList<T>

This is a template based circular list supporting any object type. We have described a use for such a utility in Chapter 8. It is initialised with a fixed number of elements. You can add elements to the end of the list (if the list is not yet full) and remove elements from its beginning (if it is not empty).

```
pCircularList<float> a(10); // circular list of floats with 10 elements
a.add(1.0f);
a.add(2.0f);
a.add(3.0f);
a.remove_begin();
printf("%f",a[0]); // prints 2.0
```

Hash Tables for Render Objects

Hash tables are perhaps not well known in the games community, and so we will give a brief introduction to them. The motivation for a hash table is efficient

Figure 11.19. Animal database.

searching. Linear search time is $O(n)$, binary search reduces the time to $O(\log n)$ but a using a hash table can result in constant time. We will describe the simplest type known as an open hash table. The construct consists of an array of data—the table and a hash function. The hash function is some mapping or function of the search target.

Consider a simple example—a data base of animals and their corresponding keepers in a zoo. We assume a maximum of 26 animals, and the hash function is derived from the first character of the animal's name as

$$\text{ascii(first\_letter)}—\text{ascii("a")}$$

If there is no vacant slot at the point given by the hash value, then we proceed down the table until we find one. After inserting the sequence on the left in Figure 11.19 we end up with the table on the right.

To search for a keeper for an animal, we hash the animal's name, access the table with the resulting index, and if there is no match, we linearly search from that point. Note the tendency for the names to bunch together in particular areas of the table. This can result in long search lengths for some names.

To avoid long search times, we have two conventional speed-ups. First, we can attempt to define a hash function that results in as wide a spread of values as possible over the table indices. The function need not be particularly meaningful.

Figure 11.20. Animal database (k = 7).

We could, for example select an arbitrary subset of the bit pattern of a key and transform this in any way to give a hash value.

Second, we can modify the simple linear search. Instead of examining locations

$$p, p+1, p+2,...,$$

for an empty slot or a match, we can proceed as:

$$p, p+d(1), p+d(2),...,$$

where d is some displacement function, the simplest being a linear one

$$d(i) = k_i$$

If we make k_i equal to 7 for example we would examine:

$$p, p+7, p+14,...,$$

and the table is now as shown in Figure 11.20.

In the previous table search lengths of up to nine were necessary, but now the longest search length involves only three comparisons. Note that if n is the size of the table, then k and n must be co-prime, otherwise not all the locations of the table will be reached for any given value.

With the simple zoo example, all animals with the same name would be distributed vertically in the hash table. In our game implementation, table slots are arrays which can expand horizontally, so the hash function returns the row and a linear search proceeds along the row. Although this arrangement is not as fast as a binary search, it handles additions and removals far more efficiently. The initial size of the hash table is set at n slots.

The integer hash table is a template class, which means you can associate an integer with any object type. The hash function we use is the classic choiceof

$$h(k) = k \bmod n$$

where k is the key and n is the number of slots in the table.

The value of n must be chosen carefully. It should not be a power of two and should be a prime number.

For the string version we derive an integer key by summing the ASCII for each character in the string.

pHashTable<T>

This is a template based hash table of integer keys. You can add multiple objects each with an associated integer key used in the hash process. It speeds up querying of objects by their associated integers.

```
myObject obj1,obj2;
pHashTable<myObject> a;
a.add(11,obj1);
a.add(12,obj2);
// get object 2 by its integer identifier
myObject obj=a.get_object(12);
```

pHashTableStr<T>

This is a template based hash table of string keys. You can add multiple objects each with an associated string key used in the hash process. It speeds up querying of objects by their associated strings.

```
myObject obj1,obj2;
pHashTableStr<myObject> a;
a.add("object1",obj1);
a.add("object2",obj2);
// get object 2 by name
myObject obj=a.get_object("object2");
```

Optimisation of GPU Systems

It does not really need to be said that optimising graphics programs to make the most efficient use of the hardware is critically important. From time to time in the text we have discussed some aspects of efficiency with respect to particular algorithms. For example, in the case of shadow volumes, we discussed the problem of the high fill rate exhibited by certain versions of that method. In this chapter, we will look at optimisation issues more generally.

Bottlenecks in the Graphics Pipeline

Pipelining is a technology where instructions are overlapped in execution. It is one of the key technologies that enable PCs to be so powerful, and as you might expect, GPUs are deeply pipelined architecture. A simple model of this concept is given in Chapter 1.

In computer graphics the term "pipeline" can refer to the sequential abstraction of rendering by geometry processing followed by all the processes necessary to produce a colour at a pixel. But we should remember that the GPU also contains pipelined architecture in the sense of the original meaning of the word—units operating in parallel.[1]

Pipelines can be seen as processing structures for data streams in which the process is split into sequential, self-contained modules that can be executed in parallel while the streams are fed into the pipeline. Such a structure benefits greatly from parallelization, increasing the throughput rate of the system. However, achieving the best possible performance for a pipeline system is usually a tricky task.

Since each module depends on the output of the previous one in the sequence, the overall throughput of the system will be capped by the performance of the slowest module in the pipeline. Such a module is called the bottleneck of the system, and the task of optimising a pipeline structure involves determining and optimising the module that represents the bottleneck. This is so because all the other modules are idle during some time, waiting for the bottleneck module to terminate its execution, and optimising any of these non-bottleneck modules would only produce more idle time while keeping the system throughput rate untouched.

Computer graphics APIs such as OpenGL and Direct3D process the streams of geometric data submitted to them with a pipeline system. The tasks involved in rendering the geometric structures into screen pixels are divided into modules in a pipeline. Therefore, optimising the performance of a graphics application such as a 3D game involves determining and optimising the bottleneck of the graphics pipeline.

....

[1] Somewhat confusingly "pipeline" is a word used both to describe hardware architecture and also to describe the abstraction of rendering—as in "the OpenGL pipeline".

The overall process in a graphics program can be divided into three high-level stages: application, geometry and rasterisation. This approach serves as an adequate abstraction that helps to determine and tackle the part of the process that comprises the bottleneck.[2]

The application stage comprises all methods that deal with the geometric data structures before they are sent down to the API. This stage is fully executed on the CPU, and if the bottleneck is located in this stage, it is said that the application is CPU-bound. The geometry stage comprises all the work performed in transforming and processing vertices passed down by the application stage to the API. All of the modern graphics cards already offer full GPU execution of the geometry stage. The rasterisation stage involves the tasks that deal with fragment processing, from the assembly of primitives from the transformed vertex data until the assignment of pixel values in the frame buffer. This stage is fully performed by the GPU. When the bottleneck is located in the geometry or rasterisation stages, it is said that the application is GPU-bound.

Because GPU hardware is evolving more quickly than CPUs, it is reasonable to expect that graphics applications will tend to become more and more CPU-bound [WLOK03]. Therefore, most of the effort in optimising the graphics pipeline must be applied to analyzing the work of the CPU and trying to find workarounds for the most costly CPU tasks involved in the graphics pipeline.

Batching

Aside from application-specific processing, the tasks performed by the CPU in the graphics pipeline mostly involve configuring state variables and submitting data to the graphics API. As we have seen in this chapter, typical games and computer graphics applications have a large amount of different objects, each with its own set of textures, materials and shaders. Given that several of these objects must be drawn together in any given frame, the CPU must make the necessary API calls for configuring the state of the GPU before submitting geometry. Each of these configure-state–submit-geometry cycles is called a batch [WLOK03].

Having too many small batches is one of the main causes of CPU bottlenecks. A batch is simply the action of grouping geometric elements with same material properties so that as many as possible can be rendered with one API call. The worst case is, of course, one API call per triangle, and the unnecessary use of large numbers of batches causes the GPU to wait and its pipeline to be less effective. Overall performance is then limited to the speed of the CPU and not the GPU. M. Wloka quotes a factor of 100 increase (from 1 M triangles per second to 100 M triangles/sec) by increasing batch size from 10 triangles to 1500 triangles.

. . . .

[2] An excellent treatment on determining the position of bottlenecks in systems is given in [CEBE04].

We must also make sure that each batch of data is compact and that we are not wasting any space. This enables us to maximize caching and transfer speed. The triangle indices list, which tells what vertices are used by each triangle, can be stored in 16-bit integers instead of 32-bit integers if batch does not have more than 65,535 vertices (most batches will not exceed this). Using triangle strips can also make the triangle indices much smaller and faster to execute. Additionally the vertex colours can be encoded in byte 8-bit per component instead of float 32-bit per component taking up one quarter of the space when colour is required at the vertices.

A batch is set up by an API call, for example `glDrawArrays()` or `glDrawIndexedPrimitive()`, which pass the specified number of triangles into the GPU. The render state calls are part of the batch and apply to all triangles in the batch.

Thus, we conclude that having a huge amount of API calls in a single frame can be one of the most unfavourable scenarios for the CPU, and reducing the number of batches by grouping together objects that share the same state configuration is always a good strategy. In this way, the number of API calls will be reduced. A single state change set of instructions is called with a large amount of geometric data, and this data will be processed in a single batch. However, even after sorting and grouping these similar objects, there can still be a large amount of batches to be sent, requiring even more aggressive batch-reducing strategies.

These strategies must rely on diminishing the main differences in object properties that force state changes, the so-called batch-breakers. For example, one of the most different properties among objects is the diffuse texture. Therefore, it would be convenient to have some strategy in order to reduce the number of texture state changes, so that objects with different textures could be joined in fewer, larger batches. One such strategy comprises joining several textures into a large map called a texture atlas.[3]

There are problems associated with this technique. The first one is that the modelled texture coordinates, from different objects and/or different parts of the same object, have to be remapped into the atlas representation. The second problem concerns mip-maps. Clearly, we cannot have mip-maps of the atlas otherwise all texels (from different objects) would eventually join together in lower levels of the mip-maps. This can be avoided by not using the smaller mip-map levels and grouping the textures in the atlas more loosely. For example if we stop the mip-maps at a 4 x 4 size, we could have 16 textures in the atlas, each in one of the 4 x 4 regions from the high-resolution atlas. In this way, no pixels from different textures will blend together (we would only have problems with mip-maps smaller than 4 x 4).

....

[3] See download.nvidia.com/developer/NVTextureSuite/Atlas_Tools/Texture_Atlas_Whitepaper.pdf.

Another strategy that offers a limited decrease in the number of batches, but does not suffer from any mip-mapping issues found in texture atlases, is to map six textures onto the faces of a cube map, and join the six sets of objects that use these textures into a single batch.

All texture atlas optimisations fail to support texture tiling and can therefore only be used on objects that do not need to repeat the texture multiple times over the object. They are especially good for character models and other highly detailed objects which access a single texture.

It is also a good strategy to increase the amount of GPU work in order to decrease the number of batches, thus decreasing the amount of CPU work. For example, packing objects with different material properties, other than the diffuse texture, into a single batch is also possible, by exploring the pixel shader's branching capabilities. The strategy consists of passing multiple materials to the pixel shader and then combining or interpolating between them internally, based on additional parameters passed per pixel (passed to the vertex shader and interpolated by the rasteriser) or in a texture map [WLOK03].

More high level considerations can be applied to reducing the number of batches in a render. One of the more important of these is to construct visibility sets [OROR04]. The idea here is that organizing objects into such sets enables an optimal construction of batches. J. O'Rorke defines four such sets:

- The visible set, V is all those objects visible from the camera. These include objects in the view frustum; but not all objects in the view frustum are members of V, as certain objects may be completely occluded.

- The lights set, L is one in which each light possesses an influence volume, a sphere, a bounding box or, in the case of a spotlight, a light frustum. We can thus consider each light influence volume for containment within the view frustum and consider L to be the set of light objects that intersect the view frustum.

- The illumination set, I is the intersection of V and L and is the set of visible objects that can see the light and are within its influence volume. I is thus determined by examining, for each object in L, if the object is also in V. If L and V are sorted, this can be done in a single linear pass through the lists.

- The shadow set, S is the set of objects (shadow casters) that must be included in a shadow pass. These include objects in I. They also include objects not in V but in the view frustum—occluded objects. Yet another category is objects outside the view frustum that cast shadows into it. S is the most difficult and expensive set to determine. However, it is a subset of L and so can be approximated by L.

O'Rorke points out that the amount of CPU processor time spent to determine these sets is a fine judgment. Clearly the calculation of V should include, as a minimum, view frustum culling, but how much effort should be expended on occlusion culling?

At the beginning of the chapter, we discussed the implementation of this structure:

```
for  each light source
  for  each object
    render(object,light source)
```

Using the above, set categorisations enable us to rewrite this pseudocode to organize batches as

```
for  each light source in L
  for each object in S
      render_shadows(objects,light source)
  for  each object in I
      render_lighting(object,light source)
```

Note that sets L and V are global, while sets I and S are different for each light source.

Optimising the GPU

Although CPU-bound applications are commonplace in our current scenario of GPUs outpacing CPUs in hardware evolution, it is not rare to stumble upon a situation where the GPU must also be optimised. Programmable graphics hardware and its accompanying flexibility open a lot of opportunities for programmers to write amazing programs, but also to use it inefficiently. Therefore, some useful tips on optimisation of vertex and pixel shaders would be desirable.

One of the most obvious considerations is that texture and frame buffer access must be optimised for optimal performance.

Vertex Program Optimisations

If vertex processing is the bottleneck in your application then obviously this can be tackled by reducing the number of vertices or by reducing the data per vertex.

To reduce the size of the vertex data, we can use triangle strips and smaller texture data (as we have already discussed in the context of batching). It is also a good strategy, if possible, to organise the geometry to access vertices in a sequential manner so as to maximize efficiency in the transformed vertex cache.

Using a geometry LOD system can also help in vertex program bottlenecked applications as it can drastically reduce the number of vertices drawn with minimum image quality loss. Objects small in screen space use lower levels of geometric detail, saving a lot of vertex processing. LOD schemes are well established, as much work has been carried out on them over the past decade. Principal amongst these schemes is Hoppe's famous Progressive Mesh [HOPP96] now incorporated in DirectX. Another similar optimisation is to use a 'shader LOD' scheme where a simpler shader is selected for distant objects with small screen space projection.

Task division between the CPU and the GPU is important. For example, if we have computation that is constant throughout the object render, this should take place in the CPU, passing the results as constants to the vertex program. It is better to compute once in CPU than recomputing the same results for every vertex drawn.

Newer GPU, support branching in vertex programs. This can be used to reduce the number of instructions executed per vertex. For example, a vertex lighting shader could take advantage of it when the vertex is back facing the light thus saving all lighting computation code for that vertex.

Pixel Shader Optimisations

The most common GPU bottleneck is the pixel shader as it is run for every fragment and thus can result in millions of executions in a frame. In general fragment shader optimisation can be approached on two fronts: reduce the complexity of the fragment shader and reduce number fragments running the fragment shader.

The first obvious strategy to adopt is to judiciously balance work between the vertex shader and the fragment shader. It goes without saying that if a property can be calculated per vertex then interpolated, then this strategy should be strictly adhered to if possible—there are many more fragments in a frame being rendered than there are vertices. For example, light vector and space transformations can be done in vertex program and have their results interpolated to fragments instead of recalculating them for all fragments. Another efficient optimisation is to store complex functions as texture maps. The texture will then work as a look-up table with all possible values for the given function. For example, this was used in omnidirectional depth maps application (Chapter 5) where we stored the functions $\texttt{acos(x/sqrt(1-y*y))}$

and $\texttt{acos(y))}$ in a texture map to avoid calculating it at all fragments as it uses complex trigonometric functions such as $\texttt{acos}$. Another example, described in Chapter 3, is complex lighting function such as anisotropic shading.

Another candidate to consider is the use of normalisation calls. It is usually not necessary to normalise a vector at each step of a calculation and many times it need only be done once. For example, transforming a vector into tangent space could require up to four normalise calls as tangent vectors will lose normalisation when linearly interpolated.

```
view  = normalize( float3(
dot(view, normalize(IN.tangent)),
dot(view, normalize(IN.binormal)),
dot(view, normalize(IN.normal)) ));
```

But using only a single normalize at the end of the calculation will be almost the same for most cases where the tessellation is not too low and camera is not too close to geometry.

```
view  = normalize( float3(
dot(view, IN.tangent),
dot(view, IN.binormal),
dot(view, IN.normal) ));
```

To reduce the number of fragments running the pixel shader, we can use an option called 'render depth first' which takes advantage of the early z-culling support found on current graphics hardware. This is described in Chapter 2 and relies on hardware double fill rate when rendering to a single buffer (colour only or depth only).

Texture Optimisations

Texture size is the most important issue for optimising texture access. Using high-resolution textures is slower and reducing the texture sizes will improve texture access performance as well as use the texture cache more efficiently. Also, colour resolution is a similar issue, and using colour components with 16 or 32 bits should be avoided or only used when necessary. Mip-mapping also improves texture access performance, as it will usually access lower mip-map levels (lower resolution versions of the texture).

Another factor that assists texture access performance is texture compression. Compressed textures will take less memory space, be faster to transfer from system to video memory and improve texture cache efficiency.

Frame Buffer Optimisations

During rendering, the frame buffer is usually accessed multiple times, and we must minimize data transfers to/from the frame buffer as much as possible. To do that, we should disable depth writes and depth tests, whenever possible, to save writes and reads from the depth buffer. For example, some sprites and particle system effects do not require depth buffer writing as they use additive blending and are drawn after opaque objects.

Most polygons drawn in a game will replace the colour in the frame buffer and no blending is needed. When setting destination blend factor to zero we save a colour buffer read for every fragment, as it will only replace the values already in colour buffer.

The colour and depth resolutions used also influence the bandwidth required for reading and writing to and from the frame buffer. We should try to avoid float buffers as they take four times more memory and bandwidth than byte versions. But when float buffers are needed and the precision is enough for your application, using half-float (16 bit) will be faster than full float (32 bit). The depth buffer can also be stored in 16 bit or 24 bits per component, and if 16-bit precision is enough for your application, it should be used.

References

[BANK94] D. C. Banks. "Illumination in Diverse Codimensions." In *Proceedings of SIGGRAPH '94, Computer Graphics Proceedings, Annual Conference Series,* edited by Andrew Glassner, pp. 327–334. New York: ACM Press, 1994

[BATC68] K. E. Batcher. "Sorting Networks and Their Applications." *AFIPS Spring Joint Computer Conference* 32 (1968), 307–314.

[BEES04] C. Beeson and K. Bjorke. "Skin in the "Dawn" Demo." In *GPU Gems*, edited by R. Fernando, pp. 45–61. Boston: Addison-Wesley, 2004

[BERG03] R. W. Berger. "Why do Images appear Darker on Some Displays." (accessed April 2005 from www.bberger.net/rwb/gamma.html).

[BIER86] E. Bier and K. Sloan. "Two-Part Texture Mapping." *IEEE Comp. Graphics and Applications* 6: 9 (1986), 40–53.

[BLIN78] J. Blinn. "Simulation of Wrinkled Surfaces." *Computer Graphics (Proc. SIGGRAPH '78)* 12:3 (1978) 286 – 292.

[BOHM82] W. Bohm. "On Cubics: A Survey." *Computer Graphics and Image Processing,* 19:3 (1982), 201–226.

[BUCK04] I. Buck and T. Purcell. "A Toolkit for Computation on GPUs." In *GPU Gems*, edited by R. Fernando, pp. 631–635. Boston: Addison-Wesley, 2004.

[BUNN04] M. Bunnell and F. Pellacici. "Shadow Map Anti-Aliasing." In *GPU Gems*, edited by R. Fernando, pp. 185–192. Boston: Addison-Wesley, 2004.

[CHAN04] E. Chan and F, Durand. "An Efficient Hybrid Shadow Rendering Algorithm". *Proceedings of the Eurographics Symposium on Rendering.* Eurographics, *2004.*

[COOK84] R. L. Cook. "Shade Trees." *Computer Graphics (Proc. SIGGRAPH '84)* 18:3 (1984), 223–231.

[COHE93] M. Cohen, S. Chen, and D. Massaro. "Modelling Coarticulation in Visual Speech." In *Models and Techniques in Computer Animation,* edited by N. Thalmann and D. Thalmann, pp. 139–156. Tokyo: Springer-Verlag, 1993.

[COHE98] M. Cohen, M. Olano and D. Manocha. "Appearance Preserving Simplification." In *Proceedings of SIGGRAPH '98, Computer Graphics Proceedings, Annual Conference Series,* edited by Michael Cohen, pp. 115–112. Reading, MA: Addison-Wesley, 1998.

[CROW77] F. Crow. "Shadow Algorithms for Computer Graphics." *Computer Graphics (Proc. SIGGRAPH '77)* 11:2 (1977), 242–248.

[DEME04] J. Demers. "Depth of Field—A Survey." In *GPU Gems,* edited by R. Fernando, pp. 375–389. Boston: Addison-Wesley, 2004.

[EBER98] D. Ebert, F. Kenton Musgrave, D. Peachey, K. Perlin, and S. Worley. *Texture and Modelling a Procedural Approach.* Boston: AP Professional, 1998.

[EDGE04] J. Edge, M. Sanchez Lorenzo, and S. Maddock. "Animating Speech from Motion Fragments." Tech. Rep. CS-04-02, Dept. Comp. Sci. University. of Sheffield, U.K. (accessed April 2005 from www.dcs.shef.ac.uk/~jedge).

[FERN01] R. Fernando, S. Fernandez, K. Bala and D. Greenberg. "Adaptive Shadow Maps." In *Proceedings of SIGGRAPH '01,* Computer Graphics Proceedings, Annual Conference Series, edited by E. Fiume, pp. 387–390. Reading, MA: Addison-Wesley, 2001.

[FERN03} R. Fernando and M. J. Kilgard. *The Cg Tutorial.* Boston: Addison-Wesley, 2003.

[GERA04] P. S. Gerasimov. "Omnidirectional Shadow Mapping." In *GPU Gems,* edited by R. Fernando, pp. 193–203. Boston: Addison-Wesley, 2004

[GREE03] S. Green. "Stupid OpenGL Shader Tricks." *Paper presented at Game Developers Conference,* San Francisco, CA, 2003.

[FINC04] M. Finch. "Effective Water Simulation from Physical Models." In *GPU Gems,* edited by R. Fernando, pp. Boston: Addison-Wesley, 2004.

[FOUR86] A. Fournier. "A Simple Model of Ocean Waves." In *Computer Graphics (Proc. SIGGRAPH '86,)* 20:4 (1986), 75–84.

[HANR93] P. Hanrahan and W. Kreuger. "Reflections from Layered Surfaces due to Sub-surface Scattering." In *Proceedings of SIGGRAPH 93, Computer Graphics Proceedings, Annual Conference Series,* edited by James T. Kajiya, pp. 1165–174, New York: ACM Press, 1993.

[HARR04] M. Harris. "Fast Fluid Dynamics Simulation on the GPU." In *GPU Gems,* edited by R. Fernando, pp. 637–665. Boston: Addison-Wesley, 2004.

[HASS80] D. Hasselmann, M. Dunckel and J. Ewing. "Directional Wave Spectra Observed during JONSWAP 1973." *J. Physical Oceanography,* (August 1980), 1264–80.

[HODG95] J. Hodgins, W. Wooten, D. Brogan, and J. O'Brien. "Animating Human Athletics." In *Proceedings of SIGGRAPH '95,* Computer Graphics Proceedings, Annual Conference Series, eduted by Robert Cook, pp. 71–78. Reading, MA: Addison-Wesley, 1995.

[JUNY01] J. Y. Noh, and U. Neumann. "Expression Cloning." In *Proceedings of SIGGRAPH 2001, Computer Graphics Proceedings, Annual Conference Series,* edited by E. Fiume, pp. 277–288. Reading, MA: Addison-Wesley, 2001.

[KANE01] T. Kaneko, T. Takahei, M. Inami, N. Kawakami, Y. Yanagida, T. Maeda and S. Tachi. "Detailed Shape Representation with Parallax Mapping." In *Proceedings ICAT 2001,* pp. 205–208.

[KING04] G. King and W. Newhall. "Efficient Omni-Directional Shadow Maps." In *Shader X3,* edited by W. Engel. Hingham, MA: Charles River Media, 2004.

[KINS65] B. Kinsman. *Wind Waves.* Engelwood Cliffs, NJ: Prentice-Hall, 1965.

[KIPF04] P. Kipfer, M. Segal and R. Westermann. "UberFlow: A GPU-Based Particle Engine." Presented at *Graphics Hardware 2004,* (accessed April 2005 from www.graphicshardware.org/Presentations/PeterKipfer.pdf).

KOZL04] S. Kozlov. "Perspective Shadow Maps: Care and Feeding." In *GPU Gems,* edited by R. Fernando, pp. 217–244. Boston: Addison-Wesley, 2004.

[KRIS96] V. Krishnamurthy and M. Levoy. "Fitting Smooth Surfaces to Dense Polygon Meshes." In *Proceedings of SIGGRAPH '96,* Computer Graphics Proceedings, Annual Conference Series, edited by Holly Rushneier, pp. 313–324. Reading, MA: Addison-Wesley, 1996.

[LATT04] L. Latta. "Building a Million-Particle System." (accessed April 2005 from www.gamasutra.com/features/20040728/latta_01.shtml).

[MARK03] W. R. Mark, R. S. Glanville, K. Akeley, M. J. Kilgard "Cg: A System for Programming Graphics Hardware in a C-Like Language." In *ACM Transactions on Graphics (Proc. ACM SIGGRAPH),* 22:3 (2003), 896–907.

[MAST87] G. Mastin, P. Watterburg and J. Mareda. "Fourier Synthesis of Ocean Scenes." *IEEE Computer Graphics and Applications* 7:3 (1987), 16–23.

[MCCO00] M. McCool. "Shadow Volume Reconstruction from Depth Maps." *ACM Trans. on Graphics* (2000), 1–25.

[McGU03] M. McGuire, J. F. Hughes, K.T. Egan, M. Kilgard. "Fast, Practical and Robust Shadows ." Tech. Report CS-03-19, Brown University, Providence, RI, 2003. (accessed April 2005 from www.cs.brown.edu/publications/ techreports/reports/CS-03-19.html).

[MERE04] M. Meredith and S. Maddock. "Individualised Character Motion Using Weighted Real-Time Inverse Kinematics." In Proceedings of GAME-ON 2004 (accessed April 2005 from www.dcs.shef.ac.uk/~mikem).

[MORE03] K. Moreland and E. Angel. "The FFT on a GPU." In *HWWS '03: Proceedings of the ACM SIGGRAPH/EUROGRAPHICS Conference on Graphics Hardware*, edited by M. Doggett et al., pp. 112–119. Aire-la-Ville, Switzerland: Eurographics Assoc., 2003. (accessed April 2005 from www.cs.unm.edu/~kmorel/documents/fftgpu/fftgpu.pdf).

[OLIV00] M. Oliveira, G. Bishop and D. McAllister. "Relief Texture Mapping." In *Proceedings of SIGGRAPH 2000, Computer Graphics Proceedings, Annual Conference Series*, edited by Kurt Akeley, pp. 359–368. Reading, MA: Addison-Wesley, 2000.

[OROR04] J. O,Rorke. "Managing Visibility for Per-Pixel Lighting." In *GPU Gems.* edited by R. Fernando. Boston: Addison-Wesley, 2004

[PEAC86] D. Peachey. "Modelling Waves and Surf." In *Computer Graphics (Proc. SIGGRAPH '86)* 20:4 (1986), 65–74.

[PETI02] S. Petitjean. "A Survey of Methods for Recovering Quadrics." *ACM Computing Surveys* 32: 2, (2002), 211-262.

[PIER64] W. Pierson and L. Moskowitz. "Spectral Form for Fully Developed Seas." *J. Geophysical Research* (Dec. 1964), 5181-5190.

[POTM83] M. Potsmesil and I. Chakravarty. "Modelling Motion Blur in Computer Generated Images." *Computer Graphics (Proc. SIGGRAPH '83)* 17:3 (1983), 389-399.

[REEV83] W. Reeves. "Particle Systems—A Technique for Modelling a Class of Fuzzy Objects." *Computer Graphics (Proc. SIGGRAPH '83)* 17:3 (1983), 359–376.

[REEV85] W. Reeves and R. Bla. "Approximate and Probabilistic Algorithms for Shading and Rendering Structured Particle Systems." *Computer Graphics (Proc. SIGGRAPH '85)* 19:3 (1985), 313–22.

[REGE04] A. Rege. "Shadow Considerations." Presented at 6800 Leagues Under the Sea. (accessed April 2005 from download.nvidia.com/developer/presentations/ 2004/6800_ Leagues/6800_Leagues_Shadows.pdf).

[REIN02] E. Reinhard, M. Stark, P. Shirley and J. Ferwerda. "Photographic Tone Reproduction for Digital Images." In *Transactions on Graphics (Proc. SIGGRAPH 2002)* 21:3 (2002), 267–276.

[REYN87] C. Reynolds. "Flocks, Herds and Schools: A Distributed Behavioral Model." *Computer Graphics (Proc. SIGGRAPH '87)* 21:4 (1987), 25-34.

[SANC04] M. Sanchez, J. Edge, and S. Maddock. "Realistic Performance-Driven Facial Animation." Tech. Rep. CS-04-10, Department of Computer Science, University of Sheffield, U.K., 2004. (accessed April 2005 from www.dcs.shef.ac.uk/graphics).

[SEDE86] T. Sedeburg and S. Parry. "Free Form Deformation of Solid Geometric Models." *Computer Graphics (Proc. SIGGRAPH '86)* 20:4 (1986), 327–334.

[SING00] K. Singh and E. Kokkevis. "Skinning Characters using Surface Oriented Free Form Deformations." In *Proc. Graphics Interface 2000*, pp. 35–42. Wellesley, MA: A K Peters, Ltd., 2002.

[SHIM03] C. Shimizu, A. Shesh and B. Chen. "Hardware Accelerated Motion Blur Generation." *EUROGRAPHICS 2003* 22: 3 (2003)

[SHIN01] H. Shin, J. Lee, M. Gleicher and S. Shin. "Computer Puppetry: An Importance Based Approach." *ACM Trans. on Graphics* 20: 2 (2001), 67–94.

[SHOE87] K. Shoemake, "Quaternion Calculus and Fast Animation." In *SIGGRAPH Course Notes*, 10, pp. 101–21. New York: ACM Press, 1987.

[STMI02] M. Stamminger and G. Drettakis. "Perspective Shadow Maps." *Transactions on Graphics (Proc. SIGGRAPH '02)* 21:3 (2002), 557–562.

[TARI03] M. Tarini, P. Cignoni and R. Scopigno. "Visibility Based Methods and Assessment for Detail-Recovery." In *Proc. of IEEE Visualization 2003*. Los Alamitos, CA: IEEE Press, 2003.

[TSO87] P. T'so and B. Barsky. "Modelling and Rendering Waves." *ACM Trans. on Graphics* 6:3 (1987), 191–214.

[VLAC04] A. Vlachos J. Isidoro and C. Oat. "Rendering Refractive and Reflective Water." (accssed April 2005 from www.ati.com/developer/shaderx/ShaderX_ RilingRefractive AndReflectiveWater.pdf).

[WANG03] Li. Wang X. Wang, X. Tong S. Lin, S. Hu B. Guo and Heung-Yeung Shum. "View-Dependent Displacement Mapping." *ACM Trans. on Graphics* 22: 3 (2003), 334–339.

[WATE87] K. Waters. "A Muscle Model for Animating 3D Faces." *Computer Graphics (Proc. SIGGRAPH '87)* 21:4 (1987), 17–24

[WATT92] A. Watt and M. Watt. *Advanced Animation and Rendering Techniques.* Harlow, UK: Addison-Wesley, 1992.

[WATT01] A. Watt and F. Policarpo. *3D Games: Real-Time Rendering and Software Technology."* New York: Addison-Wesley and ACM Press, 2001.

[WILL78] L. Williams. "Casting Curved Shadows on Curved Surfaces." Computer Graphics, (*Proc. SIGGRAPH '78*) 12:4 (1978), 270–274.

[WLOK03] M. Wloka. "Batch, Batch, Batch: What Does It Really Mean?"(accessed April 2003 from developer.nvidia.com/docs/IO/8230/BatchBatchBatch.pdf).

Index

Printed and bound by CPI Group (UK) Ltd, Croydon, CR0 4YY

23/10/2024

01778226-0001